PRAISE FOR

Travel Mania

"*Travel Mania* is a godsend. It's the perfect way to imagine I'm a seasoned traveler, without having to leave the comfort of my living room couch. Gershowitz who responds to the suggestion 'let's go' by packing her bags, hasn't quite turned me into a travel junkie, but she has hooked me on reading about a woman who just can't sit still."

—CHARLES SALZBERG,
two-time Shamus Award nominee and author of *Second Story Man*

"Buckle up! *Travel Mania* is pure adventure and passion, circling and crisscrossing our exotic globe, ever eager for the next horizon. From those pre safety-belt days in the back seat of a DeSoto to the uncertain risks of traveling during our present-day pandemic, each leg of Karen Gershowitz' life-long voyage is fueled with insights and intimacy, humor and poignancy. This is no mere itinerary or travelogue, but an inside passage."

—MARC NIESON,
author of *Schoolhouse: Lessons on Love & Landscape*

"Karen Gershowitz suffers from the only traveler's disease that's fun to have and be around: the compulsion toward travel itself. This book is full of terrific stories, revealing with richness and particularity not just places and people, but the traveler herself— complicated and often conflicted, comforted by certain traveling companions and people met on the road, driven to distraction by others, but never daunted, never able to resist the pull of another journey. This book was a delight to me during these times of shutdown and is an inspiration for the times to come."

—LON OTTO,
author of *A Nest of Hooks*, *Cover Me*, and *A Man in Trouble*

"Prepare to be swept around the world in the capable and enthusiastic company of KG. You will climb Mt. Kilimanjaro, 'poli-poli', eat the famous-for-its-revolting-smell durian in Malaysia, trek through a scirocco in the Sahara, watch bribes being passed on Moscow sidewalks, ride a felucca on the Nile, and spend New Year's Eve in Saigon. Wherever she goes, Karen is an astute observer and willing experimenter. You are in for a treat."

—CHRISTINE LEHNER,
author of *What to Wear to See the Pope* and *Absent a Miracle*

"No 'guided' tour here. The only fitting description is: page-turner. Karen gives us wondrous—whether white-knuckled or resplendent—nuggets. Her own growth as a global citizen winds through the decades and essays and leaves me wishing I might have trailed along at least a few times. I'm already looking forward to dipping in repeatedly, and without booking a single flight."

—CAROLYN LIEBERG,
author of *West with Hopeless* and *Calling the Midwest Home*

"Alone or in the company of others, Gershowitz navigates the world with an open heart and a sense of adventure. This collection covers impressive ground, and whether she's rocking out with Moroccans to the Blind Boys of Alabama, struggling up the slopes of Kilimanjaro, or doing business in Asia, her sharp eye brings the wonders of the world in focus."

—MARILYN JOHNSON,
author of *Lives in Ruins* and *This Book Is Overdue!*

"As a travel-industry professional, I've watched the world shrink as access has grown. Gershowitz's lovely travel memoir is a look back at a time when faraway places really were far away, distant cultures were very different, single women travelling alone were an unusual sight, and travelers with open hearts had extraordinary experiences. *Travel Mania* made me appreciate current travel opportunities even more."

—SUE SHAPIRO, former President of NY Skal,
former President and CEO of GIANTS consortium

TRAVEL MANIA

TRAVEL
MANIA

STORIES OF
WANDERLUST

KAREN GERSHOWITZ

Published 2021
Printed in the United States of America
Print ISBN: 978-1-64742-126-7
E-ISBN: 978-1-64742-127-4
Library of Congress Control Number: 2021900223

For information, address:
She Writes Press
1569 Solano Ave #546
Berkeley, CA 94707

Book design by Stacey Aaronson

She Writes Press is a division of SparkPoint Studio, LLC.

Included photographs are from the author's personal archive.
Names and identifying characteristics have been changed to protect the privacy of certain individuals.

To my mother, Mary Lotker Gershowitz,
who taught me to be curious about the world.

"All journeys have secret destinations
of which the traveler is unaware."
—MARTIN BUBER

TABLE OF CONTENTS

INTRODUCTION

At a farewell dinner the night before I left on a one-year journey, a friend proposed a toast: "May you have a few really terrible days, when it pours, and you get stuck in a laundromat or inch along in a ten-mile traffic jam. You'll need those days to remind you how great the rest of the trip is."

It was a reminder I didn't really need. I've spent many hours, sometimes days, bored while waiting for delayed flights or stuck inside in beautiful places unable to get out and explore because of relentless, torrential rain. While traveling in Thailand, I tore my meniscus climbing onto an elephant. In Guatemala, our Land Rover was stuck in mud so deep and viscous it took six people almost an hour to extract it. Across the world I've experienced terrifying taxi rides, pickpockets, and run-down hotels in dicey neighborhoods that have put me into a state of tense alertness. But no matter what mind-numbing or frightening events have occurred, my enthusiasm for travel remains undiminished. I am very lucky to be able to explore the globe. When I'm on the road, I wake each morning eager for the adventure to begin.

I was seventeen when I boarded a TWA flight bound for Amsterdam, my first solo adventure. I didn't return for three years. Traveling became a passion. At least a couple of trips are always in some stage of planning, and I've got a backup list of another two or three. No matter how many places I explore, my list of must-visit destinations only gets longer. For me, travel is an addiction, but one for which I don't want treatment. I've even compiled a list of places that will be easy to negotiate as I grow old and frail.

When friends are looking for a companion to explore some remote or bizarre destination, I'm often their first choice. They call prepared to twist my arm to convince me to, say, go camel trekking in the Moroccan desert in the summer when it's 110 degrees or to tool around the Galapagos Islands on a decrepit fishing boat or explore the extreme northern tip of Japan. My usual answer is, "Sure, sounds great. When were you thinking of going?" An out-of-the-way destination, especially one I know little about, is my personal drug of choice.

When I can't find anyone who's able or willing to come with me, I travel alone, often picking up traveling companions along the way. Some have become lifelong friends.

What is my favorite place? It is an impossible question to answer. At almost any given moment, I am enamored with the scene in front of my nose. Spectacular beauty, astonishing accomplishments, and warm, generous people intermixed with outrageous schlock all captivate me. Over six decades, I've experienced over ninety countries plus all fifty US states and all ten Canadian provinces. There are many cities that, over time, I've been to a dozen times or more, allowing me to witness major change and subtle shifts. As time has passed, I've learned to look more deeply for the less obvious things that define a culture.

In 2001, when I took a yearlong sabbatical and traveled around the US, I developed a website. A blog, before there were blogs, I intended it to let family and friends know where I was and what I was doing. But long before that blog and after it ended, I have always kept a travel journal. Recently I uncovered one from 1967, a time capsule from my earlier self. Those scribbled notes and outlines of events, some detailed, some sketchy, have been memory prods helping me to fill in details about trips and, occasionally, whole journeys that might have vanished forever if I hadn't written them down.

This book is a compilation of stories that explore how travel can change a life. I am an ordinary person. Through travel I've learned courage and risk-taking and succeeded at things I didn't know I could do.

Each story can be read and enjoyed independently, but taken together, I hope they convey the profound impact travel can have and the joy that can be found in exploring the world. My hope is that these stories tickle your travel bug and give you the courage to set off on your own adventures. Maybe we'll meet in Tonga, high on my must-visit list.

THE INAUSPICIOUS BEGINNINGS: 1950S

My father was a workaholic, too busy running his sponge factory to consider anything as frivolous as a long weekend or an extended vacation. But every summer, during the first two weeks of July, he shut the factory down to give his employees a vacation. My mom insisted we travel, though my father would happily have stayed home. She picked our destination and planned the itinerary. Nothing about those two-week excursions could have predicted two of the three children in my family would become passionate travelers.

I remember packing up our DeSoto Woody, filling every inch of the massive station wagon with stuff. There were clothes and footwear suitable for every potential weather condition (including snowstorms). We packed inflatable rafts, plastic flippers, and swimmies if we were headed to a lake, as well as towels and metal folding chairs with webbed plastic backs. Cardboard boxes filled with rain gear were shoved into a far corner—galoshes, umbrellas, and yellow rubber slickers so hot and sticky I don't recall any of us ever wearing them. More cardboard boxes held decks of cards, the Monopoly set, a game my brothers played with frightening intensity, and my personal favorites, Chutes and Ladders and Candyland. It took hours to pack the car, and sometimes I wondered if there'd be room for all of us once everything was loaded. Looking back, I can't imagine where all of this gear was usually stored; the five of us were a tight fit in our two-bedroom apartment.

When my father announced we were ready to go, there'd be last-minute elevator rides to the fifth floor for one final bathroom stop. Then Mickey (nine years older than me), Roy (five years older than me), and I would fight about who would sit in the middle, over the hump on the floor. It was a foregone conclusion that, as the youngest and smallest, I'd sit squashed between my brothers. But before every trip I'd cry, threaten to throw up on them, plant myself by a window, and refuse to budge. It never worked.

By the time the Woody slid away from the curb, it was late morning, no matter how early we'd woken up. My father was already in a dither, concerned about reaching our destination before nightfall. He was the only driver and must have dreaded eight to ten hours of traffic with three whining kids.

We lived in upper Manhattan, in Washington Heights. It meant nearly every vacation began with a trip over the George Washington Bridge. My brothers and I had a ritual of singing "George Washington Bridge, George Washington, Washington Bridge," from the second the car hit the on-ramp until we arrived on solid ground in New Jersey. On a typical weekend, this was annoying enough for my father. In the thick of Fourth of July traffic, it must have been torture.

After about five minutes, as we crept across the span, my father would turn around and calmly say, "That's enough." We kept singing.

"Stop."

Our voices got lower for a few minutes, whispering, "George Washington, Washington, Washington," but we persisted.

"Stop. Now. Or I'm throwing you out of the car!" He wasn't shouting, but his voice was definitely louder.

My mother didn't acknowledge either my dad or us but remained a 1950s Madame Defarge, knitting as the war raged on.

By the time we crossed the span and entered New Jersey we were all exhausted, with at least seven hours still ahead of us. That was when we'd start singing "Ninety-Nine Bottles of Beer on the Wall." My father would turn on the radio, and if he was lucky, he'd be right in time for the start of Saturday's Texaco-sponsored Metropolitan Opera broadcast. If he was even luckier, it would be *Tosca* or *La Traviata*, his favorites. He'd turn it on full volume, drowning us out before we hit "Ninety-eight bottles . . ." At about sixty-five bottles, we would have entered into the mountains, and the radio would begin to crackle and fade in and out. With one hand on the wheel and one on the tuning knob, my dad would try to extend the range of WQXR for a few more miles.

Since we traveled in the heat of summer, we always headed north. When I was six, in 1957, we drove via a circuitous route toward the Laurentian Mountains in Quebec. Our first overnight stop was at Gastown, not far from Niagara Falls. The location had been selected, I'm certain, because the motel was cheap. A child of the Depression, my father could "pinch a nickel so hard, it would scream." The name "Gastown" said it all. The drinking water, the pool, even the air smelled like rotten eggs. My parents tried to be stoic. My brothers and I had no such discipline—the stench made us gag. We held our fingers to our noses, screaming "P-eww!" and "Fart!" over and over. At dinner, none of us had an appetite. Even though my parents were only picking at their food, there were a lot of reminders from them about the starving children in China. My brothers and I didn't care. When my dad lit up one of his five-cent stogies, we remained silent. Normally the stink from those cigars would send us running from the room. In Gastown, the familiar odor, pungent though it was, was an improvement. Without air-conditioning, the room was hot and smelly. It was a long night.

The power of Niagara Falls' thundering water, the cool droplets spraying our faces, and the ice cream we hurriedly licked before it melted improved our dispositions. My brothers and I were disappointed my father wouldn't let us ride the *Maid of the Mist*, the boat that traveled under the falls. He assured us seeing the falls from both the American and Canadian sides was just as good and, of more relevance to him, free. My brothers and I weren't convinced; donning yellow slickers and riding under the roaring falls sounded exciting, but we didn't get a vote. We stopped for a quick look at the Floral Clock, then back into the car for the next leg of our journey.

Our ultimate destination was a provincial park many miles north of Montreal. As the sun was setting, we were nowhere near the cabin we'd reserved. Thinking back, I realize it must have been very late—just past summer solstice in the far north, the sun wouldn't have set until ten o'clock or so. The road wasn't great, more pebbles and ruts than macadam, few signs. Nerves were on edge. My brothers and I knew to be quiet, though a lot of elbowing and shoving went on silently. Any squeaks or squeals or giggles provoked an angry "Be quiet!" from my exhausted father. There was no *La Bohème* on the radio to soothe him, nothing but static to drown us out—so we drove in silence. We always got lost at least once on any excursion in those pre-GPS days. Mickey was an excellent map reader, but even he had no idea how far we were from the lake. There was no one to ask.

I must have fallen asleep; the car's sudden stop jolted me awake. We had pulled over to a small building, the official entrance to the park. The ranger on duty gave directions to my father, assuring him we were close. "Go to the second stop sign, make a left. You'll be in the third driveway." What he hadn't told us was it was eight miles to the first stop sign and another four to the second one.

For a family from New York City, this was serious culture shock, the first I ever experienced. I remember my father muttering, "We must have missed it, we must have missed it." My mother reassured him with five pairs of eyes on the lookout, we hadn't passed the stop sign. Twenty-five minutes later, we pulled into the driveway of the rustic cabin that would be our home for the next ten days. The powerful scent of pine, gentle lapping of wavelets at the lakeshore, and cool, fresh air emphasized how far we'd come.

We did all the usual things a family did at a cabin at a lake in 1957—swimming, canoeing, cooking out on the grill. Days were warm; nights were cool. Far away from the dangers of Manhattan, I was allowed to go outside by myself, as long as I didn't go near the lake. It was the first time I had that freedom; as a city kid there was no backyard to play in. I would go in and out, letting the screen door slam behind me, dozens of times a day. I didn't have anywhere to go, didn't really even want to be by myself; I just loved that I *could* go out and about on my own.

News was sporadic, but we did receive one snippet of information from a newly arrived family—the Northeast was suffering from a heat wave. Temperatures in New York had been over ninety degrees for a week. We were giddy in the cool. To celebrate our escape from the oppressive weather back home, my dad hauled in wood from the massive pile behind the cabin, arranged it in the fireplace, and ceremoniously lit it.

It was one of the first important travel lessons I learned: the whole world doesn't experience the same thing at the same time.

On our first trip to Canada, we *must* have passed through border control and customs, both entering and returning, but it made no impression on me. Being so young, I'm not sure I even understood the concepts of "borders" or "countries." Everyone we met spoke English, and I could read the words on signs with a little help; nothing looked or felt different from our vacations in the Catskill Mountains or the Adirondacks. "Foreign" meant my grandparents, immigrants who spoke English with a thick accent or never learned to speak it at all.

My second international trip, two years later, was once again to Canada. But this time, in Quebec City, my focus was on language—French. At age eight, I knew about French and Italian but had never heard them spoken. I grew up hearing the guttural sounds of Yiddish at home. My best friend Judy's parents spoke German. Some of my grandparents' friends would occasionally speak Russian or Polish. On our jaunts to Chinatown, the waiters spoke to each other in a strange singsong way, but they always used English with us. The chalkboards listing the specials of the day, with their odd up and down symbols, had an English translation.

Now, on our annual Fourth of July vacation, after the predictable preparations and arguments about seating arrangements and songs, we'd arrived in a magical land where everyone spoke in a melodious tongue. Once across the border, years before Canadian law decreed all signs must be bilingual, there was no English to be seen. We were immersed in French; it was beautiful, mysterious, exotic. This was a foreign country.

My father's approach to resolving the language difference was to speak louder, as if everyone in Quebec City had suffered severe hearing loss. If he just spoke loudly enough, they'd be able to direct him to the zoo or advise him on a restaurant. When volume didn't help, he'd turn to my mother in frustration. She had come armed with a small English-to-French phrase book. While she struggled to find and then slowly read the phonetically spelled-out sentence, I'd try to help by acting out what we wanted. Charades was a game at which I excelled. I'd also picked up a few important phrases—*bonjour, merci, parlez-vous anglais?*—and was happy to try them out. A child with a big smile and no fear can butcher a language horribly and still, miraculously, be understood. My enthusiasm usually made my victims smile and try especially hard to help us. Somehow, between kind people who spoke a little English and getting information from the travel guide, we managed to get around just fine.

I emerged from that trip so overconfident about my ability to communicate with anyone, I've never learned to proficiently speak another language. In foreign lands, I still rely on kind strangers, especially those who are good at charades. In retrospect, I wish I'd made a serious effort to learn other languages. Still, that early experience taught me I'd be able to negotiate the world even without understanding the local language—it made me a lot braver.

I remember one final trip across the border from my childhood. The year following our trip to Quebec, we headed to Nova Scotia. Mickey had gotten his driver's license and had been driving for about six months. My father, happy to be able to share the time behind the wheel, alternated with him as soon as we were out of city traffic. Roy and I must have teased Mickey and made jokes about the new seating arrangement—when he drove, we shared the back seat with our mom. But Mickey took his new responsibilities to heart, even yelling at us to be quiet.

For some reason I can't recall, I was in the front passenger seat and the designated navigator as we made our way into Halifax. I was a proficient map reader; it was considered by my family to be a crucial survival skill, and I can't remember a time when I couldn't read one. My guess is my parents taught me about maps at around the same time I was learning to read Dr. Seuss. As we got closer to the city, my brother Mickey asked me which way to go. I studied the map and called out a route number I was certain would get us close to our motel.

When he asked, "East or west?" I confidently replied, "East." Then we approached a traffic circle.

"There's nothing marked east. Do I go inbound or outbound?" His voice was tense, and I could see him gripping the steering wheel just a smidgen tighter.

I looked up at the sign, then studied the map. From what I could tell, we were heading from one suburb to another. Was that inbound or outbound? "I'm not sure," I said in a small voice.

He tersely repeated the question.

"I don't know, just pull over," I begged. You'd have thought I'd asked him to dance naked in front of the mayor. He screamed at me, infuriated that I couldn't give him a simple answer.

"I can't pull over, we're in a traffic circle—*inbound or outbound?*"

I began to cry. Mickey drove around the circle two or three times, cursing and yelling at me. No matter how hard I tried, I couldn't figure out which way to go. I knew giving the wrong answer would be worse than admitting I didn't know. It would have meant days or even weeks of teasing. As usual, my mother was doing her Madame Defarge act, and my father didn't want to get involved. Finally Mickey picked a ramp, exited the traffic circle, pulled over, and grabbed the map from my hands. I sniffled while he studied it intently for several minutes. He finally growled, "Stupid signs."

We proceeded in the direction he'd turned, which was incorrect. When we stopped at a gas station to get directions, we got a tip about a local fish and chips place that turned out to be the best restaurant of the entire trip. After he'd calmed down, Mickey apologized and peace was restored. We eventually found the motel, a big relief. That my big brother couldn't read the map any better than I could was an even bigger relief.

This was another crucial travel lesson: sometimes you get lost, but you don't get lost forever. Eventually you find what you're looking for, and sometimes the best part of a trip is the unexpected gem you discover while wandering.

And so began my life as a traveler.

FUELING THE PASSION: 1960S

My grandma Bella was one
of the most self-absorbed,
flamboyant people I've
known. She was also one of
my greatest inspirations.

M y brothers, cousins, and I all found Bella completely annoying;
our litany of kvetches about her could fill an encyclopedia. To
put it kindly, she wasn't the stereotypical grandma of the 1950s.
Bella never wore flowered housedresses, knitted scarves for us, or
baked apple pies. In fact, her cooking and baking went beyond bad
—it was dangerous. You could easily break a tooth if you bit into
one of her oatmeal cookies more than twenty minutes after it
emerged from the oven. For years I refused to eat strudel because I'd
been raised eating her version—rubbery dough filled with overly
sweet apricot jam, often burned at the edges. In my thirties, I spent
time in Vienna and tasted the real thing: it was revelatory.

Bella was a talker. She knew how to hijack any topic and twist it to something she wanted to discuss. In my home, all conversations abruptly ended when she entered a room. We'd try to sneak away before she could catch our eye, but if we weren't fast enough, we'd still be there an hour later. In public, she'd grab anyone in sight and, in heavily accented English, chatter away without pause. As a child, I'd be mortified when she'd do this with strangers in the park or the supermarket, but people found her delightful. Within minutes, Grandma would have a new friend. As an adult, I now marvel at both her charm and chutzpah.

But her chutzpah often went too far. Bella showed up at my brother's wedding in a sparkling silver dress with matching high heels, wearing a vast amount of fake glittery jewels on her ears, wrists, and around her neck. It would have been an unusual outfit for any wedding guest but was especially startling on someone in her late seventies. Even though the photographer spent a lot of time shooing her away, she weaseled her way into at least half of the photographs. In some of the outtakes, her broad smile, oddly reminiscent of the Cheshire Cat, can be seen peering around other members of the wedding party.

Bella had three husbands and buried them all. Harry, my mother's dad, died before I was born. From the stories I've been told, he was quite a catch—kind, good-looking, a union labor leader, and a scholar. A few years after Harry died, Grandma remarried, this time to a chicken farmer in New Jersey. He lived for only a couple of years after their marriage, and I can't remember him at all. Grandma's third husband, Izzy, she met and married in her early sixties. A dapper gentleman, he was always well-dressed, with perfect manners, and he adored Bella. Sadly, he passed away while I was young.

She never married again. I've sometimes wondered why she

didn't remarry. Perhaps when she was widowed for the third time, there simply weren't enough men in her age group. Maybe her charm had worn off a bit by that point in her life—I do remember her bossiness with Izzy (and every other family member). Perhaps she decided three husbands had been enough. But, for whatever reason, she found herself single.

When she had only her own needs to consider, Bella decided to do things she'd always dreamed about. High on her list was to see America, her adopted country. She'd arrived at Ellis Island from the Ukraine and then lived in Manhattan for decades, too poor to take a vacation. Later, she and Izzy became snowbirds, traveling every winter to Miami to escape the cold northern winters. But New York and Florida comprised her knowledge of the US, and that didn't satisfy her curiosity. About a year after Izzy's death, Bella announced to my mom and aunt she was going to see America. And she planned to go alone.

In the 1960s, this was a shocking idea. Sixty-five was considered old, and women of any age rarely traveled alone. I'm certain Mom was surprised by her mother's unexpected wanderlust. Thinking about it now, I realize she was also probably a bit jealous. But she was supportive. Mom had always been somewhat unconventional and longed to travel. I think she appreciated her mother's ambition and bravery. I always suspected she helped Bella make her dream come true by providing financial support and taking care of some logistical arrangements.

At age sixty-five, Bella boarded a Greyhound bus and set off on her adventure. Her chattiness must have been a big asset. I imagine her looking out the window and providing her seatmate with a running commentary on the scenery, the old country, her family, and whatever else popped into her mind. I'm sure she must have always had bags of treats and cookies (thankfully not home-baked) she offered to everyone seated near her. At rest stops, the driver would have gallantly helped her off the bus, for which he would have received one of Bella's dazzling smiles.

She spent six weeks visiting distant relatives and one of my mom's friends who had moved to California. Sometimes, when no one she knew lived in a place she wanted to visit, she'd stay at a cheap motel while she looked around. Every few days we'd receive a postcard; they rarely contained a message, just a signature. It was how we knew she was okay, long-distance calls being expensive. I loved getting those shiny pictures of the Grand Canyon, San Francisco, and Chicago. Bella returned with a couple of boxes filled with gifts for us. The gifts, like her cooking, were well meant but awful— T-shirts too small to fit any of us, cheesy plastic doodads, oranges that had been fresh and delicious in California but were long past their prime by the time we received them.

Her first trip was such a success she did it again the following year. Then she got more ambitious: she decided she wanted to track down long-lost relatives in her homeland. While my mom and aunt had been okay with her travels in the US, they weren't too happy about Bella traveling to the Soviet Union. In the thick of the Cold War, relations between the two countries were tense. Though she had become an American citizen and would carry a US passport, her origins were clear from her appearance and accent. I remember overhearing a lot of heated arguments in Yiddish, which I couldn't understand, but the tone and volume made their disagreement clear. In the end, as in all things, Grandma prevailed; she wore them both down.

Because Bella's English was "sketchy," I usually helped her compose letters to businesses and friends. This time she had no problem writing notes in her spidery penmanship, on tissue-thin paper, in a language I couldn't read. She mailed these aerograms to people I'd never heard of who lived in far-off places. I found the whole process intriguing, especially when the replies returned bearing colorful foreign stamps. With each letter she received, she became more excited, and her planned trip got longer. Looking back, I wonder how she located so many of her relatives—nearly a half century had passed since she'd lived there. Then again, communist Russia was hardly a mobile society. Her relatives were probably in the same houses their families had lived in for generations.

Bella departed from Idlewild Airport with several overstuffed suitcases. She brought her relatives clothing, shoes, and packaged food, items difficult to obtain in Russia at the time. The gifts would repay her relatives for their hospitality, but as important, they would demonstrate her success in America.

I can't recall how long she was gone, but it seemed an extended visit, at least a few months; after half a century, I guess they had a lot of catching up to do. We may have received a few postcards, but for most of her trip, there was no contact at all.

Unlike her journeys around the US, Bella's suitcases were lighter when she returned home: the gifts had been distributed, and there was little to buy in Russia. But she did bring back stories. Of all of the tales of shtetls and distant relatives, the one most fascinating to me was about a second or third cousin just about my age. Grandma told me she looked so much like me she could have been my sister. She even had a blurry photo, dutifully snapped with her Brownie camera, to prove it. I stared and stared at the picture. In it I saw an alternate universe, the life I might be living if my grandparents hadn't come to America.

That trip to Russia was the last of Bella's international travel adventures. But the following year, and every year after until her late seventies, she traveled back and forth to Florida on the Greyhound bus.

Among the many things Bella taught me, the most important lesson was that it is possible for a woman to be adventurous, travel alone, and not just survive but thrive. She paved the way for me to make my own journeys—if my mom allowed Bella to travel, I knew she'd permit me to do so too.

LEAVING HOME: 1970

It was my first solo trip, and I was heading overseas. My parents and brothers had accompanied me to the gate, hugging me and saying goodbye only as I handed over my boarding pass. I walked across the tarmac toward the plane; in 1969, there were no jetways. Nearing the plane, I stopped and turned around to get one last glimpse of my family, but all I could see were reflections on the building's tinted glass. I was on my own. Heading toward the plane, it felt as though the heat-softened tarmac was grabbing at the soles of my shoes. I walked slowly toward the beckoning stewardess.

Fourteen months earlier, I had been a freshman at Pratt Institute in Brooklyn. It hadn't been my preferred college; my heart had been set on art schools outside the New York City area, but no other college accepted me. It wasn't because of my grades, SAT scores, or my portfolio, which everyone assured me were superb, but because of my age: I wouldn't be seventeen, their minimum age for living in the dorm, until midway through the fall semester. The schools feared liability if, entering at that young age, I got into any kind of trouble. Growing up during the height of the baby boom in over-crowded NYC schools, I had skipped eighth grade. It may have helped the board of education by getting one more child out of the overburdened system faster, but it hadn't done me much good. At age sixteen, I was socially awkward and too young to live alone or work.

Pratt was willing to admit me on the condition I live at home. The college was within commuting distance, if one considers a three- to four-hour daily round trip on subways and buses reasonable. I was continually bleary-eyed and dragging, too scared to sleep on the subway, too harried and wound up to get much sleep at home. The one saving grace was that my best friend from high school, Cassie, also chose Pratt.

In the beginning, I loved thinking about and making art in new ways and tried to ignore the horrid logistics. Then things began to change. The spring of 1969 was tumultuous in New York. The city was filthy and dangerous. Vietnam War protests, draft card burnings, and student riots shared the nightly news with an upswing in murders, muggings, drug busts, and other violent crimes in all five boroughs. Pratt Institute, located in one of the most dangerous neighborhoods in Brooklyn, Bedford-Stuyvesant, hunkered behind fortresslike brick walls. Outside the college walls, graffiti decorated every surface, and rats scuttled through piles of trash. Bed-Stuy was home to an especially active and violent group of Black Panthers who were gathering strength and making headlines. I almost never ventured through the neighborhood alone.

One bright afternoon in early spring, Cassie and I were walking from campus to the subway station. Sensing movement behind us, we picked up our pace. The footsteps were loud and getting closer. We moved faster, nearly trotting, but not fast enough. A loud explosion rang out, a cherry bomb, I think. I grabbed for Cassie, flailing to reach her hand. A shrill, jeering voice screamed, "Black and white don't mix!" Cassie yanked at my hand, and we ran from the explosion. The voice trailing behind us called out, "Stay friends and there'll be worse to come."

As the voice had warned, things got worse. Cassie and I had been close friends all through high school and had gotten beyond the differences of our skin color. Our similar interests, likes, dislikes, and bizarre humor made the issue of race insignificant. After the cherry bombing, Cassie and I began to drift apart. Most days she sat with a group of black kids at a table on the opposite side of the cafeteria and walked through the neighborhood in the company of her new friends. Every time she and I did get together, there would be hate mail in my school mail slot the next day reminding me we were being watched. I hadn't made many new friends at Pratt and felt isolated.

While on my endless commute a few weeks later, I sat alone on the F train reading a magazine, avoiding eye contact with everyone, and ignoring the graffiti-covered walls of the subway car. Something splashed on me. I looked up. A middle-aged man was standing over me. "Help me," he rasped. He collapsed into the seat next to mine, his weight pinning me into the corner. The splash had been drops of blood. Then the blood gushed. Had he been stabbed? Shot?

I don't remember the next hour clearly. Someone must have pulled the emergency cord. In 1969, violence on the subway had become routine, and the police had a lot of experience dealing with it. They boarded the train and efficiently removed the man. Everyone who had been near him was briefly questioned about what they'd seen. Then the train got moving again. For me, the violence was horrifying. I went into a state of shock, emerging from my haze only to realize I'd missed my stop, gone to the end of the line, and was heading back through Manhattan to Brooklyn. Spattered with blood, I had the seat to myself for the entire trip, everyone carefully avoiding me.

After that incident, with bloody images always at the periphery of my consciousness, I had to force myself to ride the subway or to walk in the area outside the campus. I was on constant alert for danger but continued my daily grind. In addition to school and the commute, I'd gotten a part-time job shortly after I turned seventeen; my wages paid for art supplies. Hadassah, a women's Zionist organization, was converting their mailing list from a mechanical to a computerized process. Two afternoons a week, I sat in a windowless room filled with other college students poring over lists of names, playing "Hadassah Bingo," a way to eliminate duplicate names.

"Annie Schwartz in Miami Beach," the caller would scream out. We all scanned our lists looking for the right Annie.

"I've got her—she's on Jefferson Avenue!"

"Sadie Schwartz in Dallas," the game proceeded.

It was mindless and dull—exactly what I needed. Once an hour we got a ten-minute break. People ran off to smoke, use the bathroom, or go to the deli next door for much-needed caffeine.

One afternoon at break time, I was staring into space when a young guy came over to chat. A brief snippet of our conversation is imprinted in my memory like a tattoo.

"If you could do anything, anything at all, what would you do?" he asked.

Without hesitation I said, "I'd quit school, work for a year, save every dime, and go to Europe."

"So why don't you?"

I couldn't think of a single reason why not.

In mid-August, fifteen months later, having done exactly what I'd blurted out, I was on the tarmac leaving for Holland. The Koninklijke Academie van Beeldende Kunsten, the Royal Academy of Fine Art, in The Hague had accepted me as a transfer student.

I was anxious to leave yet terrified of going. I'd never traveled anywhere by myself—not even to nearby Connecticut. I knew not one person in Holland, didn't speak Dutch, wasn't even sure why I was going there instead of California or Florence. I'd picked Holland on a whim. My parents had recently visited Amsterdam, and I thought they'd be less opposed to my studying in a place with which they were somewhat familiar. And I liked the idea of having an ocean and six time zones between us. When my mother understood I was determined to go through with my plan, she was encouraging—it was something she would have liked to have done in her youth.

My fear of staying in New York had propelled me forward. Now, step after slow step, I made my way across the tarmac, up the stairs, down the center aisle, and into my seat. I burst into tears but willed myself to stay seated, not to run off the plane in a panic. When the doors were secured, and the plane taxied to the runway, my tears dried up. My breathing slowed, and a deep calm settled over me. Much later I understood that distance wasn't really the point; it was the act of leaving that counted, the separation from the familiar and constricting. I thought I was going to experience a foreign culture. In retrospect, I went to reinvent myself.

By early October, just two months after arriving in The Hague, I'd found a place to live, and the scant bit of Dutch I'd learned at

Berlitz had improved (besides, nearly everyone spoke fluent English). But each time I entered the art academy, it felt as though I'd time-traveled to the 1890s. At Pratt we'd been encouraged to experiment and to stretch the limits of our imaginations and materials. I'd used soda cans to create a 3-D chess set and in life-drawing class had drawn two-minute charcoal sketches capturing the spirit of the pose, if not the precise anatomy. In the academy we spent hour after dull hour standing silently at easels sketching from plaster busts or bowls of fruit. In desperation, I began to draw dust motes floating in a beam of sunlight and the patterns of raindrops streaked across dusty windows. I'd made some acquaintances, but no one I thought of as a friend. Desperately lonely, I knew I'd made a horrible mistake.

I considered returning to New York. But I couldn't. I knew what I'd be going back to. The Hague may have been a poor choice, but surely there was somewhere else, some safe yet engaging, stimulating environment. I struggled with what to do. After yet another dull afternoon sketching, when even a couple of mugs of strong coffee couldn't prevent me from continually yawning, I packed up my belongings, bought a train/ferry ticket, and headed for London. I had lasted five weeks at the Koninklijke Academie.

On the ferry, my mood reflected the North Sea's steel-gray, choppy waters. Others on the ferry must have thought I was about to be ill, but my pallid complexion and ragged breathing were caused by fear, not seasickness. I was glad to be escaping yet again, but fearful I wouldn't like London any better. Then what would I do? Still, I looked forward to being around people whose mother tongue was English, naively assuming because we shared a common language, the British would think and act just like Americans.

The Princes Square Hotel was described in *Frommer's Europe* *on $10 a Day* as inexpensive, centrally located, student-friendly accommodations. Dragging my massive suitcase, I navigated my way from the Liverpool Street train station onto the Underground and made my way to Bayswater and the hotel. The manager, Mr. Singh, told me the only available room was a small one with a shared bathroom, on the first floor, one flight up. For several long minutes, I stood frozen in place, unable to decide if I should stay. The stress of leaving Holland, aching muscles from hauling luggage, and just plain tiredness immobilized me. A flight of stairs was daunting, finding another hotel more so.

I was saved from becoming a permanent front desk fixture by a young man who cheerfully offered to carry my luggage. That was enough to convince me to take the room. I told myself I would move the next day.

As we climbed the stairs the young man gave me a quick primer on the hotel. There were few available rooms, he said, because almost everyone at the hotel was a student at the University of London. The same baby boom that had caused my progress through school so quickly in New York City had also overwhelmed London. The university dormitories couldn't accommodate everyone, and school officials suggested several hotels to late-registering students.

"Breakfast is terrible, but you can steal toast and hard-boiled eggs for lunch." He shifted the suitcase to his other hand and bumped it up step-by-step, talking as he went. "The TV is pretty useless, all wavy lines, and it fades in and out, but we all watch it anyhow. Make sure you take a bath early in the day; by evening there's never any hot water." There were lots of British students, the young man continued, as well as many other nationalities. "But you'll be the only American."

The room where he dropped me off was furnished in what could only have been castoffs—a shaky table and equally wobbly chair, a dresser marked by dozens of cigarette scorches, and a scary-looking electrical device I couldn't identify. I flopped down on the bed, surprised it was comfortable and the sheets looked clean. As I lay there in stupefied exhaustion, the floral pattern in the wallpaper transformed into gremlins laughing at me.

My room was perched on a landing between floors, so everyone going upstairs had to pass my door. In my haste to lie down, I hadn't fully closed the door. Within minutes I had visitors; word had quickly spread, and they were curious about the new American. By evening, I had eaten dinner with several new friends and decided to stay at the hotel for a few more days.

One of the students told me about an art school in the East End he thought would accept me, even though the semester had already begun. By the following evening, before I'd seen the Tower of London, Piccadilly Circus, or Buckingham Palace, I was enrolled in the Sir John Cass College of Art and had taken my first ceramics studio class.

The life I'd been imagining had begun.

THREE LEAVING LONDON: 1971

After a few months in London, I was enjoying my classes, had begun a part-time job working for the instructor, and developed a circle of friends. It was time for a holiday from my new routine.

"The car's gone," Ron howled. I wasn't really surprised; Roby had parked her ancient Fiat in what was clearly marked as a no-parking zone. She'd told me not to worry, getting coffee would take only five minutes. What could happen in five minutes? When she said it, I'd shrugged. After all, what would one more unpaid parking ticket mean? Roby, an Italian studying for her PhD at the University of London, had been parking her car illegally since she'd arrived four months before. Each morning she plucked a parking ticket from under the wiper and used it to clean her windscreen. She was disappointed when she didn't get one—her wipers didn't work well, and she hated looking through streaky glass.

Ron, Roby, and I were traveling to Paris for the winter holidays. Ron, always a worrier, began to panic. "We'll miss the ferry. Oh, my God! All my stuff is in the car. Thieves have taken it; we'll never get it back. Oh, my God!" While he worked himself into a frenzy, Roby calmly approached a bobby (policeman). After she explained our plight, the bobby used his walkie-talkie to call in the information.

"Miss, your car has been impounded. You'll have to go pick it up in Islington."

I flashed on all those parking tickets and silently swore under my breath. Ron was right: we'd never get our stuff back. We were students with very limited resources; between us we couldn't begin to pay what Roby owed.

The three of us had met by chance, living at the Princes Square Hotel at the height of baby boomers entering college. The seedy hotel had been transformed by the University of London into student housing to accommodate the overflow. Greasy eggs and soggy cornflakes for breakfast every morning, furniture that seemed ready to collapse at any moment, and evenings spent watching one small TV with a wavery image had created a strong bond among the thirty or so students living there. I was eighteen, and it was my first experience living in a community of my peers. It became an adventure, and the living conditions seemed only a minor inconvenience. I reveled in both my freedom and new friends. But as winter break approached, and everyone shared their plans for holiday time, my elation sunk into dread. Left by myself, the hotel's dim lighting and cramped quarters would merely be damp, dirty, and depressing rather than inspiration for endless jokes. When Roby proposed I join her to visit friends at the Sorbonne, I didn't hesitate in saying, "Yes!"

In our excitement planning our getaway, Ron had somehow invited himself. My friend Michael had repeatedly told me to uninvite Ron. "He's a right bloody twit. It won't take two days for him to send you right 'round the bend." I protested; while Ron was a bit naive and childlike, he wasn't a bad sort.

While saying goodbye earlier that morning, Michael was still trying to convince me to dump Ron. "Bloody Midlands wanker—I don't know how he manages to get around London without getting lost and going home to cry to Mummy."

I'd nodded and ignored him.

"Really, it's not too late to chuck him out."

I'd nodded again.

"Well, don't come back and complain. You're going to have a bloody awful time, and I won't listen to it."

Despite Michael's warnings and a small inner voice murmuring, *He's right, it's a bad idea—a really bad idea*, the three of us had climbed in the car and set off. Now I wondered if we'd even make it out of London.

"So where exactly is Islington, and how do we get there?" I asked the bobby. He gave us directions, and off we went to the Tube to retrieve the car.

On the long ride to Islington, we considered how we might extricate it while still holding onto some cash for the trip. Roby, in her airy, nonchalant manner assured us, "No worry. I get the car. I talk to them. You see."

I wondered if the car was worth what the parking fines were likely to be. And had they actually brought it to the pound? Or had they taken one look and just towed it to the dump? The teensy white Fiat was adorned with multicolored streaks of paint from cars she'd sideswiped. The front headlight was secured to the frame with black-and-white-checked electrical tape, as was a portion of the rear fender and a side panel. Fascinated by people and the city, Roby spent more time looking at the sights than at the road. Worse yet, she kept forgetting to drive on the left. A few harrowing drives with her had metaphorically put the first gray hairs on my head. Going the wrong direction around a London traffic circle must have cut a year or two off my life expectancy.

Despite being less than a half mile from where we'd exited the Tube, the walk to the pound took nearly an hour. There were no signs, and we seemed to be going in circles. Though I knew she had no idea where she was headed, Roby strode confidently along, clacking her high heels on the pavement. Ron slunk along a few steps behind her. Nearly six feet tall, he seemed to shrink into himself and looked as if at any moment he might begin to cry. I began to think of him as a seven-year-old in a nineteen-year-old's body.

I stopped the few people we passed, and they gave conflicting directions. It was only when we saw a car being towed and followed it that we finally found the entrance to the pound.

Pointing her finger at Ron, then jabbing him with it, Roby said, "You let me talk. You say nothing. Nothing. You understand?"

"Yes, I understand," Ron mewled softly.

She crooked her finger at me. "You come with me. You also say nothing unless I tell you to. You understand?"

At the front gate, she explained to the officer there had been some mistake and her car had been towed. She went on to tell him we were headed to the ferry for Calais and then on to Paris. It took a lot of self-restraint to keep me from throttling Roby. Knowing we were about to head out of the country, the police would never release the car.

While the officer shuffled through a pile of papers, Roby smiled and chatted. She was tall and striking, with dark sultry looks, a mane of shiny jet-black hair, and tight jeans. She turned on the charm in a way I never thought possible, except maybe by Gina Lollobrigida in the movies. While another officer tore himself away to bring the car around, the desk officer said, "That will be a hundred fifty pounds to release your car."

In 1970 that was a lot of money, more than I had with me for the entire ten days. "How much is that in lire?" Roby asked sweetly as she pulled out a checkbook.

With a rueful smile the young officer told her, "I'm sorry, we can't take a foreign check."

Roby's eyes opened wide, and she fluttered her long black eyelashes. "What am I to do? Only lire, no pounds."

"Sorry, miss, we can't take your check."

One lone tear slid down her cheek. "My momma, she's meeting us in Paris." The officer fidgeted a bit but didn't relent. Roby's eyes softened, and more tears flowed. "Without the car, I can't visit my momma."

Her momma? That was pouring it on a bit thick. The plan was to crash at a friend's flat and party for a week. Next she'd say her momma was sick and if we didn't get to Paris today, her mother would die without her saying goodbye.

"Maybe I could pay you when I get back?" Roby asked hopefully. When the officer didn't immediately say no or, as I would have done, laugh at her, Roby pressed on. "I'll be back in a week. I promise, cross my heart, I will pay the hundred fifty pounds." With that she put her hand on her chest and ever so subtlety caressed her breast.

The officer's eyes lingered as he murmured, "It's most irregular, but . . ."

"I'm a good Catholic." Roby moved her hand just enough to fish out a gold cross from under her sweater. "Lord Jesus is my witness, I pay you when I return." I followed her gaze to his left hand; there was no wedding band. "And maybe we go to dinner?"

Ten minutes later, Roby was in the driver's seat, and we were headed toward the ferry. It was a typical drive with Roby—I spent my time alternating between navigating, yelling at Roby to "Keep left, dammit, I don't want to get killed. Left. Left," and replaying the scene at the pound. While I would love to be able to pull off such an audacious con, could I ever summon the nerve or sultriness to do it? I decided not. Maybe it was an Italian thing. My American accent just wouldn't work. Neither would my American forthrightness and compulsion for honesty. And, even with my best effort, my short curly hair would never have the same impact as Roby's suggestive flipping of her long lustrous locks.

Ron fretted because they knew his name. Since he was the only Brit in the car, they'd come after him for Roby's unpaid fines. He sniffled and sniggled until Roby turned 180 degrees to face him in the back seat and shouted, "Basta! Enough! Be quiet!" I grabbed the steering wheel as the car lurched. Surely, we wouldn't make it to Paris alive. And even if Roby and I did, Ron wouldn't—we'd throw him off the ferry in the middle of the channel.

In Dover, we got lost several times before arriving at the terminal, tired, hungry, and grumpy. The ferry on which we had a reservation had departed long before. There'd be a two-hour wait. Roby ordered Ron, "Go for a walk. Don't come back until the ferry go." I was hoping she'd pull another con and we'd leave without him. I was ready to heed Michael's warning and ditch Ron at the first opportunity. But no, she and I choked down dried-out cheese sandwiches and lukewarm tea with milk from the commissary while she licked her lips and described brioche, croissants, and other culinary delights of Paris.

I finally began to relax and even began to get excited. Warm yeast-scented brioche. The Louvre. The Eiffel Tower. With no more driving on the left and on roads with which Roby was familiar, we might make it to Paris after all.

CAPTURING JAPAN: 1974

After three years in Europe, attending classes and working, I decided it was time to return to the US and get my college degree. I visited the American consulate in London and researched art programs, willing to live anywhere in the States except New York.

The Kansas City Art Institute seemed to have a good ceramics program, was willing to accept me without an interview, and would grant me credit for my time in London. Initially, living in the Midwest produced extreme culture shock—I'd been used to going to Paris for the weekend, not Omaha. But after a year there, I came to love the school.

When I returned to Kansas City after a summer vacation visiting friends in London, the culture shock wasn't nearly as disorienting as it had been during my first transition. Still, it only took a couple of weeks for me to become antsy and to begin pondering my next adventure.

Ken Ferguson, chairman of the ceramics department and ever-present figure in the studio where I worked, had spent his summer traveling in Japan. From the moment classes began, he regaled us with stories of the pottery studios he'd visited and the fabulous artwork he'd seen and artists he'd met. There didn't seem to be a corner of the country or a famous potter with whom he hadn't connected. However, show-and-tell was mostly tell, with only a few tea bowls, teapots, and plates he'd brought home as tangible evidence of his adventures. The one photo he did pass around showed him standing next to Shōji Hamada, one arm casually draped over his shoulder. Hamada, one of the most celebrated artists in Japan, had been designated as a national living treasure by his government. Standing next to six-foot-six Ken, who at about three hundred pounds dwarfed almost everyone, Hamada looked like a porcelain miniature. The snapshot was later pinned to a corkboard in the ceramics studio.

Every time I passed the photo, I would glance at it and smile and feel an itch to travel. But travel was definitely not in my budget. I was living on student loans and the meager proceeds from two part-time jobs and eating a lot of spaghetti dinners. Still, I began thinking there had to be some way to make it happen.

Not long into the semester, a close friend, Jim, told me of his plans to spend eight months in Japan, beginning in January. A few years earlier, his family had hosted an exchange student, Yasue Nakatani, from Osaka. Jim had been writing to her ever since. When Yasue's parents learned of Jim's desire to visit, they offered to help him find a place to live in Kyoto. After hearing me chatter constantly about Japan, Jim promised to put me up and find other places for me to stay throughout the country. Now lodgings were taken care of, and, if I was careful, the cost of food wouldn't be excessive. But flights and railway fares in Japan seemed prohibitive.

For weeks I puzzled about how to get enough money for transportation. Nothing I came up with seemed both realistic and sufficient. I knew my parents wouldn't fund the trip, nor could I get a loan. Yet another job was out of the question. I began to conjure up vaguely criminal activity, like stealing all the abandoned mugs, teapots, and bowls in the ceramic studio and selling them at the weekly farmers market. Reason prevailed; I knew I'd get caught.

One day Ken was talking about a particular type of wood-burning kiln he'd seen used in a small village in Kyushu, one of the southern Japanese islands. He drew pictures of multiple chambers snaking up the side of a mountain, but none of us could really picture the details he was keen to have us understand. I had a sudden flash of inspiration. The Kansas City Art Institute *needed* to have a library of photos illustrating Japanese studios, potters, their pots and kilns. I was just the person to make it happen.

I wrote a long letter to the college administrators explaining that, if the college would pay for my transportation and the film, I'd follow Ken's itinerary from the previous summer, taking photos everywhere I went. When I returned, I'd hand over the film. I wasn't sure they'd really consider funding this, but it was worth a try—after all, they encouraged creativity, and this was certainly a novel idea.

Much to my surprise, within a couple of weeks both Ken and the dean asked me to provide a detailed proposal and budget. A month after I submitted it, they gave approval, though they asked me to not mention the "scholarship" they were awarding me, so as not to receive a flood of copycat student requests.

While I couldn't talk about how I was paying for the trip, the excitement of traveling to Japan was too much for me to contain. I'm sure the entire student body, all five hundred, heard about my plans. Lisa, a fellow ceramics student but not an especially close friend, asked if she could accompany me. Having a travel companion in a country where I could neither speak nor read the language seemed a good idea. She even offered to take Japanese lessons, something I had no time to pursue and couldn't afford.

For the next several months, I prepped constantly for the trip, at times more focused on it than classes. Lisa and I pored over Ken's itinerary, as well as train schedules, youth hostel locations, and any other information we could get our hands on. As our departure drew closer, Ken suggested a photograph of the three of us together. Showing the picture at the studios we planned to visit would help to smooth the way. As in the photo with Shōji Hamada, Ken towered over us.

A few days before the end of spring semester and our departure date, Ken called across the studio to me. "Gershowitz. Come into my office."

I looked up from the potter's wheel wondering what was up.

"And make sure you wash your hands. Really well," he continued.

While scrubbing up, I assumed he had a choice bit of advice for me; he'd been casually dribbling out tidbits for weeks. What could he have in mind that had to be done in his office and with clean hands?

"Okay, Gershowitz. I thought about it and decided you'd need this." He handed over a small cardboard tube.

I removed the cap from one end and carefully slid out a thick sheet of paper. As I unrolled it, several teachers and classmates crowded into the room. There, on creamy parchment, was a scroll proclaiming the support of the Kansas City Art Institute. It had ornate calligraphy, a hand-drawn border, and a bright gold seal trailing a blue ribbon embossed with the seal of the college. I was stunned and barely had the breath to stammer out, "Thanks. It's wonderful, great."

Ken grinned, pleased.

I stared at it thoughtfully and then got up my nerve to ask, "But it's in English. How will they know what it is?"

"Don't worry. They just like official-looking documents; the more elaborate, the better. Somehow that makes it authentic. When you show them the picture with us together and this, they'll be happy to show you around."

In mid-May of 1974, Lisa and I left for San Francisco, our point of departure for Tokyo. We'd arranged to share a ride with another student who was happy to have extra drivers and the gas money we contributed. Our route took us through Denver and Boulder, Salt Lake City and Reno, along one of the dullest stretches of road imaginable. It got so bad we began to take bets on how many miles it would be until the next bend in the road. We didn't stop along the way—there was no money to spare for a motel. I kept reminding myself there was an excellent reason to put myself through this torture—the pot at the end of the rainbow would be Tokyo.

After two days of endless driving, we arrived in San Francisco. Lisa took off to visit a family friend; we'd meet at the airport for our flight. My friend Gary, who'd been my upstairs neighbor in Kansas City and was now living in San Francisco, had offered to put me up for the week prior to our departure. Although his roommate had initially agreed, he now abruptly objected. After a nasty argument, Gary promised him I'd stay for only a single night.

"Gary, what are we going to do for the rest of the week? I haven't got a single cent I can spare to stay somewhere else."

"My brother Ronnie lives in LA. We'll go visit him."

"But you don't have a car."

"No problem, we'll hitchhike."

And so we did. Gary, it turns out, had been hitching to classes in Oakland every day for the entire semester. He'd taken a sheet of cardboard, cut out the shape of a raised thumb, and written the message "Home to Mom" in large letters. That sign was our lucky rabbit's foot on the way down to LA, unfailingly getting us rides.

For four days we stayed with Ronnie, "plumber to the stars," and his family. On absolutely no money, we managed to visit Disneyland, swim in the Pacific, and get stuck in a most horrific traffic jam—the quintessential Los Angeles vacation. Then it was time to return to San Francisco for my flight to Tokyo.

Hitching to San Francisco, the magic sign didn't seem to be quite as magical. We'd get short rides and then wait for long stretches before another car stopped. As the hours passed, my anxiety increased. If I missed the plane, how would I ever explain it to Lisa, Jim, my family, the college? Would I have to repay the plane fare? I stood by the side of the road while Gary hid. Gary stuck his thumb out while I made myself scarce. We danced, pulled silly faces, tried to look as charming as possible. Even with every hitchhiking trick imaginable, our progress was molasses-like, while my frustration grew and near panic set in. I arrived at the airport only one hour before the flight took off. When I finally made my way through immigration and reached the departure gate, our flight was almost at the end of the boarding process. I hadn't had any way to contact Lisa, who'd been praying for my arrival and cursing me. She hugged me and dragged me onto the plane. I was a wreck.

Once airborne, it took less than thirty minutes for me to fall into a deep sleep. The tension of getting to San Francisco had exhausted me. As I was peacefully asleep, the ten-hour flight to Japan seemed to take no time at all.

Fortunately, Narita Airport had many signs in English. Without them, I doubt in our travel-weary state we could have navigated our way to the train and into the city.

For the first few days we gently eased ourselves into the culture. The staff at the youth hostel was eager to practice their English. With garbled instructions (think of poorly translated leaflets describing how to put together a bicycle) and a lot of pointing, they explained how to take a traditional Japanese bath and use the vending machines. When one of the staff saw we weren't sure what to do with the artfully arranged ingredients on our breakfast tray, she demonstrated. We watched as she cracked the raw egg into the steaming bowl of rice and stirred well, which cooked the egg, and then sprinkled seasoning on top. With a deft use of chopsticks, she then wrapped a sheet of nori (seaweed) around a small mound of the rice mixture and popped it into her mouth. After a couple of tries we could both do it with ease. It was a far cry from cornflakes, but tasty and filling.

Early on in our trip it became obvious Lisa's Japanese conversation lessons had been futile. She would carefully enunciate "How do we get to . . . ?" in Japanese, but then never understood the response, no matter how slowly and carefully the person spoke. Instead, before we left each morning, we would ask a staff member at the youth hostel to write a card in Japanese listing our destination. We'd show the card to people on the street, and, given the cultural mandate of politeness, they would always point us in the right direction, sometimes even leading us there.

The subway system got us to museums, the Ginza shopping and entertainment district, and the Imperial Palace. In comparison to the graffiti-covered subway cars of NYC it was a pleasure to ride the clean, fast, and efficient Tokyo transit system. What the two cities shared was overcrowding, though at least in Tokyo I got shoved onto the subway car by white-gloved attendants rather than other passengers. It was something of a surprise, however, to realize that at five foot eight, I was often able to peer over a sea of heads, towering over everyone in the densely packed subway car.

Signs in English popped up in unlikely places all over the city. There was no pattern as to where they would appear. Some signs butchered the language so badly they left us befuddled. What exactly did "More right need, manager get" mean? I'd always heard the Japanese can't distinguish between *l* and *r*, and signs scattered around the city proved the point. We saw a huge neon sign: "Hotel Plesident." The "Croak Room" was near the entrance of a museum, and "Rock Smith" was understandable because it was next to a display of keys. Hip-looking teens wore logo T-shirts that often got the spelling right but were emblazoned with totally unfathomable messages: "Cheer Me Up, Groovy Reality," "Monkey Doze Yesterday," "Playing Work—Hop." While often baffled by their meaning, at least we could read them. Written Japanese has thousands of indecipherable (to us) ideographs. Most of the time, we stumbled around the city like functional illiterates, looking for clues to help us find our way. I gained a lot of empathy for those who can't read, completely understanding their frustration.

Despite our inability to read a menu, we discovered ordering food was easy. Many restaurants had front windows filled with realistic-looking plastic replicas of the foods they offered. We would lead the server outside and point at a bowl of noodles or a plate of tempura. Given my childhood passion for Japanese food, I felt comfortable making selections. Sometimes the replicas looked better than the real food served. Occasionally we'd be surprised by some ingredient like slippery, salty seaweed we hadn't noticed in the display. But at least we wouldn't starve as we traveled around Japan.

Coffee, to which I was and remain addicted, was a bit more

problematic; it isn't a part of the Japanese tradition. The youth hostel didn't serve coffee in the morning, and in restaurants it was frighteningly expensive. When it became obvious buying coffee would deplete my spare cash, I had a mild panic attack—crashing headaches would definitely detract from this journey. And tea, no matter the variety, just didn't do it for me in the morning. On our second day, we discovered a Kentucky Fried Chicken outlet selling decent American coffee at a reasonable price. I've never, before or since, so appreciated an American fast food joint. It did make me laugh, however, that the statue of Colonel Sanders standing outside the front door had distinctly Asian eyes.

After almost a week in Tokyo, we'd adjusted to the time difference and felt comfortable enough to begin the main purpose of our journey—visiting pottery studios. The studios were almost always in rural areas, far from typical tourist haunts. Fortunately, Japan had an excellent public transportation system, and navigating the trains and buses proved to be manageable. Our presence on local transport in rural areas almost always created a scene. My curly hair and height provoked stares of amazement. Children would giggle and point at Lisa's dirty blond hair. The most daring shyly reached up to touch it, amazed it was real. Whole packs of kids would smile at us, say, "Hello," then hold up an imaginary object and in a loud and clear voice say, "This is a pencil."

At first, Lisa and I thought perhaps they wanted us to give them one. After the tenth or twelfth child had done this, we would smile back and say, "And this is a pen." We had no idea what was going on. Much later we discovered that "This is a pencil" was the punch line to an ongoing gag on a popular children's TV show.

Our arrival at the first ceramic studio set a pattern for most of the visits we made. I can only imagine the surprise the local potters felt when they saw two young American women, hauling back-packs, walking to their front gate. Despite our novelty, we were al-ways greeted with a polite smile. When, using both hands as I'd been taught to do, I presented the ornate certificate and the photo of us with Ken, the smiles broadened.

"Ah so, Kansas City!"

As Ken had predicted, we were warmly welcomed at every stu-dio. The first order of business was always ceremonial tea. I learned to loathe the acid-green tea. It had the same effect as eating an unripe persimmon—my mouth would pucker, and I had to resist spitting or choking. Politeness always prevailed, and I somehow managed to down the entire vile cup. Ceremony completed, we would be given a tour of the studio. Few of the potters spoke English, but we knew enough to see what they were doing. They showed us everything—how they prepared the clay and threw pots; the drying, glazing, and decorating processes; the kilns being loaded, fired, and unloaded. And we saw the final product—beautifully crafted teapots, bowls, canisters, and plates. In each studio, I took dozens of photos and meticulous notes.

In one very remote studio, the master potter pointed to the potter's wheel with a flourish and waved his hand to suggest I try it. I gamely sat down, and he handed me a lump of clay. With little effort, I centered the smooth porcelain and pulled it up into a tall cylinder, then shaped it into a fluted vase. When done, I looked up and saw him gaping. He began to applaud. Lisa and I looked at each other baffled. Wouldn't he expect a student of Ken's to be able to throw a pot? He excitedly jabbered something, then signaled for me to stay where I was and ran off. Minutes later he returned with a crowd of people. After a slight bow, he handed me another ball of clay and motioned for me to throw another pot. This time I got a thunderous ovation. It was when Lisa and I realized my audience was all male that we began to understand. Women would sometimes decorate pots, but they never, ever threw them. This was the first time anyone at the studio had ever seen a woman at a potter's wheel. I hoped that perhaps my demonstration would somehow pave the way for females in the studio to begin throwing pots.

Forty rolls of film later, Lisa and I made our way to Kyoto on the Shinkansen, the high-speed train that barreled through the countryside at more than a hundred miles per hour. It moved so fast we couldn't see much of anything, but we were both eager to spend time with Jim and were willing to sacrifice the view. He met us at the train station and brought us to his lodgings, a traditional Japanese room in a low building, situated in the middle of a temple garden. At one time it had been a residence for acolytes while they were being trained. Because the temple was in need of money, they now rented the rooms to outsiders. Jim's room had shoji screen doors that filtered the light and gave everything in the room a warm glow. He slid them open to let in the cool air and give us a view of the garden. The sweet scent of roses perfumed the air. Surrounding the room was a narrow wooden porch. Years of soft socks padding along it had burnished the wood. We sat on cushions on the tatami mats covering the floor, drinking in the serenity and catching up.

At first glance, Jim appeared much as he always had, but when I looked more closely, I saw he'd undergone a subtle transformation. Japanese food had left him thin and a bit gaunt looking. He'd grown a moustache, and while still wearing a typical college student's jeans and T-shirt, he'd added a few distinctly Japanese touches. Relaxing in his room he often wore a *yukata*, a loose cotton kimono. Lined up at the front door were pairs of *zori* (similar to our flip-flops but with colorful cloth straps) and *geta*, shoes unlike any I'd seen before. They resembled zori but had wooden soles and two blocks of wood attached horizontally across the bottom.

"Geta are great in the rain. They're like wearing mini-stilts," Jim explained. "Everyone used to wear them to keep their feet above the mud. Now you don't see them all that often."

"Don't you fall over wearing them?" Lisa asked.

Jim laughed. "The first couple of times I went out walking I must have looked drunk. But then I got used to them. In bad weather they're quite practical."

During the six months he'd been in the country he'd been painting, studying Japanese, and learning how to play the *shakuhachi*, a traditional bamboo flute used for meditation. The food had become as familiar to him as it was to me. And he'd been making friends—through his friend Yasue, Japanese lessons, and simply by being out and about in his neighborhood. Westerners tended to stick to the tourist attractions, so his presence in a residential area provoked much curiosity. In 1974, Japan had a very closed society, and non-Japanese, including the Koreans who have lived there for more than a hundred years, were considered *gaijin* (foreigners). Jim would be out painting in a garden or crowded market and be approached by brave Japanese students who thought meeting a *hijō ni kimyōna gaijin* (very strange foreigner) would be interesting. Jim was open to these encounters and over time had made several friends. But, he said, "We never fully understand each other. I probably get one out of every eleven words."

He told us he'd arranged for us to stay with Yasue's family in Osaka, where he'd lived when he first arrived. His first couple of weeks at their home had been culture shock for both him and the Nakatanis. Jim's family was a purveyor of fine meats in Boston. As a gift to his hosts, he'd brought over a box of steaks, packed in dry ice. The first afternoon he'd been woken from a nap by a persistent *thump, thump, thump.* When he went to investigate, he'd found Mrs. Nakatani pounding the steak ferociously with a Coke bottle. While Kobe beef is extraordinarily tender, most of the meat available to ordinary folk tended to be quite tough. Any cut of beef was extremely expensive in Japan and not a part of the typical diet, so Mrs. Nakatani had no idea how to prepare her gift. She'd consulted a cookbook and followed the instructions in an attempt to tenderize the beef. By the time Jim showed up, the two-inch steaks had been flattened to about a half inch.

"I tried to explain to Mrs. Nakatani pounding wasn't necessary. But I didn't get my point across, and she just kept at it. My father would have had a heart attack if he'd seen the end result."

Jim went on, "But that night we evened the score. Yasue showed me how to take a traditional bath. It's a time-consuming ritual, meant to be relaxing as much as cleansing."

Lisa and I nodded; we'd experienced a bath and the accompanying explanation at the youth hostel in Tokyo.

"Yasue explained to me the same bathwater is used by everyone in the family, so it was important I completely scrub before entering the bathtub. Yasue switched on the heater, handed me soap and a brush, and left. Not wanting to offend anyone, I spent a long time washing. When I lifted the lid on the tub, a cloud of steam engulfed the small room." Jim paused for dramatic effect and refilled our glasses. "I stuck a toe into the water and was shocked by the heat," he said. "Then I tried again, and that time my foot came out bright red. When I looked more closely, I saw small bubbles forming around the edges. I thought, gee, the Japanese really like hot baths."

"Did you get into the tub?" I asked.

"No, I just couldn't do it." Jim said. "Instead, I dressed and found Yasue. She followed me back to the bath. When we opened the door the water was at a rolling boil."

"Like cannibals getting the pot ready," Lisa joked.

"Just about. When Yasue saw the tub her face flushed, and she looked mortified. She'd forgotten to tell me one small detail—I was supposed to shut off the heater after five minutes. She'd almost boiled her guest alive."

Lisa and I laughed. By comparison, our cultural mishaps had been minor.

At the monastery, a young businessman named Mr. Suzuki lived in the room next door to Jim. He spoke a little English and liked practicing with him. He was probably surprised Jim would have two females staying with him but tried to maintain a sophisticated facade. We received a cheerful "Good morning" every time we saw him, regardless of the hour. One evening we invited him over to have a drink with us. We had a couple of bottles of cheap wine, and Mr. Suzuki brought over a fifth of scotch. Within an hour, we were all more than a little tipsy. Jim was especially happy to have friends with whom he had a lot in common and, perhaps even more importantly, who spoke fluent English. I'm afraid we left our guest to fend for himself. Jim, Lisa, and I talked fast and over each other. The conversation meandered from recent art institute gossip to Japanese traditions to what we all missed from home. At one point we turned to toxic drinks and poisons in food.

"Alcohol will do anyone in."

"Especially if you drink this much."

"Think about Pernod; they banned it in France."

"But it doesn't have to be booze. Saccharine is the worst. It will kill you."

Jim turned to Mr. Suzuki. "Do you understand what we're talking about?"

"A little," he slurred. "You're talking about cherry blossoms." Mr. Suzuki had heard the word *saccharine* as *sakura*.

At that point we gave up talking, turned up the music, and danced. Mr. Suzuki, having consumed most of the scotch by himself, was so drunk all his attempts at sophistication and inhibitions had faded. He danced along with us, whirling and whooping.

The next day, despite hangovers that felt as if a dragon were breathing flames inside our skulls, we visited the Temple of the Golden Pavilion. Walking on paths that skirted perfectly manicured woods and sitting quietly meditating near the raked pebble gardens was the perfect antidote to our evening of excess.

Long before I'd traveled to Japan, I'd seen and admired examples of bonsai, miniature trees trained to grow into perfectly shaped specimens. Strolling along the temple paths, I realized every tree in the woods, no matter how large, had been pruned in the same way as bonsai. They were exquisitely formed. Some branches were propped up with carved supports, lashed to the branch with ropes that formed decorative patterns. Paths had been swept and raked, every leaf and twig meticulously removed. Gently flowing fountains and birdsong provided a musical accompaniment.

On the sloping lawn, caretakers trimmed the grass *with scissors*. There wasn't a cigarette butt or scrap of paper anywhere. Rocks had been placed to enhance the overall aesthetic. The closer I looked, the more it seemed that what at first glance looked natural was, in a sense, man-made. Ken, my professor in Kansas City, had taught that an important part of the Japanese aesthetic is the belief that perfection isn't possible or even desirable. All human creations must contain some small, deliberate flaw. Every pot, no matter how experienced and revered the potter, had some miniscule scratch or an almost imperceptible bump. When I looked around the woods very hard, I'd find some tiny imperfection—a slightly out-of-line stepping-stone or uneven weave in the rope lashings. The level of care was as breathtaking as the garden.

Lisa and I boarded another high-speed Shinkansen train and followed Ken's itinerary, zigzagging across the south of Honshu, the main Japanese island. We spent a day or two at half a dozen different studios; at each one I took yet more photos and notes. Traveling by slow train, we arrived on Kyushu, a mostly rural island further south. Until then, even in areas with few tourists, we'd always been able to find someone who spoke some English. In Kyushu, no one spoke a single word of it.

Here, there would often only be a single restaurant in a village, and they didn't have those wonderful food replicas we'd come to rely on. Instead, the waiter would lead us back to the kitchen and show us what was available. Despite that, we frequently didn't have a clue as to how the fish or tofu or chicken would be prepared or even exactly what type of food the waiter was showing us. In one restaurant the owner's small children peeked out from behind a curtain and pointed and giggled while we ate until Mom noticed and took them away. The one time we heard any English was walking to the youth hostel after dinner. A man, clearly very drunk, followed us screaming at full volume, "I wuv you! I wuv you!"

Everywhere we went, the ceramicists were gracious. The rolls of film and my notebooks were filling up.

On our way north, back to Tokyo, we stopped off in Osaka to see the Nakatanis. Yasue was away at college, but Mr. and Mrs. Nakatani gave us a warm welcome. Though they spoke not a word of English, and our Japanese was hardly enough to have a conversation, we got along well. Mr. Nakatani acted as chauffeur, driving us to every gallery and pottery studio within a twenty-mile radius. Mrs. Nakatani gave us cooking lessons, teaching us how to roll sushi, make tempura batter, and then dip and fry vegetables in it. For one dinner she'd prepared a special surprise for us—a traditional Japanese New Year's meal, the equivalent of cooking a Thanksgiving feast complete with all the trimmings. This included more than a dozen courses, each served on an elegant ceramic platter and each with a specific wish for the New Year. *Toshikoshi soba,* made from extra-long noodles, symbolized long life. A golden-hued, sweet egg omelet was a hope for many sunny days. A plate brimming with baby sardines and sprinkled with sesame seeds asked for a bountiful harvest. Other dishes represented wealth, health, and happiness.

Mrs. Nakatani invited her friends and relatives to meet us for an hour of bowing and smiling. They then dressed Lisa and me in traditional kimonos for a photo session. Lisa is about the height of most Japanese, and the kimono fit her perfectly. The kimono I wore came only to my knees rather than my ankles, which produced fits of good-natured laughter.

Only years later, when friends were transferred to Tokyo by their employer, did I come to appreciate how extraordinary our visit had been. My friends, who are warm and open, hadn't once set foot in anyone's home in the two years they lived in the country. All entertaining had been done in restaurants. Their experience was the norm; the Japanese rarely invite foreigners to visit them at home.

We'd brought small American gifts, replicas of the Statue of Liberty and packets of jelly beans. These couldn't begin to repay the Nakatanis' hospitality. Lisa and I fretted about this, wanting to do something special for them. After seeing Mr. Nakatani watching a game on TV and listening to him excitedly chatter about "*basu-baru*," I had an idea. When I returned to New York I bought a Yankees baseball cap and shirt and mailed them to him. Yasue wrote to us, saying her father was thrilled by the gift—he wore the cap constantly like a small child who refused to remove a favored item of clothing. For Mrs. Nakatani, Lisa bought some American cookware, unlike anything we'd seen in Japan. I did wonder, thinking about her experience with the steaks, how she figured out how to use the garlic press, lemon squeezer, and other gadgets.

On our last morning in Osaka, the Nakatanis drove us to the train. Boarding the train with us, they proceeded to urgently speak with everyone in our vicinity. I assumed they'd been asking our fellow travelers to take care of us and make sure we got off at the right station in Tokyo. Then they handed us an enormous bundle of food and exited seconds before the train began to move.

Coming back to Tokyo after our adventures in the countryside felt like a return to the familiar. Perhaps it was the hustle and bustle in the train station, seeing the occasional sign in English, or simply noticing a Western-style restaurant that set off cravings we hadn't had in weeks. We were suddenly desperate for a burger or sandwich and hurried over to the "international" restaurant. Seeing knives and forks on the tables felt almost shocking. The menu was in English, a first since we'd arrived six weeks earlier. I don't remember what we ate, only that even the pale facsimile of Ameri-European cuisine was very welcome.

What I do remember is the middle-aged Japanese gentleman who sat at a table across from us. When they served his plate of lamb chop with mashed potatoes and peas, he picked up the fork and knife and sat for a few minutes unsure of how to attack this strange meal. Lisa and I couldn't help but discreetly look. It was an odd twist on having people stare at us while we ate with chopsticks. As he started to cut into the meat, it slid across the plate, causing a fusillade of peas to shoot across the table. He turned flame red and glanced in our direction, hoping, I'm sure, that we hadn't noticed. To save him further embarrassment, we politely averted our eyes.

After a taste of Western food, we were now craving familiar sweets. In the basement of the Takashimaya department store, their famed food hall was enormous, filled with food we couldn't even begin to identify. All around us we heard squeals of "*Oishi,*" which we knew meant "delicious." After eating numerous mystery meals we'd sometimes had to choke down, it was hard to think of fermented soybeans, gnarled seaweed, or bits and pieces of unidentifiable sea life as delicious.

An enormous glass case was filled with the most gorgeous-looking chocolates I'd seen outside of Switzerland. We rushed over. For the first time during the trip, we didn't think about price. Pointing at one piece after another, we stopped only when the shop girl indicated the box was full. We could hardly stand still while she carefully tied on a ribbon and rang up our purchase.

Outside, we found a bench and tore away the ribbon. I sighed in anticipation and bit into a dark chocolate morsel piped with an elaborate design in white frosting.

"Ugh. That's disgusting."

Lisa had just bitten into her first piece. "Yecch! What is this stuff?"

I carefully examined the chocolate and its sickly sweet, gooey, gritty filling. "It's red bean paste." I groaned and flung the remainder of the piece into the shopping bag.

Lisa tossed her piece away and then reached for a second one. This time she licked the chocolate shell off, stopping when she came to the red bean paste center. We proceeded to do the same for every piece in the box.

After our episode with the chocolate, both Lisa and I were ready to go home. Our food cravings had intensified, and our desire for other English-speaking company had become acute. Equally important, I'd fulfilled my promise—one hundred and fifty rolls of film and ten notebooks captured the best of Japan's ceramic studios.

Two decades later, I began to regularly visit Tokyo for work. During the intervening years, the city had transformed, becoming more westernized. Coffee was readily available, English was everywhere, international brands dominated the stores, and many of the older, traditional buildings had been replaced by gleaming skyscrapers. Despite exchanging youth hostels for some of the finest hotels in the city and dining with clients at fashionable restaurants without display plastic food replicas, I found myself reminiscing about the Japan of my youth and the potteries and rural areas I visited.

WILL WORK FOR TRAVEL

All through graduate school, I had the gnawing sense that ceramics wasn't the best possible career choice for someone who loved to travel. Though teaching would provide vacation time and sufficient funds, I knew I didn't have the patience to teach. Most studio potters are self-employed factory workers, monotonously turning out mugs and bowls, plates and pots to earn a living. The finest do so at a very high level, but even then, only one in a hundred potters earn enough money for the kind of travel I envisioned. So, despite many years of study and a real love of the craft, I decided to rethink my career.

I got advice from a rookie career counselor, and though I knew nothing about her suggested occupation, marketing turned out to be the perfect choice for me. I've enjoyed being a marketing professional for more than forty years. It is intellectually stimulating, pays well, and, most importantly, requires lots of travel. Some business travel has allowed me to see and experience parts of the world I would never have been privy to as a tourist.

FIRST BUSINESS TRIP

In 1977, after a year of working at a small marketing research firm, my boss asked me to go on my first business trip. I was thrilled. With someone else paying the expenses, I didn't care that my destination was Omaha. What I failed to anticipate was that my earliest business trips would be reminiscent of my childhood travel experiences—highly instructional but not always fun.

Arriving in Omaha, I was met by my contact, a chatty, middle-aged woman. Dressed in a beige sweater set and long shapeless skirt, with her hair in a severe bun and wearing no makeup, she looked like a 1970s version of Auntie Em from *The Wizard of Oz*.

"This your first trip to Omaha?" she asked.

"Yes."

"Well then, let me give you a quick city tour before we head to the office." She beamed with pleasure. "Most people from the coasts think they've come to the middle of nowhere, but there's lots of interesting sights. You'll love it." As we pulled out of the airport, she said the first place we *must* visit was Boys Town.

As we drove into Boys Town, Auntie Em explained it had been founded by Father Flanagan as a refuge for difficult boys. "The Academy Award–winning film, you know, the one starring Spencer Tracy and Mickey Rooney, well, after that, everyone 'round the world knew about it." I nodded, having a vague recollection of having seen the film many years before. We drove up and down street after street of nondescript split-level homes. "This is where the boys live. Isn't it wonderful?" I nodded again, agreeing—but thinking, *Well yes, better than some Gothic nightmare of an institution, but couldn't they at least plant a few flowers?* The streets of identical houses reminded me of Levittown.

After we'd examined the neighborhood thoroughly, she drove toward an industrial area. With great passion she said, "These stockyards used to be the largest in the country, even surpassing Chicago's." I looked out onto old, tired-looking slaughterhouses and thought, *Get me out of here.* The car kicked up clouds of dust, partly obscuring the view. Full of trivia about the yards, she rambled on about the number of cattle processed annually and the percent of Omaha's population employed there while we examined the train tracks and every structure on the property. When I spied an enormous wooden enclosure with a stark one-word sign—"DEAD"—I'd had enough. "We really need to get to the office and start our meeting."

Auntie Em reluctantly turned out of the stockyards. "Omaha is such a great city," she gushed as she drove. "Did you know this is where the TV dinner was created?" Somehow that didn't surprise me at all.

The next evening, meetings concluded, I was happy to return to New York.

One month later, I needed to return to Omaha. Auntie Em again greeted me at the airport and with a bright smile chirped, "How about a quick city tour before we head to the office?" She'd obviously forgotten I'd been in her city recently. "Most people from the coasts think they've come to the middle of nowhere, but there's lots of interesting sights. You'll love it." I knew better.

GAMING THE SYSTEM

After two years and many uninspiring trips, I changed jobs in 1980, moving to the credit card division of American Express. I was warned I'd be spending at least 25 percent of my time traveling. Despite the dullness of my business travel to date, when my corporate American Express card was delivered to me, it felt like the best gift ever.

True to what I had been told, the travel began almost immediately. There were so many trips they began to blur together: an endless loop of airplanes, hotel rooms, taxis, and conference rooms. When I could, I'd try to take a few extra days to see Dallas or Atlanta or whatever other city I found myself in. But, in short order, unless I'd never been to the city before, all I wanted by the end of the meetings was to go home to friends, family, and my own bed.

American Express required exhaustively thorough expense reports. On my return flights I sorted receipts and filled in forms, and as soon as I was back in the office, I compiled everything. At the end of each month, I promptly turned in the completed report.

The billing department, however, wasn't as efficient. Every couple of months I'd get a phone call from someone at American Express following up on a late payment on my corporate card.

"Ms. Gershowitz, this is the fourth time payment for your card has been late."

"Sorry. I turn in everything on time to accounts payable; I'm not sure what else I can do." I tried to hide the frustration I felt at wasting so much time on paperwork. "I've been following up and trying to make sure everything gets processed, but . . ."

"Well, American Express does not allow any delinquency, no matter what the reason," she said sharply. "You may not extend payments. If your payment record doesn't improve, we'll have to cancel your card."

"Okay, I guess I won't be able to travel for American Express anymore."

"You work for American Express?" The woman at the other end of the phone sounded incredulous. She paused a moment and must have looked more carefully at my account information before she said, "Oh, you do." Another long pause. "Well, I'll let it ride for now, but don't let it happen again." She said this as though I could control the accounting department. If only I could.

After months of threatening phone calls, I went to the head of my department. Explaining the situation, I asked, "What do I do to get them to stop?"

"No problem, do what I do. Let corporate travel book your flights and directly charge it to the department."

"And hotels and meals?"

"I get large advances and pay for everything with cash."

"You don't use your card?" I asked incredulously.

"Nope."

MAKING IT WORK

In 1982, I was hired by Emery Air Freight. (A company similar to FedEx, it is now defunct.) Jim, my boss, wanted me to see the operations end of the business. On my third day, I flew to the company's central hub in Dayton, Ohio, where the nightly action took place.

At midnight, the sky shone with a stream of planes, steady as the Christmastime flow into LaGuardia. Eighty cargo jets arrived from cities across the country. As Jim explained, "East Coast arrives first, West Coast last, following the time zones. They depart in the same order." From our vantage point at a strategically positioned viewing window, I watched as planes taxied to the football-field-sized building and were secured in place. Within seconds, each one was surrounded by equipment and crew, and the unloading process began.

Jim led me back into the building. Standing on a catwalk over the main sorting facility, I could see dozens of fully loaded forklifts racing across the massive room. I was astounded they didn't collide. Long conveyor belts snaked this way and that, mechanical arms dropping envelopes and small parcels into bins. Workers reached periodically into the reject bin, read the label, pasted on a corrected label, and inserted it back onto the conveyor. Lights flashed, sirens shrilled, people dashed between moving vehicles and around other equipment.

This vivid scene of organized chaos thrilled me. It was the first business trip I'd taken that had allowed me, as an insider, to see a place and event closed to most people. Though I'd relied upon air delivery for years, it had never occurred to me to think about how it worked.

For three and a half hours, there was no break in the activity level or the speed. By four in the morning, all the planes had been fully loaded and were back in the air, and the facility went into hibernation for the next twenty hours.

SMARTASS

Emery owned the fleet of airplanes that used the Dayton hub for domestic deliveries. But it also did business internationally, using space on commercial carriers. American Airlines, Northwest, BOAC, Lufthansa, and others were indebted to Emery for their business. As a consequence, Emery employees flying any of those airlines were very well cared for. Our tickets were not just free; they were almost always first class.

On my first international business trip, Jim and I flew Lufthansa to Frankfurt in the front of the plane. For Jim, "flying first" wasn't a novelty; prior to joining Emery, he'd been an executive at American Airlines. But for me, first class had always been out of reach. On overseas flights for personal travel, I'd sometimes peeked into the business class cabin to see how the privileged flew, but I'd never even seen a first class cabin.

It was better than my best fantasy. Not only were the seats spacious, the flight attendants gracious, and the goody bags brimming with high-end lotions and potions, we also had a celebrity in our midst—Henry Kissinger. But, as I looked at my cabin-mates, I real-

ized I was the only female in first and the youngest by at least fifteen years. This pattern held true on most subsequent flights for at
least a decade; other than the occasional spouse, I was usually the
only woman in first class.

Emery handled a lot of freight going to Europe, but it couldn't
seem to convince businesses to use the company to ship goods to
the US. We'd spoken with the staff in the Frankfurt office prior to
our visit. They'd told us that while prices were very competitive, the
service excellent, and people they called on seemed interested, the
salespeople couldn't generate activity. My job was to conduct research to understand the reasons for this disparity and to help develop strategies to increase inbound US business.

As soon as Jim and I arrived at Emery's European headquarters
I asked to see all forms used by customers and all the local marketing materials. The European head of sales brought over a pile of
brochures and customs documents looking much like what the
company used in the States. I flipped through them and then said,
"I'd like to see everything, even if I can't read them."

"This is everything."

"But, but . . . it's all in English," I sputtered.

"Well, we work with American companies, so everything is in
English," he told me a bit peevishly.

I couldn't contain my astonishment and blurted, "You think
the guys in the shipping department speak fluent English? You
think they bring in expats to work in shipping?" I held up a three-
page customs document printed in a miniscule typeface. "Could
you fill this out in a language that wasn't yours?"

He gave me a blank stare.

I scanned the top page. "I mean, if you were German, what
would you make of . . ." I pointed to a line on the form, ". . . Any

agreement covering transportation of the goods described herein with other than due dispatch, or for specific time, must be endorsed on this bill of lading and signed by the parties hereto."

"Oh. Yeah. See what you mean." He scowled.

I read a few more convoluted, legalese sentences from the document.

"I get it. I get it."

Thirty minutes into my visit, I'd solved the problem we had traveled thousands of miles to address. But I hadn't endeared myself to my European counterparts. I had been too young and too inexperienced to be tactful. Jim, who had silently watched this exchange, later laughed and coached me on how I could have better handled the situation.

That evening, our hosts took Jim and me out for dinner to a local beer garden. At the time, I was not eating meat, which I explained to the head of the Frankfurt office. He promised he'd order for me, no problem. When our dinners were served, the waiters placed enormous plates heaped with a slab of roasted meat, mashed potatoes, and sauerkraut and other trimmings in front of Jim and the others. A few minutes later another waiter, with overly elaborate care that directed all attention to me, placed an equally large plate in front of me. In the center of it were two fried eggs surrounded by a lot of empty space. This was payback time.

FINDING TRUE LOVE: 1978

I'd returned to New York and worked as a marketing researcher for a few years when I met Bob. We'd been dating for nine months when he asked if I'd like to join him on a business trip to Colorado. He'd be in Denver for about a week, but if I came at the end for a long weekend, he'd rent a car and we could explore Boulder and do some hiking in the mountains. This was the first time Bob would travel out of town since we'd met. During that same period, I'd been on numerous business trips and gone to London to visit friends. He had refused invitations to travel with me, which I'd chalked up to it being too early in our relationship. When he asked me to join him, I was thrilled.

On my flight from New York to Denver, I began to think of myself as a jet-setter, a person who could hop on a plane for a long weekend jaunt. And, now that Bob and I would finally be traveling together, I fantasized about other places we could explore together. I would show him all my favorite London haunts. We could spend a weekend in Paris or Florence or on the Amalfi Coast. Maybe we would go even further and spend a couple of weeks in Asia, Australia, or South America.

When I arrived on Thursday night, we were both exhausted— me from flying to a different time zone after working all day, he from long hours at a dull conference. Neither the fluorescent-lit hotel coffee shop where we ate nor the utilitarian guest room decorated in faded orange and mud brown did much to enhance the mood. Bob flicked on the TV and, zombie-like, watched a talk show. I kissed him goodnight perfunctorily and passed out. Our first evening was as romantic as a visit to the accountant.

The next morning was sunny with a bright blue sky and, despite Denver's reputation for smog, clear. Tossing our bags into the trunk, we took off for Boulder. Hand in hand, we walked for hours through the University of Colorado campus and on a narrow path alongside the stream running through town. For a city boy, Bob knew a lot about plants and pointed out unusual ferns and flowers. We strolled around the farmers market, making a meal of abundant local wine, cheese, fruit, and bread samples. On the pedestrian mall, we poked around quaint boutiques and admired crafts and antiques. In the evening, Bob requested a bottle of my favorite wine. Our B and B oozed charm, every room filled with tasteful antiques, vases of flowers, and local artwork. We made good use of the very comfortable bed. I was finally fulfilling my image of a weekend traveling with my boyfriend.

On Saturday, Bob suggested we visit the remains of a mining community, now a ghost town. He was engaged by the history; I loved the crumbling, photogenic buildings. While we were ambling around the ruins, Bob told me he'd made a dinner reservation at a restaurant recommended by his colleagues. He promised I would love it. After the previous couple of guys I'd dated who relied on me to do all our planning, this made a welcome change.

The reservation was for six, which I thought a bit early. It made me think of visiting my grandmother in Miami Beach and going out for the early-bird special. But happy he'd arranged it, I didn't question the time. I dressed carefully, putting on a low-cut top, short skirt, and heels. Applying a little mascara, lipstick, and a dab of perfume, I was ready.

On the drive up the steep, twisting road leading to the restaurant, I alternated between admiring panoramas of the city that grew more expansive as we ascended the mountain and panicking we'd fall over the cliff—there were no guardrails.

From our table, the city of Boulder spread out far below us. The sky was enormous, with a pale moon edging its way over the horizon. As if on a timer perfectly tuned to setting the mood, the sky turned golden as we sipped wine. Over dinner, the stars blinked on, twinkling in the fading light.

Bob ordered buffalo rather than his usual beef. I read that as a sign of his openness to new things. When he placed a forkful in my mouth, I agreed it was delicious, not gamy as we'd both imagined.

After talking about what we'd seen that day, Bob told me more about his childhood and family. I realized our family histories had much in common. His father and mine had both served in the Pacific during World War II and had told similar stories about their experiences. Until that evening I'd told him little about my eccentric relatives. I was relieved when my stories amused rather than upset him.

As we were sipping coffee, a waiter whispered, "Quick, come to the parking lot, *now!*" We ran out just in time to see two massive black bears ambling across the pavement. I grabbed Bob's arm; what a treat!

Back at the B and B, we didn't get much sleep. I was falling in love. The whole day registered several notches above my best fantasies. I hoped this would be the first of many such adventures.

On the flight back to New York on Sunday morning, I wondered aloud, "Where should we go to next?"

"Maybe The Cloisters?"

Laughing, I replied, "I meant somewhere a bit more exotic than that." Bob said that while the weekend had been fun, "I'd be just as happy staying at home."

I was dumbfounded. How had we experienced the weekend so terribly differently? Turning in my seat to stare at him, I asked, "Didn't you like exploring?"

"Hell, I haven't seen three quarters of the neighborhoods in the city."

"Well, yes," I agreed. "But there aren't mountains like that in the city. And the restaurant . . ."

"It was nice, but there are lots of great restaurants in New York."

"Not with bears in the parking lot."

I grew increasingly despondent as Bob complained about packing, flights, and strange beds, and repeated he wasn't really interested in leaving New York. "You mean you don't want to travel at all?" I finally asked.

"Nope, not really."

I didn't know how to respond. Not wanting to travel was unimaginable to me. I dropped the subject—for the moment.

Over the next few months, we spent as much time together as we could, cooking dinner, visiting museums, going to movies and theater. And we talked endlessly. When I had problems with my boss, he patiently listened to my complaints. With his many years of business experience, he became a mentor, helping me to amicably resolve some difficult issues.

At every opportunity, I tried to persuade him to go somewhere, anywhere, with me. I made connections to his love of history, food, and theater. I embellished stories from my own travels so they might appeal to his interests. His response was always the same. Travel simply didn't interest him.

He met my family, and I met his. Trying to be casual about it, I grilled his mom, attempting to uncover any reasons why he was so anti-travel.

"When Bob was growing up, what did he do during the summer when school was out?"

She laughed. "He loved day camp, but after one summer at sleep-away he refused to ever go again."

"Any idea why?"

"Absolutely no clue, but he was adamant about it." She continued, "He loved our family vacations at the shore."

"Did you ever travel on vacation?"

"Not very much, never seemed to have the time. It's tough when you own a small business. But I sure would have loved to travel more." She smiled wistfully and continued, "Maybe when he retires."

From my perspective, nothing adequately explained Bob's lack of interest in travel. In my mind it meant I'd be able, with time and patience, to convince him how much fun seeing the world could be.

On each business trip I tacked on a couple of days so I could wander about new cities.

"I wish you wouldn't do that," Bob said after one extended business trip. "I miss you when you're away."

"So join me. It would be much more fun if you would." I explained that, for me, travel was like food and breathing—a necessity—and I was not about to give it up.

As always, he emphatically ended the conversation with the words "I really don't like to travel."

What had been a niggling annoyance grew into a source of

major friction between us. Despite his consistent refusals, I persisted in trying to change his mind. I felt like a harpy but couldn't help myself.

About six months after our Colorado trip, I told him I had two weeks of vacation and was planning to go to Mexico. I hoped he would join me, for any or all of it, but I was going whether he accompanied me or not. Bob chose not to come, and I ended up going with my friend Barbara.

We visited Mexico City and saw the archeological sites of Chichen Itza and Uxmal on the Yucatán. By chance we came upon a cloud of monarch butterflies during their annual migration, hundreds of thousands of them—bright orange grace in motion. We ventured into small towns to track down carpet weavers, potters, jewelers, and other craftspeople I'd read about. To all appearances I was having a good time, but inwardly I fumed it was Barbara, not Bob, traveling with me.

When we arrived on Cozumel (then, an untouched, perfect romantic island), my frustration and growing anger turned to action. I flirted with every cute guy I met. If Bob wouldn't join me, I'd still have a good time; maybe I'd even meet someone else. Someone who liked to travel. One guy spent a day snorkeling with me. Another took me on a ride around the island on his motorcycle. I abandoned Barbara to have drinks and dinners with the guys I'd met. This created some guilt but not enough to stop me. I rationalized that Barbara was a chain smoker who refused to stop even at meals, and I had the right to escape.

On the final day, while catching a few last rays of sun, I talked with a young American couple sprawled on nearby lounge chairs. They were from New Jersey. "What do you do?" I asked. She was a teacher; he, Dave, was a computer scientist.

"Really? So's my boyfriend."

"What does he do?" Dave asked.

"I've got to be honest, I'm not sure of the specifics. But he works in aerospace. I think it has to do with tracking systems."

"You're kidding! That's exactly what I do. What's his name?"

It turned out not only did Dave know Bob, but he worked two offices away, on the same project.

Uh-oh!

Back in New York, I told Bob about the trip, carefully omitting my flirtations on the beach. Once again, I told him how much I'd missed him and how the trip would have been a lot more fun with him, rather than with Barbara. "Maybe next time," he said non-committally.

A few days later, Bob mentioned he and Dave had spoken. "Dave told me you were seeing other guys there," he said. "It wasn't just Barbara you spent time with."

"It really wasn't anything. Just trying to get away from Barbara and her omnipresent smoking. If you'd been with me, I wouldn't have done that."

"But I'm probably not going to travel with you much, and I sure don't like the idea of you traveling if that's what's going to happen."

"So you won't go with me, and I'm not supposed to travel without you?" In frustration and with nothing left to say, I stormed out and slammed the door behind me.

For the next few weeks I stewed about the situation. I liked Bob a lot, maybe even loved him. But could I ever settle down with a man who didn't like to travel? One who didn't want me to travel? I tried to envision our future, my future.

After much introspection, I realized I was more passionate about travel than about Bob. I hoped I would meet someone else, someone who also loved to travel. But my curiosity and need for adventure could only be fulfilled by seeing the world. I knew my true love.

ON ICE: ALASKA, 1981

I had taken a job as a marketing researcher at American Express because it would look great on my résumé. But the corporation valued the bottom line far more than it valued any employee—one of their favorite descriptions for people was "fungible," a polite way of saying replaceable.

After two years, I was hoping to be fungible and decided if I did something outrageous they'd fire me. I'd collect unemployment insurance for a while and take a long, much-needed break before looking for another position.

Alaska had been on my radar for a few years. It seemed to be one of the least visited, most pristine place within the US. After poring through guidebooks and travel brochures, I found an affordable camping trip that leisurely meandered through the Yukon and Alaska and ended with a cruise down the Inside Passage. The tour lasted a full month, long enough, I hoped, to get me fired. If not, the trip would at least satisfy my need for an extended travel fix.

N o one at American Express took off for a month unless they were nearing death or had contracted something so contagious it threatened the entire workforce. If you were junior, you got two weeks. If you were an executive, you wouldn't dare take your full month for fear of being branded a slacker, or worse yet, no one even noticing you were gone. With that in mind, I blithely announced to my boss: "I've booked a trip to Alaska in June. I'll be gone for just over a month."

"You what?" my boss asked, disbelieving what she'd just heard. I repeated my intention.

"You can't do that."

"You don't need to pay for the extra vacation time," I said. "I'll be happy to take an unpaid leave of absence."

"But . . . but, you just can't!" she sputtered.

Just watch me, I thought. I pointed out I was planning far enough in advance to make sure my peers would be up to speed on all of my projects before I departed and assured her everything would go smoothly in my absence. Eventually she understood I wasn't asking for permission; I intended to take this trip no matter what. Employees had been leaving her department in droves for months, which reflected poorly on her. Hoping to stanch the flow, she agreed that if human resources approved my plan, she'd okay it too. She made me swear I would stay for six months on my return. I swore.

Human resources had no idea what to do about this request. They'd never heard of anyone doing anything like this. I repeated that in addition to my regular vacation, I would take two weeks without pay. Then I pointed out the section in the employee handbook permitting, with a supervisor's permission, up to three months of unpaid leave. They reluctantly agreed to see what they could do. After getting approval from at least six different levels of management, they gave my plan their blessing.

My leave arranged, I started packing. The list of required items was daunting, especially since travelers were allowed exactly one medium-size duffel bag and one daypack. Had this luggage been exclusively for clothing, toiletries, and the usual bits and pieces, it would have been easy. But the recommended minimum necessities included a sleeping bag suitable for temperatures to minus thirty degrees, a down vest, hiking boots, a heavy sweater, gloves, at least three spray cans of bug repellant, and nearly as much sunscreen. The tour company also reminded participants to bring a passport and to check into visa requirements. This final instruction seemed a bit odd, but as I was working long hours and exhausted, I didn't consider the implications.

When I first signed up, the trip looked like many of the adventure trips I'd read about—camping, hiking, and touring. The photographs showed smiling tourists about my age hiking on scenic trails with snow-covered mountains in the distance, camping by a pristine lake, and roasting marshmallows over a blazing fire. Nothing about the brochure gave the slightest hint the company catered almost exclusively to Europeans. When I met up with my travel companions in Vancouver, I was the only American in a group of ten. That explained the mention of passports and visas.

The first evening we met for dinner to "meet and greet." Our group was comprised of eight tourists, a driver, and a guide. Thirty years later, the names and faces of our Canadian guide and driver have been erased from my memory, but I clearly remember my first impressions of my fellow travelers.

In addition to me, there were two women. One was a national security police officer from Holland in superb physical shape with an expression that screamed, "Don't mess with me!" I was certain she could single-handedly apprehend the most violent of criminals with ease. The other woman was Australian and the antithesis of the cop. Pasty and out of shape, she looked as if she'd spent the previous year in the deepest recesses of a dank saloon. She drank too much that night and, as it turned out, every subsequent one.

The five men included two Germans, who both immediately latched onto Ms. Aussie. The threesome slipped out early from dinner to stock up on booze, wanting to be certain they'd have sufficient supplies of whiskey and gin when we left for the wilderness early the next morning. The threesome spent much of the trip in a semi-stupor. Two friends from the Netherlands were inseparable and the least likely pair imaginable. One guy was short, rail thin, and wimpy, with the charisma of a potato. His buddy was at least six foot six, well muscled, and talked nonstop. In addition to the required gear, he'd brought along a set of weights that he used religiously. The final member of our group was a Frenchman. I watched him observing the group; his scowling suggested his reaction to the prospect of spending four weeks in the wilds with this crew. The bland, tasteless food we'd been served for dinner put him in a foul mood, and he stomped off to buy edible provisions.

This ragamuffin group bonded during endless hours in the van. We were surprisingly tolerant of each other's quirks, and there were many.

On the second day of the trip, the scrawny Dutchman purchased a ten-gallon hat. Since there was nowhere to stow it, and this was to be his prized souvenir, he wore it constantly, still encased in its protective covering. The plastic-wrapped hat was the nearest thing to wearing a "kick me" sign pinned to his back. His buddy was enamored of huge trucks. He constantly pleaded with our van driver to stop so he could take a photo of an especially large or flashy vehicle. I think he went home with twenty rolls of pictures of trucks, dotted with a stray photo of the landscape and wildlife.

The Frenchman, perhaps because he wasn't able to get food that satisfied him, went into sexual predator mode, particularly toward the cop. He was fascinated that she was licensed to carry a gun, and this information was prominently printed in her passport.

"Can you really carry a gun across borders?" he'd ask over and over.

"Yes, and if you don't stop asking me, I'll buy one here and use it. On you."

"Ooh la la, I love the way you talk dirty," he crooned, with a sweet smile that helped to soften the words.

"I'm also a black belt in judo; I don't need a gun. Just back off," she'd snap with just enough of an edge to make it clear she wasn't kidding. This exchange went on day and night for the entire trip. He got nowhere. She made sure he never got into her tent. Away from him, she and I chuckled conspiratorially about his attempts.

While the human company wasn't ideal, I was awed by the snowcapped Canadian Rockies: fields of wildflower-covered tundra; bears, moose, and elk wandering across meadows; and star-studded skies undimmed by man-made light. Experiencing this beauty in the company of foreigners added another dimension. All were well traveled, but apart from the Aussie, none had ever seen such broad, unpopulated expanses of land. I'd been in the West many times. Seeing this landscape through their eyes was like seeing it again for the first time. The farther north we traveled, the greater their astonishment. At times, while we stood admiring the wilderness, the group would settle into hushed reverence.

As the trip progressed, the days stretched longer. Sleeping in tents became more difficult, even with eyeshades; the dark of night lasted only a couple of hours. After a few days of insomnia caused by the white nights, we all became crazed from lack of sleep. We bickered and laughed, cried and screamed for no reason. People would fall asleep mid-sentence. English would slide into Dutch or German and from there descend into gibberish.

Summer solstice coincided with the northernmost point of our journey. At about one in the morning, we watched the sun sink into the horizon. Then, before disappearing completely, it began to reemerge. The cycle of sunset and sunrise happened within about five minutes. In total, there had been about thirty minutes of twilight.

Crazy making as the constant daylight was, I knew if I were ever to return in December, the interminable darkness would make me suicidal. I wondered how anyone survived the long northern winters. Wandering through a small village one day, I got into conversation with a local. "How do people manage?" I asked.

"We sleep a lot."

"Well sure, but how much can you possibly sleep?"

"When we're not sleeping, we're drinking." He smiled broadly. "That's about it."

"Oh, come on, you must do *something,*" I pressed him, not believing they didn't do anything productive for months on end.

"Lots of babies arrive late summer." He paused. "Once there's even a couple of hours of light, we do go out. But really, we kind of go into hibernation."

That clinched it: the far north was not for me.

We often camped far out in the wilderness. The plus was being in spectacular, unspoiled places, but it was difficult because we lacked most amenities. There were no showers; whenever we set up camp near a stream or lake, we'd all take a plunge into icy water. Despite gallons of bug repellent, mosquitoes the size of hummingbirds tortured us. The constant threat of grizzly bears required extraordinary measures to prevent any ursine raiding of our campsite. Disposing of trash and human waste was always a problem. It isn't possible to dig pit toilets in the tundra, and the unique methods our guide employed to keep our campsite clean, like sprinkling a sparse shovelful of surface dirt over the toilet area periodically, wouldn't pass current standards of environmentalism.

Denali National Park was a highlight of the trip, but we were scheduled to stay for only two days and then head to Anchorage. The cop and I had little interest in being in a city, so we peeled off from the group, telling the guide we'd stay at the park campground for a couple extra days, then take a train and meet them.

Mt. McKinley's summit, as is usually the case, was shrouded by clouds: for three days we never caught even a peek. We hiked, took guided ranger walks, and luxuriated in the campsite's hot showers and being apart from the rest of the group. On our last day, we were deep in the park, in an area accessed only by bus service provided by the rangers. The clouds had played peekaboo with the mountain all day, providing tantalizing glimpses, but we hadn't had a clear view.

As evening approached and only two return shuttles remained, we had to make a decision: wait at the visitor center in hopes of a break in the clouds and take the last bus or assume we wouldn't get a clear view and take the earlier bus. We opted to leave earlier. As our bus neared the campsite, a stream of police cars and ambulances with sirens screaming and lights flashing sped past us, heading in the direction we'd come from.

Later, we learned the bus behind us had pulled over so passengers could have a clear view of a mother bear and her cubs. The ground beneath the vehicle had given way, and it rolled down a steep slope. Two of the passengers were killed, everyone else seriously injured. The information shocked me. For many weeks I could not escape thinking about the fragility of life and my own mortality. It was the first time (but not the last) pure chance saved me from disaster.

The group heard about the bus accident. It was headline news all over Alaska, and they were terrified we'd been among those killed. When we rejoined them, the group's relief was palpable, and we received a hero's welcome.

The final leg of our journey was on board the Alaskan state ferry, which we boarded in Haines. True to the tour's ambiance, we didn't have cabins. Instead, we pitched our tents on deck, along with dozens of other young adventurers. From the minute we boarded, a raucous party atmosphere reigned. Now, not only did the sunlight impede my sleep, but the sounds of drunken revelers ensured I'd spend five days fighting for catnaps and struggling to stay awake. I was torn between wanting to quietly soak in the natural beauty and join in the party.

When someone spotted a massive blue iceberg floating past the boat, or a pod of playful seals swam alongside us, everyone gathered near the railing. Periodically we would hear a sound like gunshots or thunder, and a massive chunk of ice would fall from high on a glacier and crash into the sea, creating an explosion of water and a huge wave. We all hooted and clapped.

When the ferry docked in Fairbanks, I made my one splurge of the trip, a sightseeing flight over the glaciers. The view from the six-seater plane was a pristine crazy quilt of intense blues and greens, stitched together with black ridges. There wasn't a sign of human activity. I'd expected to see a lot of white, so I was surprised and captivated by the patterns and expansive range of subtle colors that went far beyond anything I'd ever seen, even from the best of artists. As the flight progressed, I experienced a near out-of-body state, feeling as though I'd left Earth and traveled to another planet. I was mesmerized; the one-hour flight felt as though it ended almost immediately after we took off.

The ferry made its way down the Washington State coast on July Fourth. As the sky darkened, everyone gathered on deck to view the fireworks blazing in one small town after another, culminating in a huge display as we docked in Seattle. It felt like a personal welcome home.

Postscript: When I returned to American Express, they paid me for the extra two weeks—no one in accounting could figure out how to suspend my paycheck. And those high up the chain of command had been impressed by my gutsiness in demanding such extravagant leave: one month later, I received a huge promotion and a raise. I stayed for the six months I'd promised, then left the company.

HER FINAL GIFT:
PUERTO RICO, 1982

I associate many of my major life events with travel. Travel has been a way to celebrate birthdays, new jobs, and other milestones. I've rewarded myself for hard work by taking off to far away destinations for rest and revitalization. After relationship breakups and other disappointments, visiting less developed countries helped me to put things into perspective and remind me of all I have. However, the confluence of travel and major life events hasn't always been by my choosing.

I was between jobs—leaving American Express and heading to Emery Air Freight to become director of marketing research. It was a perfect opportunity to take time off from working and satisfy my growing thirst for travel. First, my boyfriend and I went to Hawaii, for recuperative sunshine in the middle of winter. Then, a friend and I toured Spain. The week before I was to head up to Connecticut to start the new job, my mom and I flew to Puerto Rico.

The destination had been her choice—a direct, affordable flight, she'd said. Though part of the US, it seemed foreign enough without really being foreign. Wrapped up in my own job and life, I didn't question her reasons. Being thirty will do that to you. I later realized she wanted to be sure she could get emergency medical help if she needed it.

Mom had been ill for a long time, really my whole life. She had type 1 diabetes, and I can't remember a time when she hadn't been insulin dependent. She'd also battled every possible incapacitating side effect. She'd been diagnosed with the disease during her pregnancy with my brother Roy, though I suspect she'd been living with it for longer than that. Between Roy's and my birth, she'd had two miscarriages. Even though she knew it was risky, she'd been determined to have one more child—she wanted a daughter.

Despite her illness, she had loved going to new places and having adventures. When I offered her the opportunity to travel with me, she jumped at it.

Traveling to San Juan proved a real strain on her. Getting through the airport seemed to take forever as we walked at a painfully slow pace. After a few minutes she asked to sit down and rest, and then popped a couple of the nitroglycerin pills she always kept handy. She'd developed heart problems but had refused to have bypass surgery, even though her father had died of a massive heart attack at fifty-seven. I think the fact that she'd lived longer than he had—she was sixty-four when she'd been informed of her heart issues—made her feel as though she'd somehow eluded the disease. Two years before she'd been told of the need for a bypass, she'd had major eye surgery for diabetic macular edema. Her sight had been restored, but the recuperation had taken a huge toll, and she couldn't face going through such pain again. Despite my family imploring her to at least consider surgery, she had told us and the doctors flat out she wouldn't do it.

When we arrived at the hotel, she revived a bit. The pastel-colored cabanas, warm breeze, and endless white beach against the turquoise sea fulfilled our desires for a tropical resort. Sitting at an outdoor table shaded by a large umbrella, we ate salads and drank iced tea. I noticed she was having difficulty swallowing food. She chewed each small morsel for a very long time. Occasionally, she'd stop to cough and clear her throat. My throat went dry as I watched her struggle to swallow and catch her breath. Between bites we talked. I had been busy with work and was living in New York City, so I only saw her once every couple of weeks, though we spoke frequently on the phone. When we did get together, there always seemed to be other people around.

Now she talked about my father and brothers and told me stories about when she was in her twenties, living in Greenwich Village while she attended Cooper Union in pursuit of an architecture degree. She'd been quite the bohemian in the 1930s. She'd lost her virginity at age sixteen and could remember every detail of her tryst with the curly-haired boy who'd been the first of her lovers. We sat for hours, barely moving as the stories kept coming. I heard tales about my leftist grandfather, who'd died the year before I was born. As she spoke, I noticed urgency in her telling of these stories, though she was clearly becoming increasingly tired. Leaving most of the food on her plate, she finally said she needed a nap. The short distance to the elevator and from the elevator to the room required two rest breaks and more nitro pills.

I knew, deep in my soul, my mother was dying, and not as in "We'll all die someday." Her death would be soon. My mother had taught me to be an atheist. But I began to pray. I prayed she wouldn't die in Puerto Rico.

The nap revived her a bit, so we made plans with the concierge for an island tour the next day. We'd see Morro Castle, some isolated beaches, and the rain forest. I had no idea how my mother would manage this, but she insisted she'd be fine.

I vaguely remember only bits of the day, but etched in my memory was my mother's delight in seeing the rain forest. She'd never been in one before and grinned like a small child on Christmas morning as we drove up the damp verdant road into thick vegetation. She urged me to go with the group for a hike through the forest while she remained on the bus. Torn between wanting to see the rain forest and worrying about her, I left with the group only after I realized she had become friends with the bus driver. He assured me he would watch over her. As I meandered down the path, I heard her directing him to bring her sample leaves and flowers so she could examine them closely.

That evening, after yet another long nap and what seemed to be an increasing frequency in her swallowing nitro pills, we set off for a nearby restaurant. Purported to serve some of the best local seafood, the menu was full of surprises. My mom insisted on ordering a vast quantity of food, even though she couldn't swallow and I'd lost my appetite. She wanted to taste everything. She'd never eaten snails, so we requested a plate of snails in garlic and butter. We both hated it but told each other at least we'd tried. Ceviche came next, followed by grouper and baby octopus—all tastes we loved. And, of course, we ate rice and beans. The waiter seemed to sense this was a special occasion for us. He hovered just enough to be able to answer my mother's questions about ingredients and preparation yet was discreet enough to stay far away when we were deep in conversation.

My mother, once again, told me stories I'd never heard before. I learned details about her parents, cousins, aunts, and uncles. About when my brothers were small children. About when I was an infant. I finally got the courage to ask, "Mom, why are you telling me all of this now?"

"I don't have much time left, and you should know these things."

"What are you talking about?" I asked, though I knew exactly what she was saying.

"I'm dying. Surely you can see that. But don't worry, everything will be okay. You'll be okay."

I held back the tears welling up.

"It's okay," she said. "I'm not scared. I had a good life, and it's my time to go."

Now I was openly sobbing while she explained what she'd done to make sure everything was in order. Then she made me promise to do whatever it took to keep the family together. And, most importantly, she told me I must live my life in a way that would make me happy. "Do not compromise; do not do what others want. That's my one regret. I love you and your brothers, but I shouldn't have married your father."

While I knew what she meant—they'd had a rough marriage— I couldn't respond.

A taxi drove us the four blocks back to the hotel. My mother was so worn out she didn't even attempt to walk them, even after popping nitro like peanuts. With some help, I managed to get her to the room and into bed. Then I went down to the concierge and had him change our flight so we would return to New York the next day. I didn't know if she'd make it home.

We arrived home without a problem. Two days after we returned, my mother had a massive heart attack. She went quickly and, as I was repeatedly reassured, painlessly.

I've been asked if I think people can determine when they die; I always answer yes. Through many months of tears, I reflected that my mother had willed herself to hold on so we could have some final time together. It was a gift she gave me, and herself. She showed me how to live every minute fully. She taught me how to leave life with grace.

CLIMBING: TANZANIA, 1983

Ever since I was a small child and first visited the Bronx Zoo, I had wanted to see elephants, giraffes, and lions in the wild. A trip to Africa was a necessity.

When my friend Diane and I discussed possible trips, we agreed that our destination should be as far from the usual tourist routes as possible. Her vision included climbing Kilimanjaro, the highest mountain on the African continent.

Climbing Kili had never been part of my fantasies of an African adventure, and I was hesitant; at over nineteen thousand feet, Kili isn't in the same class as Everest (over twenty-nine thousand feet) but is still challenging compared to any mountain I'd previously tackled.

After Diane assured me Kili doesn't require technical climbing, I said, "Sure, why not?" I like to hike.

P rior to planning for this trip, I knew almost nothing about Tanzania. Beyond the fact that it was in Africa, I didn't have a clue as to its location. The terrain, weather, culture, and nearly everything else about the country were a mystery to me. Inquisitive by nature, a market researcher by profession, and believing books never give the whole story, I asked everyone what they knew about Tanzania and

Kili. Besides, I was excited. The pending trip to Africa was such a thrill, I had to share my plans with everyone.

More people have trekked on Kilimanjaro than one would imagine. Within a couple of weeks, I learned of a colleague, a client, and a friend who'd made the climb. The colleague described the trip in a mystical way. His eyes were aglitter as he rambled on in rapturous terms about the inner peace it brought and his sense of well-being. His main refrain, "It's a high," didn't mean "high" in the altitude sense. Though I loved his enthusiasm, what I really wanted were practicalities about the climb; he never said a word about that.

A friend was a bit more prosaic; he told me the climb takes five days, and the base camp is covered in flowers. But when I tried to wheedle out nitty-gritty information, he drifted into blissful reveries. What I wanted to know was how hard is the climb? Do they have oxygen at the top, just in case? What do you have to carry with you? What happens if you don't make it? What's the food like?

My client, Sue, provided the rapturous look I'd come to expect plus more practical details. Her first warning was, "It's freezing cold on the top. Bring the warmest clothes you have. Don't forget thermal underwear, down vests, insulated socks and gloves, a hat, and earmuffs." She shivered in remembrance. "Think bitter cold day in January on the riverfront with a stiff wind blowing."

Tanzania is on the equator; freezing cold hadn't even occurred to me. My failure to recognize that Kilimanjaro's altitude negated its location proved I wasn't quite the experienced traveler I imagined myself to be.

Her next comment concerned the food. "It's lousy." She suggested I bring at least a dozen rolls of Life Savers.

She assured me sherpas would carry all our gear, and we'd only need a day pack with our immediate necessities. That sounded good. Then she mentioned how important it is to go slowly because of the altitude. "It was tough for me to breathe whenever I walked at even a normal pace." I figured that would be fine; I had every intention of a slow trek. Then I gulped. Sue ran marathons. If she had gone slowly, snails would be rushing past me.

Then the killer comment: "If you can't make the last few steep feet at the top, the sherpas will get behind you and push."

I would not suffer that indignity. Although at thirty-two, I was physically fit and worked out regularly, a few days after we spoke, I ramped up my exercise schedule. I began a strict regimen of swimming and walking. Frantically. Fanatically. When not at work, my waking hours were consumed by exercising. I swam a mile in the morning, walked several miles at noon, and ended the day back in the pool. When determined, I get crazed.

As the trip drew near, I read the list of suggested items sent by the tour company. I, who normally travel with one small carry-on bag, would be bringing enough stuff for the entire population of a small town—summer clothes for the safari, cold weather gear for the mountain, boots, sneakers, a zillion rolls of Life Savers, bug goo, sun goo, medication for every conceivable ailment, toilet paper, a collection of camera gear, extra glasses, hats, pens, pads, books.

Two days before departure, a telegram arrived from the tour company. The tour leaders had sent a list of items unavailable in Tanzania. They requested we bring as much as we could carry for use on the trip, including cans of tuna, yeast, pepper, sardines, hard salami, Bacitracin, tissues. By the time I left for the airport, my duffel bag looked nine months pregnant. Fortunately, all that exercise had paid off. I'd never been in such good shape. I was fit and ready for Kili. My proof: I could lift my two-ton non-rolling duffel.

In 1983, the border between Kenya and Tanzania was closed.

But Murphy's Law or scheduling stupidity determined that our flight stopped first in Nairobi. To make the flight acceptable to government authorities, we had to fly from Kenya to Rwanda before landing in Tanzania. In Rwanda, officials ordered everyone off the plane. Two hundred of us walked to a compact hut with no air-conditioning. A few lucky people snagged a seat on splintered benches. The rest of us stood, and then sank onto the filthy floor while we waited for a change of flight crews. Fatigue, crying babies, heat, and the crush of people made me reconsider whether this trip was such a good idea. I fixated on Kilimanjaro and wondered if I'd make it to the top. Two hours later we reboarded the plane, now with a new flight number, and proceeded to Arusha in Tanzania.

It is almost impossible to stay in shape while on a tented photo safari—a detail I'd never considered. When camping in the middle of a game preserve, you don't go for a casual stroll. In the middle of one night we heard a terrific noise—a lioness killing a buffalo about two hundred yards from our camp. Another evening, an elephant nearly walked through the cook tent. The local baboons thought it great fun to rip apart any gear they found lying around.

Diane and I were the only ones planning to climb Kilimanjaro; the other six had come to Africa just for the wildlife. On morning and evening drives through the Serengeti and Ngorongoro Crater all of us learned to be totally silent as we peered at packs of lions lounging, hyenas drinking at the rim of a lake, and zebra and dik-diks (small antelope) strolling across a grassy plain. One woman, a fanatic birder, spent most of her time training her binoculars on lilac-breasted rollers and red-and-yellow barbets while the rest of us thrilled to see hippos and elephants.

Midday, in the intense heat, Diane and I would do jumping jacks while our travel companions relaxed and kibitzed, commenting, "You're out of your minds." But no matter how much they teased about our fitness program, "They'll push you up the mountain" echoed in my mind, and I kept going.

Our overland camping trip in Tanzania took us deep into Maasai territory. For six hours, our Land Rover plodded through bathtub-sized potholes, bounced over washboard ruts, and created dust storms in its wake. My fellow tourists, the guides, driver, and I all covered our noses and mouths with bandanas, which made the hot air even more oppressive. But that was the only way to breathe. As rivulets of sweat mixed with the dust, I began to feel encased in a full-body mudpack. I wasn't surprised to hear very few tourists visited the area.

When our group of eight arrived at the tour company's compound—two small, unadorned whitewashed buildings and an outhouse—we dumped our belongings, changed into bathing suits, and ran for the river to scrub off the grime. Our guides told us to be careful to not let any water enter our mouths, as the river was rife with giardia. They warned, "In the mildest form you'll get severe abdominal cramps and nausea. In severe cases it can cause death." And, they added, "Watch out for snakes; there are water moccasins. But don't worry, we haven't lost anyone yet."

We hesitated, just for a moment, and waded in.

Luxuriating in the cool, quickly flowing water, we soaped up and splashed each other while tightly keeping our mouths shut and maintaining a watchful eye for snakes. It took us a while to notice we had human company. Standing on shore were five young Maasai men. At least six feet tall and rail thin, their bodies painted in ocher-and-white patterns, they wore only loincloths and beaded necklaces. The long spears they clutched were somewhat alarming. An offense being the best defense, we smiled, waved, and called out hello. At first we got no response; they simply stared, no doubt as surprised by us as we were by them. For many long minutes they watched us, confused by what they were seeing. Then, as we continued to wave and smile, one young man's face broke out into a broad grin, and he waved back at us.

One of the warriors stared more intently than the others, seemingly both baffled and intrigued. Handing his spear to a friend and whispering something in his ear, he inched his way into the river, combing his hands through the flowing water. When he was waist-deep he pointed to the soap. Receiving the slippery bar, he examined it. We demonstrated, rubbing the bar up and down our arms until it foamed, then rinsing the soap off. Imitating what he had just watched, he began to soap up. The red ocher foamed pink, then bled off his body, making the river look like a crime scene. He stared at the pink bubbles, then laughed, delighted by this new sensation.

Next he pointed to the shampoo—he was going to try the whole experience. He'd been carefully observing us and immediately dumped about half a bottle on his hair and began to massage it in. Bright red soap bubbles grew around his head. On shore, his friends began to howl with laughter. He ducked under the water and burst up, the red bubbles clustering around his body, then rushing downstream like a flock of small birds.

His hair was still covered in shampoo and bubbles, and he began to look alarmed. The ocher, we realized, was mixed with fat or oil to make it stay in place. The more he rubbed, the more red bubbles he created. On shore, his friends continued to laugh, stamping their feet and banging their spears into the ground. We stayed with him in the river, concerned that if we stranded him, no good would come of it. By the time he'd successfully rinsed his hair, we were blue with cold and he'd been transformed into a very ordinary-looking teenager.

The next day, the young men came back, this time accompanied by what must have been half of their small village—twenty people or so. We spent the morning examining each other. The young women were adorned with intricate bead-and-wire earrings and necklaces. The flat metal-and-bead crescents around their necks moved rhythmically when they danced. I took out a drawing pad and drew a sketch of my house. One brave young woman shyly asked for the pad and pencil, and then drew a picture of her home, complete with wooden enclosure surrounding her compound.

We brought out cameras, but they waved us away, covering their faces—they didn't want their photos taken. That was until we offered to barter. The tour company had suggested we bring things to trade, and we'd all come prepared. We gave them T-shirts, mini-flashlights, bandanas, and whatever else we could scrape together. In exchange, we took photos and received beaded earrings.

The young men from the river, now our friends, were excited about the T-shirts. At the first opportunity they slipped them on and proudly showed them off. My favorite image of the day is our Maasai friend from the river, his ocher body paint restored, his fist tightly wrapped around his spear, wearing a T-shirt that read, "When God made man, She was only kidding."

After two and a half weeks on safari, Diane and I arrived at Kilimanjaro's base camp. On our way there, we got our first look at Kili. Majestic and snowcapped, it rose high above the hot, dry landscape. It's a very large mountain. Fear bubbled up. I pushed it down. There was no turning back.

The jumping off place for the climb was a hotel remaining from British rule. In the formal garden, roses grew next to native poinsettia trees. High tea, complete with cucumber sandwiches and ginger biscuits on porcelain plates, was served each afternoon. The place exuded well-worn gentility. Everyone was terribly polite.

After checking in, the desk clerk told us to relax, rest, and come by at four to get the gear we would need. At five we would have an "official" greeting and an explanation of what would happen over the next five days. We were instructed to dress for dinner, though that merely meant clean clothes.

Despite the veneer of British niceties, we were still in Africa; only a trickle of brown-tinged water came from the faucet. So much for clean clothes.

When we reported to the equipment shed, a weathered man handed us a list of needed items. We scanned the list. Most of the clothing we'd brought with us, but we hadn't known about several items or they'd been too bulky to pack, like a smaller duffel. The room he led us into looked as though it had been ransacked by incompetent thieves: gear strewn about randomly, piles of unmatched boots and socks. What had happened to that oh-so-important British order? He grabbed duffel bags off one of the tallest piles and tossed them to us. He explained sherpas would carry the duffels, and our luggage would remain at the hotel. Then he left us to sort through the equipment and find what we needed. The duffel he'd tossed me had so many holes I feared it would leak my possessions all the way up the mountain.

Looking for what we needed reminded us of pawing through the leftovers of a rummage sale. Most items appeared to be British army surplus from World War II. We had a lot of the required items, so we didn't need to decide which of the dirty, patched, threadbare woolen socks, gloves, and hats to take. I found a heavy brown parka to cover all my layers. With a down vest, turtleneck, and sweater under it, I resembled a bear.

After examining and trying on several woolen over-pants, I narrowed my choices to two. One pair fit well with nothing under them, but another traveler picking through the same pile assured me I'd freeze if I wore them. My second option was baggy royal-blue knickers. I opted for the knickers, though even with tights and jeans under them, I needed a belt cinched tight to keep them from sliding down to my knees. Diane's selections were equally awful. Tall and thin, she had a choice between well-fitting but too-short clothes or the right-length items but too large. In a photo of us in our hiking ensembles, we resemble a pair of circus clowns complete with goofy grins.

The most important article of gear was a walking stick. Staff helped us pick the perfect height from the extensive collection.

At five o'clock, we joined a group of thirty people in the day parlor for our official introduction, given by a woman in her early eighties. After welcoming us, she said she'd been up Kili more than thirty times, most recently the year before. This was encouraging; if she could do it, so could I. Gracious and forthright, she described the five days and showed us the route on a map. Then we practiced using the walking stick—grab it mid-length on the way up the mountain, and at the knob on top for the way down. Her most essential piece of advice: go slowly. About every third sentence she repeated this information. She told us to go slow from the beginning of the climb—even on the easy parts. The word in Swahili, which she assured us we would hear frequently, is *poli*. "*Poli, poli, poli*. That's how to get to the top." It became a kind of mantra.

Dinnertime arrived. In a glance, I picked out who would start the climb the next day and who'd just come down. Those going up exuded nervous energy, chattering away and trying to find out from those who'd come down what the experience had been like. The expression on the ones just down I recognized. It was the same as what I'd seen on my friend's face when he talked about the trip back in New York—rapturous and high. They didn't say much, just smiled sagely.

The next morning, day one of our climb, we met our hiking companions: four Italian doctors from Sardinia—Mario, Marco, Franco, and Isabella. They all spoke a few words of English. Diane and I did not speak Italian, unless you consider ciao, pizza, pasta, basta, espresso, and *cara mia* speaking Italian. Despite our language incompatibility, we communicated well. Within a few minutes, we got on famously; they began to teach us Italian as we taught them English, using inventive sound effects and charades.

Our guide and sherpas introduced themselves. Short and stocky, the guide had a gold front tooth and a huge smile. In broken English, he re-explained the trek and uttered the first of many "*poli, poli*" we would hear over the next five days.

The first day, we hiked in shorts and T-shirts. The hike starts at an elevation of about six thousand feet through lush rain forest. Though uphill for six hours, the trail wasn't steep. In fact, the hike was relatively easy. We walked at a comfortable pace, passed several times by locals running on the trail. As we climbed higher, the landscape became less verdant. It also got colder as the day progressed; by the time we reached the first huts, we'd climbed over three thousand feet to an elevation of nine thousand feet.

We arrived at the huts in the late afternoon. After exploring the area, we settled in and got to know each other. Franco took his pulse and let out a long low whistle to demonstrate what he heard. Diane's pulse elicited a slow *chi-chi-chi-chi-chi* like a train pulling into a station. Mine got the sound you make when you slap your thighs trying to imitate a horse trotting. These nonthreatening sounds made us giggle.

Dinner came, served on linen tablecloths with linen napkins. Nothing matched, but we thought it a classy touch. The food was edible, but just barely: a starchy, mushy stew. As Mario, Marco, Franco, and Isabella first saw and then tasted the food, distress and revulsion crossed their faces. They struggled to swallow the taste-less but necessary sustenance. At nightfall, the temperature dropped sharply, and we all snuggled in our sleeping bags, exhausted.

The second day started early. After breakfast we again walked through rain forest. A couple of hours after we started, the sherpas came from behind, passed us, and were quickly out of sight. They'd left the cabins long after we did, as they had to clean up from our breakfast, eat their own, and repack everything. We figured they'd left at least an hour after we did. They'd covered the same territory in half the time while carrying all the gear. Most were barefoot. Even at this lower altitude, we weren't moving fast.

Midmorning, we passed through an area of scrubby brush and dense fog. An hour later, we emerged into clear, clean open air. With a start, I realized we had just walked through a layer of clouds. We were now hiking above the clouds. The air was thinner and breathing more difficult. *Poli, poli, poli* became a constant theme. But really, there was no choice except to go slowly. Diane and I didn't speak much; our conversations were limited to exchanges like:

"If we walk for twenty minutes without stopping, we can have a Life Saver."

"How about fifteen minutes?"

"Sold."

At lunch break, it was time to take pulses. Franco now made

sounds like a small motor racing: *mmm-mmm-mmm*, or in one case, like a watch gone berserk: *ticka-ticka-ticka-ticka*. The sounds were a bit unnerving.

We trudged on a well-worn path through thinning vegetation. The higher we climbed, the scragglier the plant life. By late afternoon, we arrived at the second set of huts. On Kilimanjaro, at 12,500 feet, we should have been in the middle of nowhere. Instead, a cluster of A-frame cabins spread across the landscape. The air had become much colder. We layered sweaters and vests.

Huddled in a cabin, we ate dinner. The linen napkins became a running joke. It was obvious we would have the same napkin, unwashed, at every meal. We made a big deal about getting "our" napkin. The varying patterns, shapes, and holes made it easy to sort them. By the second day, we made a small ritual of presenting the napkins and pouring tea. We also had running contests guessing what would be for dinner—spaghetti alfredo, linguini *alla nonna*, eggplant parmigiana, cannolis. We always lost: every meal was an unappetizing stew of mysterious ingredients, but just thinking about real food cheered us up.

These huts are the crossroads where people ascending and descending the "tourist" route sleep, and where technical climbers stop before leaving for more difficult ascents. The communal room, large enough to hold seventy or eighty people, was like the UN. People from across the globe climb Kili, and they were chattering in dozens of languages.

Franco, taking our pulses, now made sounds resembling a train at full speed. We pleaded with him not to demonstrate how fast our hearts were racing; it was unsettling. But he persisted, and his sound effects got ever more inventive.

Several people told us about the gorgeous sunsets. We bundled up and went to the courtyard to look. As the day neared its end, I watched the sun sink down into the clouds, not into the horizon. All around us, the layer of white fluffy clouds was luminous red and gold. The colors shimmered and gradually deepened into darker crimson and purples. Then, as if a switch had flipped, it went black. Within minutes, the sky was awash in stars, more than I'd ever seen.

Day three was endless, cold, and unnerving. In the morning, we walked through the last of the scrub and came onto what looked like a moonscape—large stones, soft sand, and no vegetation. For three or four hours, we plodded along with little to see. Dust kicked up all around. At this altitude, with the clouds below, moisture was scarce. The air became thinner, our pace slower and slower. Short of breath, we didn't talk much. Life Saver breaks came more frequently. I never appreciated the name "Life Saver" quite so much.

Walking sticks became important. Until then I'd been swinging or dragging it along. Now I leaned on it, grateful to have something to rest against.

At lunch we got our first glimpse of that day's destination, the cabins at 15,500 feet. We cheered up, as they didn't look very far away—we'd probably be there in an hour or two. But, Kafkaesque, for the next four hours, the cabins didn't seem to get any closer. We walked and walked, the effects of the altitude making us a little headachy and nauseated. The destination stayed far away, elusive. We became discouraged, but there was no choice—just put one foot in front of the other, ever so slowly—*poli, poli*. The trail is not steep; it is a mild, steady incline, but at that altitude we might have been scaling a cliff.

At long last we arrived at the huts, exhausted. The thermometer outside the building showed thirty-three degrees. Inside was only marginally warmer. Without saying a word, each of us rolled out our sleeping bag and climbed in.

Although my head was propped on my daypack, I could have sworn my feet were higher than my head. Blood rushed into my head, and an excruciating headache settled in. Totally exhausted, I was sound asleep by four thirty in the afternoon.

At midnight, the guide woke us to eat and get ready for the final ascent. Our dinner/breakfast was *ugali* (maize gruel) and tea: it's the only thing people can usually keep down. Mario, Marco, Franco, and Isabella looked at the ugali and shook their heads sadly. No one would let Franco take their pulse, so he took his own. His sound effect resembled an out-of-control freight train.

At one o'clock, wearing every stitch of clothing we had, we gathered outside the hut to begin the final ascent. Starting at that ungodly hour is so climbers will be at the mountaintop for as short a period as possible. It's timed so that if you make it to the top, you see the sunrise. After a brief rest period, you come down, recuperate for a few minutes at the cabin, then hike to the cabins at 12,500 feet. It's a long, hard day; it would be even if the altitude were not so extreme. The odds of making it to the top are one in three.

In pitch-blackness, a sherpa led the group with a single small lantern, and another followed at the end. Each of us was accompanied by a sherpa. Though our first opportunity to spend time with them, at that hour in the cold and altitude, we didn't do much socializing. Like a chain gang, we scuffled along. In front, the shadowy figure of a sherpa, no sounds except for hard breathing and shuffling. My head pounded from blood coursing through it. My breathing was shallow and fast.

After about an hour we heard retching; the altitude had

claimed Marco. The only cure for altitude sickness is to return to a lower altitude. The minute he began to retch, his sherpa took him by the elbow and led him down. At that altitude, death is a real possibility, and they don't give you a choice.

Another hour, and the trail became steeper. Scree—slippery gray, powdery gravel—meant that for every two steps forward, you slid back one. We walked for ten minutes, rested for five. I walked in a trancelike state, all my energy focused on moving forward, my mind empty of all thought.

Another half hour and I felt bile climbing the back of my throat. I tried to hold it back—I was going to the top. But the retching wouldn't be held back; a firm hand grabbed my elbow and turned me around. I was too ill and exhausted to feel disappointment, relief, or anything else. I stumbled, scrambled, and slid my way back to the cabins, where I collapsed into deep sleep. When I woke a couple of hours later, Franco and Mario had also come back and were asleep next to me.

Diane and Isabella made it to the top. One-third, as predicted.

The return trip was uneventful. We made our way down the mountain, more alert and cheerful as the altitude decreased. On the evening of day five we arrived at the base camp, eager to take baths —but, of course, there was no water. We had a "celebratory" dinner, not saying much, not eating much, but smiling benignly. Franco did a final pulse check and uniformly made contented kitten purring sounds.

The challenge I had set for myself pushed me to my limits, both in preparation for and during the climb. I'd never thought of myself as physically adventurous; with this experience, I proved to myself I could keep up if I set my mind to it. During moments on the final struggle to the summit, I'd experienced a complete emptying of my mind, a Zen state usually achieved only after years of intensive practice.

Though disappointed I hadn't achieved the summit, I know that wasn't important. What mattered both on this trek and in life was not the destination but the journey.

At day's end we relaxed in the hotel's common room. People getting ready to start up the mountain the next day peppered us with questions. We smiled rapturously and said, "It's great."

THE ELEPHANT TREK:
THAILAND, 1985

I've made it a point to try different modes of transportation wherever my travels take me—no trip is complete without a ride on the local subway, bus, or whatever form of transport the local population uses to get around. I've sailed on feluccas on the Nile, flown over the Australian outback in a tiny four-seat prop plane, ascended mountainsides all over the globe on funiculars, and taken wild rides in motorized motorcycle taxis in Saigon (cyclo) and Bangkok (tuk-tuk). But for me, the most memorable forms of transportation have been the four-legged kind.

I have an acute fear of falling, a bona fide phobia. Should I have to walk on a log across a stream while hiking or even climb a tall ladder to change a light bulb, my breathing gets ragged. I freeze in place, unable to go forward or backward, and begin to laugh, hysterically.

The thought of sitting atop a very tall elephant, traversing

rough terrain, terrified me. But after reading descriptions of elephant trekking from Mae Hong Son in northern Thailand—sitting
high above the ground with an unimpeded view of an unspoiled
landscape, watching elephants cavort in the river, and being allowed
to sleep in a local home—I was determined to overcome my fears.
So, prior to heading to Thailand, I prepared myself with three hypnosis sessions that promised to significantly lessen, if not eliminate,
my phobia.

Every night for the week leading up to my trek, as I traveled
through Bangkok and Chang Mai, I dutifully played the hypnosis
tapes given to me by the hypnotist. I was prepared.

At the orientation meeting, I learned getting on an elephant in
the wild requires balance, dexterity, and speed. I lack all three. I'd
imagined a ladder would be used to climb onto the animal's broad
back. Instead I watched, panic-stricken, as the *mahout* (the handler) demonstrated how to mount an elephant. First, he made a
hand signal to the elephant, who dutifully knelt down. Then, plac-
ing his foot on the elephant's massive knee, he leaned into the crea-
ture's hide and used his hands to balance himself. Finally, grabbing
the wooden seat strapped onto the animal's back, he hauled himself
up. The whole maneuver took about ten seconds. The elephant
stood up to her full height, and the mahout towered over us, flashing a huge smile and waving. He leapt off and did it again, saying,
"Easy! Easy!"

I almost gave up before I started, even though I'd already paid
for the three-day trip. Our guide, Pim, a sweet, very young Thai
woman, called encouragement as one by one my fellow trekkers
made the precarious ascent onto one of the hulking animals. To a
person, they sighed with relief once they were safely atop the elephant and were raised high into the air, two travelers per animal.

When my turn came, I kept repeating to myself, *You've had hypnosis, you've had hypnosis.* I surprised myself by quickly and easily climbing up, then held onto the seat with a death grip as Maeyo, my four-legged transportation, followed her mahout's command, rose to her feet, and began to walk forward. The mahout sat in front of us, bareback on the elephant's broad neck, his legs dangling loosely in front of her ears.

Our caravan of six mature elephants, plus a baby accompanying his mama, started down a dirt path through dense vegetation. I was relieved that I felt comfortable moving along at treetop level, even though I was sitting on a narrow bench with a low back and nothing to keep me from pitching over the side. The ground was fairly level, the pace slow, and within minutes fear was replaced by the excitement of the trek. I watched the baby, full of energy and utterly adorable, run ahead until pulled back into place by mama's gentle trunk and deep snorts. The mahouts talked gently with their charges, and there seemed to be good rapport between humans and elephants.

Elephants had been used for hundreds of years for heavy labor, helping to clear land and transport goods. But as soon as powerful machinery arrived in northern Thailand, their work disappeared. Tourist treks help to ensure the survival of the species; they bring in enough money to maintain the elephants and save them from poachers. I saw echoes of Maeyo's former profession. Every few minutes, she would reach over and yank a branch off a tree, as casually as pulling up a daisy, and slowly munch on her large snack as she ambled along. Her strength and dexterity were impressive. I settled in, very grateful the hypnosis was allowing me to experience this adventure.

That was, until we started to climb a steep mountain, at least that's what it felt like. It was probably just a gentle hill, but with only a very low seatback, there wasn't much to keep me from toppling backwards. My body tensed, and my death grip returned. But, once again, it didn't take long before I became accustomed to the motion and relaxed. Going downhill, pitched forward, felt even more precarious. But by the time we stopped for lunch, I'd gotten used to every manner of elephant motion and was confident I'd manage the three days just fine. Not that I had much choice: once in the jungle, there were no roads to return to the starting point.

Our picnic lunch was spread out under broad trees beside a river in a grassy area filled with fragrant wildflowers. Before the mahouts sat down to eat, they bathed the elephants. One by one, their charges waded into the shallow edge of the river, and the mahout, using a long-handled brush, soaped and scrubbed the animal from the tip of their trunk down to each of their toes. The elephants loved it, squirting themselves with water to wash off the soap and occasionally playfully spraying their mahout. Like puppies and kittens, they especially seemed to like having their ears brushed. As the mahouts ate their lunches, one particularly rascally elephant watched her trainer carefully and, when he was deep in conversation, reached over with her trunk and snatched a piece of fruit. For the first time, I saw for myself what I'd often read about. The elephant's eyes shone with intelligence and mischief.

After lunch, mounting Maeyo didn't seem quite as daunting. I scrambled up without much difficulty. For the remainder of the day, I reveled in having conquered my fear.

At lunch the second day, our guide, Pim, casually asked if any of us would like to try smoking opium that night. *Hell yes!* I thought. We were deep into the Golden Triangle, purported to be the source of the world's best opium. I couldn't turn down a chance like that; I knew I might never have the opportunity again. And, with only a single night of smoking, I reasoned the likelihood of my becoming addicted was near zero. Managing not to appear over-interested, I told her yes.

After dinner, Pim escorted me and a fellow traveler up a long winding path to the small village. We were introduced to a group of old men, lying prone on blankets in a grassy area a little way off from the tribe's homes. Their wrinkled faces crinkled with smiles as we said hello. Their eyes were shiny and a bit glazed as they motioned for us to join them on the blankets. Several smoked long, thin pipes I assumed were filled with opium. After a few minutes of pleasantries translated by Pim, a young boy brought over a water pipe. That was how they smoked opium; the other pipes contained tobacco.

It took a while for me to get the hang of the water pipe. I've never been a smoker, and when I first tried to inhale, I coughed and choked, much to the amusement of the men. I finally managed to draw the smoke deeply into my lungs. I waited for something to happen. Nothing. So I inhaled again. Still no reaction. One more hit, and Pim insisted I stop. We hung out for a while longer and then ambled back to our group. I kept waiting for a high, to get giddy, hungry, or stoned in some obvious way. I never did. I later realized that, despite very uncomfortable bedding, noises from nearby animals, snoring of my fellow humans, and a strong stench from animal manure, the opium had allowed me to be totally content and drift peacefully into a deep sleep.

On the final morning of the trek, I was the first in line to mount my elephant. When I placed my foot onto Maeyo's knee, my leg didn't feel secure and I hesitated. Before I had a chance to reposition my leg, hands pushed me from behind, trying to shove me up and onto the seat. At the same moment, I heard an audible snap and felt immediate, excruciating pain.

Several aspirin and a cold pack (produced by the guide) later, the line of elephants proceeded down the final leg of our journey. I didn't enjoy the ride nearly as much, my mind preoccupied with trying to ignore the sensation of someone stabbing at my knee with a knife. The joint swelled, grew very hot, and turned deep red. Dismounting required the assistance of several people, and the pain grew exponentially. In desperation, I asked Pim if there was somewhere I could smoke opium again, thinking it might be more effective than aspirin at keeping the throbbing and stabbing at bay. None was available, or else she didn't want me to become addicted.

I traveled for another week in the south of Thailand, swallowing aspirin like popcorn. By the time I boarded the plane for the flight home, I'd become accustomed to the constant low-level pain and simply ignored it.

One week after I returned to New York, my knee gave out, and I crumbled to the floor during an exercise class. At the emergency room, I was diagnosed with a hairline leg fracture, and, far more serious, a badly torn meniscus. Surgery and a long recuperation followed.

My fear of falling returned. Fortunately, it didn't impart a fear of travel. Accidents can happen anywhere. Instead of in a car or walking across an intersection in Manhattan, I just happened to be on an elephant.

MAROONED: GALAPAGOS ISLANDS, ECUADOR, 1986

Working long hours for many months, I was ready for a change of pace, a trip that would provide peace, quiet, and serenity. But I had learned from several excursions to Caribbean islands that lolling about on a beach leaves me sunburned and bored.

While my friend Diane and I were investigating various locales, we came upon a trip to the Galapagos Islands offered by the same company that we'd traveled with to Tanzania and Mount Kilimanjaro. That trip had been rugged, but our small group of traveling companions congenial, guides knowledgeable, and we'd traveled far off the usual tourist routes.

The remoteness of the Galapagos and their unique wildlife that had attracted Charles Darwin nearly two hundred years before now attracted us.

Waves slapping the splintered dock and shrieking seagulls muffled the low chatter of my fellow travelers as I stood looking out at blue-gray ocean. Apart from a few small uninhabited islands scattered across the water, none of which we could see from this vantage point, we were hundreds of miles from anywhere. That morning Diane and I had flown from Quito into Baltra, one of the few inhabited islands of the Galapagos. Now, on the dock, our guide pointed out a distant boat to our group of six. It looked very small, too small for a twelve-day journey with six passengers, a guide, and three crew members hopping across the open waters of the Pacific Ocean. This was not what I had in mind when I signed up for the trip. I had envisioned a modest but modern, seaworthy vessel—definitely something more luxurious than a small, converted fishing boat.

As the dinghy plowed across roiling water toward our boat, I noticed paint peeling on the hull and a general shabbiness that made my heart sink. As we drew closer, we were given instructions on how to safely make the transfer to the boat. "We'll help you, but you need to move fast. And make sure your hands are in the boat at all times. And whatever you do, do *not* hold onto the edge."

I watched as waves made the dinghy bob up and down furiously, while the boat did the same. They never seemed to do it in sync. I immediately understood the instruction about keeping our hands away from the edge. If the two boats moved together they would smash, if not guillotine, anything that got between them. Waiting for my turn to make the transfer, a knot grew in my stomach as I tried to gauge when the two would pass at a reasonable distance so I could take a fast step with one leg and then the other before the two craft precariously separated again. If I didn't time it right, I would either end up in the water or crushed between the boats.

Once my fellow travelers and I had safely made it on board, a crew member led us to our cabins. We squeezed down a steep ladder from the deck into a small, dim space off of which doors opened to the passenger and guide's quarters and a teensy, shared bathroom. Looking into the bathroom, I saw a narrow, shallow sink, a toilet with no lid, and a handheld sprayer, which I assumed constituted the shower. The sickly green of the tiled floor and walls did nothing to dispel the gloom settling in over me.

Diane and I were assigned a cabin that, except for one tiny salt-encrusted porthole, resembled a two-tiered coffin. Two berths were wedged into a narrow, dark space. The powerful flashlight I'd thought to pack was going to be very handy; it was clear I would be using it frequently, even on sunny days.

I tried to open the porthole to allow fresh air in, hoping to replace the dank, musty smell, but salt had cemented the window closed. The only storage space was below the lower berth and on a few pegs located at either end of the cabin. The space between the wall and the bunks was just wide enough to stand in if you were parallel with the beds. Standing sideways was impossible. Once in our bunks, we'd have to stay flat; there was no headspace to sit up. I wondered how we'd change our clothes.

Quickly leaving the claustrophobic space, Diane and I climbed up to meet our new companions on the top deck. Gulping deep breaths of fresh air, I decided this open deck would be my go-to place.

A middle-aged man and his teenage daughter sat rigidly on battered wooden deck chairs, engaged in a heated discussion. She was trying to convince him to abandon ship immediately.

"Give it a chance, Anna," he said. "We won't be spending much time in the cabin at all."

She interrupted. "I want to get off. Now."

In a soothing tone, he continued, "We'll be seeing blue-footed boobies and iguanas and sea lions. And great stars at night."

"There are no people. This boat is a dump." Then she repeated, screaming this time, "I want off! *Now!*"

"Oh, come on, Anna. You wanted to come on this trip. Be reasonable, we can't just turn around and go home."

"I want off. Now." It became a chant, in increasing volume. "I. Want. Off. Now." "*I. Want. Off. Now!*"

I looked for a place to escape. There wasn't one. So much for the top deck becoming my refuge.

The other pair of travelers had been sitting quietly observing the argument. The two women were about our age and looked to be more game than the father-daughter duo for what we'd all sized up would be a challenging journey. They introduced themselves to us as Maria and Claire from Montana. On hearing that Diane and I lived in New York City, Maria stage-whispered to her friend, "Liberals."

Within a few minutes of introducing ourselves, Maria told us she was a divorced, church-going Catholic who spent as much time as possible camping and hunting big game. Coming to the Galapagos, she told us, was the opportunity of a lifetime to see unusual species.

Diane, a lapsed Catholic from Tennessee, had moved to New York to become an artist and embraced all things avant-garde. Within minutes, the two were dominating the conversation, which rapidly moved from pleasantries about our trip to serious sniping.

"You're twenty-eight and single? Why's that?" Maria asked Diane.

"You're divorced and a Catholic?" Diane responded. "Why's that?"

Diane pegged Maria as an intolerant hypocrite. She tried to ignore her, but it seemed Maria relished a good fight and spat out proclamations she surely knew would be anathema to us. Diane rose to the bait every time Maria opened her mouth.

"If I had my guns with me, this would be a great place for shooting."

"If you had your guns with you, I'd dump them into the ocean."

Within an hour, they could scarcely say more than "pass the salt" to each other without it devolving into an argument.

Claire and I tried to make ourselves scarce and fade into the woodwork. It was going to be a very long twelve days.

Fortunately, the squabbling ceased when our guide, Tom, appeared. He described his background as chief naturalist at the Charles Darwin Tortoise Research Sanctuary for the previous five years. He asked us to tell each other a bit more about ourselves. By this point the captain and crew of three were scurrying around the decks, pulling up anchor and getting us underway. Anna, wearing a sour face, pointedly looked out to sea, refusing to acknowledge direct questions from Tom or her dad, Ed. For her, this trip had *no* redeeming qualities and she wasn't going to let any of us forget it. Diane and Maria declared a temporary cease-fire.

"We'll be heading first for Santa Cruz, the only other inhabited island in the Galapagos. We'll be getting there later today." Tom went on to describe our itinerary and daily activities. "And because we're such a small group we can spend more time or less as you choose, assuming conditions are okay."

Anna finally responded, "Does that mean we can fly back to Quito?"

Tom laughed, "No, afraid not. Once we're out in open water, we won't be seeing civilization until we return here."

The sullen scowl Anna directed toward her father caused all of us, including Tom, to look out to sea.

When introductions were over, I buried my nose in a book, hoping to avoid everyone and silently praying I had enough reading material to sustain me for the trip.

In Santa Cruz, we made another treacherous transfer in choppy water from boat to dinghy and headed to shore. Tom explained we'd be making a "wet landing." "When we get close to shore, one at a time you'll drop both legs over the edge of the boat and jump." I went first and plunged in, glad the water was shallow and clear.

I gasped.

What he'd failed to mention was the water was frigid. The Galapagos are located at the confluence of five major ocean currents, four of which are bitterly cold. I ran for dry land, holding my shoes above my head. Tom tossed me my backpack.

Within minutes, the torment of the previous few hours evaporated. Nests of blue-footed boobies lined the path, their feet such an intense turquoise they appeared to have been painted. They squawked as we approached, then settled down. The baby boobies were adorable little fuzz balls that looked like rebellious teenagers with uncontrollable hairdos. These teens were better behaved than Anna, our teenage human companion.

We hiked through pitch-black lava tunnels deep below the surface and admired unfamiliar, lush greenery above ground. The shoreline teemed with life: bright orange crabs skittering sideways across the sand, endless varieties of birds, and packs of sea lions resting their massive bodies in the cool sand. Their snorts and snores provided a soundtrack for our walk. I was fascinated by the ancient, crude-looking lizards, sweating salt through their pores and resembling miniature escapees from a low-budget science fiction film. Because there are no natural, large predators on the islands the wildlife are fearless of humans. We could get within inches of most species.

Back on the boat, I watched frigate birds swoop down from the sky and, in one neatly choreographed motion, pluck a fish from the sea. Over the next eleven days, watching them became a favorite activity. Focusing on the birds' antics helped me to avoid interacting with my fellow travelers.

A bell rang to call us to dinner—lobsters I'd just seen pulled from the sea.

"Sweetie, grab me a Coke," Ed, Anna's dad, asked Claire. Pointing at Diane, he said, "Would you mind getting up and getting me another napkin, honey?" Grabbing a tray of food from me before I'd served myself, he murmured, "Now don't eat all of it, you want to keep your figure." Then he snatched a second helping for himself before everyone had had their first serving.

After watching his gentle handling of his daughter when we'd first arrived, I was dumbfounded by Ed's behavior toward everyone else. He behaved as though he were the only paying passenger, and the rest of us were part of the crew, whom he treated like indentured servants. I'd felt sorry for him earlier. Now I wanted to encourage Anna to drive him crazy.

By day two, we all replied to Ed's requests with "Get it yourself" or, more often, "Fuck off." Even that didn't slow down his demands.

I'd told Diane to just ignore Maria, and I'm pretty sure Claire had a similar talk with her friend. Those were futile conversations. Though Diane and Maria tried their hardest not to say anything to each other, they were frequently sparring. The two fought about religion, books and authors, environmentalism, style, the media. Frankly, there wasn't a single topic that couldn't provoke intense disagreement.

After that first meal, when I was able, I'd eat on deck. If that wasn't possible, I'd gobble it down. Though it was the freshest seafood I'd ever eaten and delicious, the ongoing skirmishes were nausea inducing.

At night, the skies were awash with more stars than I'd ever imagined. Five hundred miles from the closest population center, there were no lights or smog to diminish their brightness. I'd stay in my bunk writing my journal while the others were sky gazing. Then when they went to sleep, I'd go to the top deck and look through the high-powered telescope Tom had brought. The absolute quiet restored my sense of well-being. Despite the freezing temp—it was hard to believe it could get this cold on the equator—the vast expanse of sky was a relief from the airless, cramped cabin. Shivering, I saw the Southern Cross for the first time as well as other constellations I'd only ever seen in a planetarium.

The days and nights fell into a predictable pattern.

Every day we explored a different island. As we arrived at each, I prayed for wet water landings because dry landings were much scarier. With the agility of a cat, a crew member would leap from the furiously bobbing dinghy onto a slimy rock or seriously decrepit dock. With him on land, each of us would in turn grab his hand for support and make the precarious leap onto the island. While they did their best to calm my fears and steady me, the prospect of sliding into the water, smashing a leg, or harming myself in some other creative way was always at the edge of my consciousness. I forced myself not to think about what might happen if an accident occurred.

My balance was usually good enough that I didn't fall in, though my traveling companions occasionally got doused head to toe. Several landings involved not only negotiating rocks but stepping over sunbathing seals who didn't like being disturbed. They'd snort and sputter but, as I was relieved to discover, rarely actually moved.

Once safely on land, we hiked to see the few remaining tortoises and observed the Galapagos penguins and nesting sea turtles. A few islands, like Isabela, were hundreds of square miles and "frequently" visited, which meant one or two boats would arrive each day and there were clear trails to follow. We'd spend a half day or so exploring them. Most of the islands we visited, though large, had few trails, and we were limited as to where we were permitted to walk.

We braved frigid water, wearing bathing suits rather than wet suits, to swim with playful seals. Condors took death-defying leaps from cliffs before they opened their five-foot wingspans and caught an updraft.

On most islands, our small group comprised the only humans in sight. We often walked where any previous groups' footprints had been erased by wind or rain. Usually we either couldn't see any of the other islands or they were just dots on the horizon. The isolation made each excursion feel fresh and as if we were true explorers.

Every night we were provided with a fresh-from-the-sea dinner, which I ate with extreme speed. Eating amid a group whose members had come to detest each other was the best diet aid I've known. After dinner I'd write my journal until others had gone to bed, and then, bundled in nearly every piece of clothing I had with me, I'd stargaze.

On the few nights the ocean was rough, we all hung out in the open air, hoping to stave off seasickness. I was one of the few who never became ill.

When I could avoid people, I was mesmerized by the natural surroundings. Having no people, buildings, cultural sites, or events forced me to look at the smallest details of my surroundings. By trip's end, my observation skills were PhD-worthy. I understood how Darwin had been able to describe minute differences between species.

But on the boat there wasn't any way to escape my fellow travelers. I couldn't go for a walk. There was either total silence on board—we had arrived at the point where we didn't want to speak with each other—or else there was yelling. The crew, all Spanish speaking, didn't know quite what was being said, but they knew enough to keep what little distance they could from all of us.

I've been told by friends who visited the Galapagos recently that the boats are now modern and comfortable, and landings are quite easy. The boats have stabilizers, and people are less likely to become seasick. Truth is, in retrospect and having survived it, I loved the ruggedness of the trip and that we were so often alone on the islands. If only it had been a more congenial group, it would have been the perfect journey.

DURIAN: MALAYSIA, 1987

> While traveling, I always like to
> sample the local cuisine. Some foods
> I fall in love with and crave but
> can't get when home. Others simply
> leave a lasting impression.

While on my first few trips to Southeast Asia I'd seen and smelled, but never tried, durian, a native fruit. The smell— stench, really—was something I wasn't sure I'd ever be able to overcome. It was like something had died and been left to rot for weeks. Though considered a delicacy throughout the region, durian is often described as "stinky fruit" and forbidden in most public places. Several hotels had prominently displayed large notices in their lobby, with reminders in rooms, "NO STINKY FRUIT AL-LOWED."

I'd asked a few locals about durian and had received mixed re-views; the smell was off-putting even to some people who'd grown up with it, while others described it as a favorite.

Walking through a market in Kuching, on the island of Borneo, I knew durian were present long before I saw them; the distinctive odor had hit me as soon as I'd neared the area. Sequestered in a far corner, the fruit had drawn crowds of people who were buying and then eating it on the spot. Though curious, I resisted tasting it and continued to circle the market, admiring artfully stacked piles of tomatoes, squash, onions, and heaps of greens. Chickens squawked in bamboo carriers. Towering piles of white rice resembled granular snow. Tubs of spices released clouds of powerful scent, crowding out the sickening durian smell.

Clutching a sack of just-ripe rambutan, a sweet fruit I'd come to love, I circled back and again passed near the durian sellers. One particularly enthusiastic salesman beckoned to me. I smiled. He pointed to a pyramid of bulbous melon-like durian and said in clear English, "Taste it. Free." Around him other sellers and buyers watched for my reaction. I gave in, thinking now or never.

The vendor hacked a chunk off a large fruit, wrapped it in a napkin, and handed it to me. I looked at it for a long moment. Then, holding my nose, I tentatively took a tiny bite. I was unprepared for the creamy, pudding-like texture and sweet taste, so very different from the smell. My face must have lit up in pleased surprise. The vendor smiled back at me. "You buy?" I knew I couldn't bring it back to my hotel room, but grateful his insistence had gotten me over my fear, I nodded yes and then overpaid. Around us other vendors clucked in what sounded like admiration, whether for him or me, I wasn't sure.

WINGING IT: VENEZUELA, 1989

Linda and I have been friends for
more than thirty years. For most
of her career, her work required
even more international travel
than mine. On vacation, we've
explored the world together.

Guatemala sounded great, a country not frequented by many tourists, full of impressive Mayan ruins, gorgeous scenery, and, best of all, a local contact who would provide lots of tips. At least that was what Linda and I had hoped for during our planning. We were both working crazy hours, me as a partner in a marketing research firm, Linda as an international information specialist.

Both of us regularly globe-trotted for business. You'd think, given our travel schedules, we'd both want to find a beach and not move from it for a couple of weeks. But no, we still enjoyed traveling for fun. When possible, we combined business trips with vacation, allowing clients to pay the airfare. That was how Guatemala came to be our destination: Linda needed to visit a government office in Guatemala City. The plan was she'd work for a week, and then I would join her. Together we'd head off to the lake district and mountains.

A few days before Linda was scheduled to depart, she received a phone call from her Guatemalan contact.

"You need to change your travel plans."

"But why? I've got tickets, and I'm all set."

"Just trust me, don't come now," her contact said urgently. Then, in a voice just above a whisper, he added, "It won't be safe for you."

When Linda relayed this conversation to me, we both pondered what was behind it. As far as we knew, Guatemala had been stable over the past few years. But then, the governments of many Central American countries had been tenuous for a long time. We were certain there must be some type of political problem. Our greatest concern was if it wouldn't be safe for her to work there, it surely wouldn't be safe as a tourist destination. But we'd blocked off vacation time, which had been difficult to do, and neither of us were willing to waste it. We needed a Plan B.

I went to my travel agent and asked for suggestions. Her choices—last-minute cruises, Caribbean Islands, or winter in Europe—were all unappealing. We craved warm weather and sunshine, but we also wanted adventure. I asked about flights to other Central and South American cities. Caracas, a cheap, relatively short flight seemed a good fit, and the airline would allow us to change our routing for a modest fee. One brief call to Linda and it was settled; we'd leave for Venezuela in ten days.

Three days later there were news reports of an attempted coup and riots in Guatemala City.

We both knew Spanish was spoken in Venezuela and the country had a lot of oil, but that was about the extent of our knowledge. In those pre-Internet days, there weren't a lot of options for getting information. The encyclopedia provided basic data about the country, population statistics and GDP, but nothing usable as a travel guide. We made a reservation for the first two nights in Caracas, but apart from that we had no other plans or useful information. Usually I've read at least some background on my destination, so I have some idea of what I might want to experience, but there were no brochures, maps, or other tourist handouts to be had. Was I ready for that much uncertainty?

The day before departure I trekked to a shop in Manhattan that specialized in travel gear and information and paid an exorbitant price for the one book they had about the country: *Venezuela Alive!*

On the flight to Caracas, I read the guide cover to cover. According to *Alive!* we could not have chosen a more ideal destination—Caracas, the book crowed, combined historic colonial neighborhoods with an ultramodern city center. The beaches were a forty-five-minute drive, the mountains a short flight away. Angel Falls, tucked deep in the jungle, should not be missed. The author gushed about the fabulous food, the nightlife, and the shopping. And it was all affordable, even cheap. Though I was used to guidebook hyperbole, this description surprised me. If Venezuela was even half as nice as the author's rosy picture, why wasn't it a more popular tourist destination?

The first day, walking around Caracas, we weren't impressed. Yes, it did have Spanish-style colonial neighborhoods and modern skyscrapers, but everything looked a bit old and tired. It felt interchangeable with other Latin American cities. I felt a gnawing concern I'd become jaded. Had my many travels robbed me of a sense of discovery and wonder? We decided to get out of the city quickly. Perhaps deep in the mountains or on the beaches, I'd regain the deliciousness of exploring a new place.

There was a travel agency in our hotel. Despite my childlike Spanish, Linda's inability to speak Spanish at all, and the agent's minimal English, we came up with an itinerary. First we'd fly to Mérida, a colonial town high in the Andes. Then she suggested Margarita Island.

"Es una hermosa playa blanca," she said. "Ees a jewel, *un regalo."* Her face lit up. I translated for Linda, "A beautiful white beach, a jewel, a gift."

That sounded worth visiting, though I'd become skeptical about over-the-top descriptions. The one place I really wanted to see, the "unmissable" Angel Falls, was far out of our budget. The flight would cost more than the ticket from New York.

The agent couldn't get through on the phone to book a hotel for us in Mérida, but she assured us, *"Fácil, no sera una problema."* On arriving in the airport in Mérida we found a signboard listing local hotels. We scanned the photos, picked out a few key words like *restaurante* and *piscina,* then randomly selected one and called. A short cab ride later and we arrived at a charming and inexpensive inn.

Mérida is perched near the highest point in the Venezuelan Andes. The air felt thinner, cooler, fresher. The grounds of the inn were vibrant, a profusion of greenery and flowers crowding the patio as if the jungle were waiting to reclaim it. As we relaxed with cool drinks, Linda and I noticed something odd—almost everyone around us, staff and patrons, was speaking Italian, not Spanish. We consulted the guidebook to see if it could shed any light on why this might be. Not a word about Italians living in the area.

That evening, at the recommendation of the hotel proprietor, we took a taxi into town to a restaurant he enthusiastically recommended, Il Duce. The Italian influence was beginning to make sense. But were these Italians who'd fled from Mussolini? Or, more likely, had they been sympathizers who'd left at the end of the war? We never did find out.

Near the restaurant were shops crammed with local ceramics, folk carvings, jewelry, and weavings. There were tiny, handmade ceramic beads strung together in unusual patterns. We were entranced by the thousands of miniature ceramic sculptures that captured scenes from everyday life: crowded buses, shop fronts brimming with stacks of fruit, sheepherders, and more. We were amazed at how much we were enjoying ourselves in a city, "a jewel of a city," to use the travel agent's description, that we hadn't even heard of two days before.

At Il Duce, I had the best pasta I've eaten anywhere outside of Italy. While Linda and I lingered over our wine, discussing what we would do over the next few days, Mama emerged from the kitchen. She was a short, rotund woman with coal-black hair streaked with gray, tied in a tight bun. Her clothes harkened back to the 1950s—a shirtwaist dress covered by a floral apron dusted in flour. This was authentic home cooking, and Mama made an appearance to prove it.

The next day, we hired a taxi and local driver to show us the surrounding area. I say it as a simple fact, but the conversation that got us to our "tour" was a bit like the Abbott and Costello "Who's on First?" routine. My Spanish, while serviceable to ask basic directions, order meals, and exchange pleasantries, wasn't up to the subtleties of the driver's questions. I had only the scantiest understanding of the choices offered. It went something like:

"We can go up into the Andes, to the *palabra no comprendo* (incomprehensible word), but it is a long way away." He smiled. "Or we can go to the lake, where there is *palabra no comprendo, muy bonito, es un lugar especial.* Which do you prefer?"

"Say again, more slowly, what is at the Andes? And at the lake?"

"It is the *palabra no comprendo* of the Andes, there is *palabra no comprendo* and very nice *palabra no comprendo*. *Le gustara mucho*." He looked at me inquisitively. I understood we'd like it very much, but I had no idea what "it" was. Eventually he just took us to places he liked and hoped we'd like them too.

I'm not certain exactly where we went that day, but the scenery was gorgeous. The driver tried unceasingly to please us. When he heard us commenting about the small shops along the road, he stopped at one, owned by "*mi buen amigo Carlos*." He came in with us and introduced us to Carlos, a man with the friendliest smile I'd ever seen. We sampled a variety of homemade hot sauces that packed a real punch. When we found one that didn't totally burn our taste buds, Carlos ladled out the fiery yellow-and-red speckled sauce into glass bottles. We tried to explain we needed to carry the sauce back on the airplane and an old coke bottle stoppered with wax paper and cord wouldn't really work, but he couldn't understand us. What followed was a masterpiece of sign language and verbal improvisation. Eventually we got twist-on lids sealed with wax.

The following day we arranged through the hotel to take a tour with someone who, the proprietor assured us, spoke excellent English. Our guide, Helmut, was a German man who'd gone to Venezuela on vacation, fallen in love with the country and a local woman, and never returned home. He was a leftover hippie who earned cash by taking tourists to see the sights, using his own, somewhat dilapidated car. His guide skills, to be kind, were extremely limited.

Helmut pointed out buildings and plants, though he was hazy about most details. We had hoped he could enlighten us on the Italian presence in the area, but he had no idea. Most questions went unanswered. We did, however, finally figure out where the taxi driver had wanted to take us the previous day—the marker at the highest point in the Venezuelan Andes and a cable car that climbed the side of the mountain. At the top there were nature and hiking trails, but the wind was so fierce we declined. For lunch Helmut took us to what can only be described as a folly. The replica of a Gothic castle, complete with moat, sat ostentatiously in the middle of an otherwise ordinary town. Helmut could only tell us some rich man had built it. The restaurant, of course, served Italian food.

After a few more days of relaxing and wandering around the area, we were off to Margarita Island.

At the island's tiny airport, I had a terrible sense of déjà vu. We were picked up by a van emblazoned with the resort's logo—it felt as though we were heading off to Club Med. A few years before, I'd gone to a Club Med on Guadeloupe. I'd been exhausted and wanted to be freed from making even a single decision for a week. After two days there, I was nearly screaming to get away. The camp-like atmosphere and vapidly smiling, oversolicitous staff felt grating rather than soothing.

This resort was a little run-down. Our "suite" had a distinctly musty smell, and the furniture teetered a bit. But the atmosphere was very laid-back. No one wanted us to sing songs or join in the festivities, though the splashy bougainvillea, unlimited (and strong) free margaritas and piña coladas, and ongoing music did provide a party-like atmosphere. The clientele were mainly Venezuelan, mixed with a few Europeans. We were the only Americans.

After a single day of lounging at the pool and eating the plentiful but mediocre food, we needed to escape. Linda and I headed off to what turned out to be the most beautiful stretch of beach either of us had ever seen—mile after mile of sugary white sand, warm water, and palm trees. For a miniscule fee, we rented lounge chairs, umbrellas, and tables, which were set up far from other people; lying on our chaises, we had an unobstructed view of aquamarine ocean. The only sounds were the crashing of waves on the shore. Unlike other beaches we'd been to around the world, there were no vendors trying to sell us things. The staff of a nearby restaurant visited us about once an hour, taking drink and food orders and then magically returning minutes later. They served some of the freshest fish we'd ever eaten, and the potent margaritas kept us in a mild stupor. It felt as though we had discovered Shangri-la—how was it we were nearly alone in this beautiful, pristine place?

For the next three days, we ate breakfast at the resort and then headed to our magic beach, returning only after sunset. We woozily read through local real estate and tourist information, dreaming about renting a house near the water. By the end of our Plan B vacation, I was so relaxed it was as if I'd spent a week at a meditation retreat.

On the return flight to freezing New York and reality, I reflected on our trip. No expectations and little information had made everything (except for Caracas) fresh and exciting. I had enjoyed taking in the sights with my own senses with no filtering of what I was seeing and experiencing through the lens of a guidebook or someone else's comments. It deepened my confidence I'd be able to navigate my way through most places, even without advance planning. That has led me to even more remote destinations.

IMMERSION: INDONESIA, 1992

Over seventeen thousand islands comprise Indonesia; they have different customs, languages, foods, and religions. I became intrigued with this "patched together" country.

To celebrate my fortieth birthday, I took a sabbatical that included a three-month journey through Indonesia. Fascinated by Indonesia's deeply rooted traditions, fantastical architecture, and sophisticated art and crafts, I planned my itinerary.

Those three months were filled with unexpected and unforgettable experiences. The more I traveled, the less interested I became in visiting the usual tourist sites. What captured my attention were ways to interact with the local population. Taking cooking classes, spending time at markets and local shops, getting a massage, visiting neighborhoods and parks outside city centers, and finding the places where the locals go to be entertained became my favorite ways to spend a day.

A NEW ME

I left for Indonesia a happily single woman. After two weeks, I had acquired a husband and two children.

It became clear I needed a "family" after my first few days on the island of Sumatra, the start of my Indonesian journey. Within minutes of meeting anyone, I'd be asked, "What is your name?" followed by, "Are you married? Do you have children?"

"I'm single. No kids."

"Oh." A look of profound sadness would wash over the questioner's face. No matter how well they spoke English or how sophisticated they appeared, it was as if they'd instantly lost the ability to speak.

I'd struggle to keep the conversation going. Questions flew out of me. Were they married? Did they have kids? What were their kids' names, ages, and what did they like to do best? Did they have pets? I'd tell them about my planned itinerary and my home in New York. Since kids seemed to be a favorite topic, I'd talk at length about my niece and nephews. This all prolonged our time together, but we never really connected. Lack of a husband and kids of my own was like having an orangutan draped around my shoulder chomping on a banana. No one could take their attention away from it.

Generally, traveling alone in other countries creates lots of opportunities to meet people. It's one of the main reasons I often take off to foreign lands on my own. Over the years I've learned how to approach people and turn the most casual of greetings into a half-hour conversation. Telling people I am from New York often does the trick—no matter how remote the location, most people know of and are fascinated by the city. They've seen movies shot in the city or have a friend or relative who lives there, and they sense I'm genuinely curious to find out what they've heard about New York. When I ask what they think is the biggest difference between New York and where they live, they mention food, crowds, skyscrapers, or subways. If I'm lucky and skillful, I can turn a discussion about food into a shared lunch or an invitation to see their home. A mention of the Statue of Liberty might yield a personal tour of their hometown. I'm never the least bit bashful accepting an offer.

For a few days after my arrival in Sumatra, no matter what I tried, I couldn't get past the first few pleasantries with anyone local. I had to do something different. A small white lie seemed appropriate: I bought a simple silver band in the local market to assume the identity of a married woman. Once away from the shopkeeper (not wanting anyone to see me so blatantly taking on my new identity), I slid the band onto my left ring finger.

Marty, my on-again, off-again boyfriend, was elevated to husband status—at least for conversational purposes. Ring on finger, story at the ready, I now had the "correct" answer for, "Are you married? Do you have children?" I concocted a tale about leaving Marty at home with our children, Abby and Gabe (my niece and nephew), while I was on sabbatical doing research, but rarely used it. No one questioned why they weren't with me. Perhaps it was a language barrier. More surprisingly, no one ever asked to see a photo. Anything was acceptable as long as they heard the "right" answer about my family status. A husband and two children (a boy and a girl) is the ideal in Indonesia.

From then on I was a married woman. While I knew I didn't really have a husband and kids, a lifestyle I'd definitely rejected in my twenties, I comfortably slipped into the role. Because I'd spent years with Marty it was easy to talk about his likes and dislikes, and I knew what the kids were doing at school. True pride in Abby and Gabe allowed me to convincingly brag about their achievements.

Invitations began to flow. While I sat reading in a park, a family "adopted" me. The teenage sons practiced English while they led me through open farmland to see a bat cave. I was introduced to their neighbors and invited to join them for several meals. The husband helped me buy a bus ticket and asked other travelers to look out for me. They did, buying food for me at rest stops and pointing out especially nice views. The cultural barrier had been broken.

At first, I told only Indonesians about "my family." Then, to avoid confusion, other tourists got the same story. Besides, trying on this new lifestyle was fun. My virtual family had some real benefits with none of the problems of a real one. We never had fights, I didn't have to cook for or pick up after them, they didn't feel upset or rejected that I'd left them to travel, and my time and money were my own.

All was going well until I met Federico and Daniela, a couple from Italy. They'd seen me sitting alone, staring out at the jagged mountain peaks and toylike fishing boats on the island of Sulawesi. Thinking I'd like some company and, I suspect, looking for company themselves, they introduced themselves. Within minutes we were laughing and chattering away animatedly. Over a shared lunch, we compared notes about where we'd been and determined that over the next week we were planning roughly the same itinerary. Then the conversation turned to family. Their two children were exactly the same ages as mine.

As the week progressed, the three of us became good friends—our shared experiences and similarities between our families became a real bond. On the night before our paths were to diverge, Federico asked for my address and phone number.

"I travel to New York on business every couple of years."

Why, oh why hadn't he told me earlier? What would I do when he showed up in New York and I couldn't produce Marty, Abby, and Gabe? And I could never bring him home: four people clearly don't live in my tiny house. I gave him my contact information and silently debated whether I should tell them the truth. Nah. When the time came, I'd deal with it. I got away with my deception because, fortunately, my only contact with Federico and Daniela were Christmas cards for the next few years.

But fear of getting caught in a tall tale kept me honest until a few years later, when I passed myself off as a divorcée. Socially acceptable, there didn't seem to be any downside to this white lie—I didn't even need to buy a ring. More importantly, if a travel companion showed up in New York I wouldn't need to produce a husband. More recently on solo trips, I've become a widow.

FAST FOOD

I was on my way from Medan to Lake Toba on the island of Sumatra. A woman from London and I had joined forces to lower the cost of a taxi, the only way to make the trip, a long and slow drive over poorly constructed and maintained roads.

The driver eased the car to a stop by the side of the road. On all our other stops, there had been fabulous views, and he rightly assumed we'd want to take photos. This time, however, nothing was in sight except a few roadside vendors. He pointed at one and led us over, his English and our Indonesian not being up to the task of explaining anything. After a quick discussion, the vendor unsheathed his machete and selected three small pineapples from a towering pile. In a flash the fruit was chopped into perfectly sized cubes and placed into plastic bags. This side-of-the-road fruit vendor seemed to be the Indonesian version of stopping at McDonald's for a quick pick-me-up on a long drive. When we tried to pay, the driver waved our money away. The pineapple was a gift: I guess we hadn't been as good at negotiating our fare as we'd thought.

The plastic bag, the local version of a KFC bucket, made the fruit easily portable. Unable to resist, we reached in immediately. My first bite brought involuntary sighs of pleasure. It was the sweetest, freshest fruit I'd ever eaten. Sticky juice dripped down my chin and onto my T-shirt. I didn't care.

After a couple of days exploring Lake Toba, I was ready to move on. No one wanted to share a taxi, so I opted for the overnight bus to Bukittinggi. The bus was packed but, as promised, comfortable. There were reclining chairs, air-conditioning, and pillows, as well as a TV blasting raucous music videos from a VCR. Earplugs just muted the din. This being the deluxe local transport, most passengers were wealthy Indonesians, many of them students heading home on a school break. Sprinkled into the mix were a few young European backpackers. Nearly everyone smoked clove cigarettes, creating a thick haze of pungent smoke. A couple of Excedrin took the edge off a looming headache.

For the first two hours, while it was light, views of lush green terraced rice paddies, small towns, and steep mountains kept me entertained. Mesmerized by the scenery, the vibration of the motor, and the muted buzz of voices through my earplugs, I fell into a near trance. A sharp stop jolted me back to consciousness. Ahead of us, filling the narrow road, was another bus. I could hear impatient honking from behind us. Our driver got out and had a short conversation with the driver of the approaching bus. Their bus backed up a few feet and hugged the side of the mountain. I held my breath as we inched past them, forcing myself to look straight ahead and not think about tumbling down the cliff to our right. I don't think I exhaled until I could see clear road filling the windshield. After that, the scenery didn't seem nearly as benign.

My seatmate, equally frightened by the treacherous road,

turned to me. "You are tourist, yes?" Surprised that he spoke in English, but grateful for the distraction, I enthusiastically began to talk. For the first time since I'd arrived in Indonesia I told my tale of being on sabbatical. The young man, Budi, was a student returning home from a visit with his sister. "It is good to talk English with American. Is good if I practice?"

"Of course."

While happy to speak with him, I realized he might ask questions about my teaching. While outwardly listening to what he was saying, I was busy expanding my story—I would tell him I taught architecture at a community college and was in Indonesia looking at examples of the local buildings. A plausible story given that Indonesia is well known for distinctive regional styles, and I had spent considerable time looking at and reading about them. But he never asked. He was much more interested in hearing about New York City and my impressions of his country.

At dinnertime, we pulled up next to four buses. Budi translated the driver's announcement that we'd have a thirty-minute break. When the door was opened, a surge of hot, moist air rushed aboard. Stepping into the darkness, I surveyed the scene. This wasn't like any of the rest stops I'd been to along the New Jersey Turnpike. The building was a large tentlike structure—a roof held up by sturdy poles, the sides open to the crushing humidity and all manner of bugs. Crowds of people swarmed around, stretching their legs, getting food, and looking for somewhere to sit, illuminated by a few bare, low-watt light bulbs suspended from the ceiling. Deep shadows darkened most of the space. The din of travelers talking and the clatter from the kitchen made me glad I hadn't removed my earplugs.

A single neon-lit stand was the only place selling food. Clouds of aromatic smoke billowed around it. The throng surrounding the counter, half-shrouded by the greasy haze, was especially daunting. There wasn't a single sign in English. I was glad I'd tucked food into my shoulder bag. But I didn't need it. Budi caught my eye and motioned for me to follow. After searching the overflowing seating area, he found two unoccupied chairs at a large communal table. He signaled for me to sit and wait. A few minutes later, he returned carrying two plates of *nasi goreng* (fried rice with an egg).

"Sorry," he said, "but this was only food."

"No problem. And thanks so much." Then I took my first bite. In the gloom I must have bitten directly into a chili pepper. I could feel my face flush and rivulets of sweat stream down my already damp face. Frantically I pawed through my bag for a bottle of water. I would have stopped eating after the first bite, but I couldn't disappoint my new friend. One forkful at a time, examined by flashlight for chili chunks, I picked my way through the meal. Thankfully, Budi was not offended. I was grateful we had to reboard the bus before I finished the whole thing.

A few days later, I flew to the island of Java. There I joined a "mini-tour" to see the small inland villages. We were five foreigners in a van heading east with Paul, our tour guide, and a driver. Paul had lived briefly in the US and really liked Americans. However, few Americans ever joined his tour, so he was pleased I was part of the group. We spent a lot of time chatting, comparing travel experiences.

We stopped overnight in Bandung, a small, unremarkable inland city, but it was Paul's hometown, and he wanted us to see it. On Java even the smallest hamlets are overpopulated. The crowds in the local shopping district made Macy's on Christmas Eve seem deserted. Close by the shops was a warren of tiny food stalls. Smoke from charcoal grills weakened the already dim light: everything beyond the radius of the twenty-watt bulbs disappeared in darkness. The spicy aroma from cooking meat and vegetables, curries, onions, and garlic blanketed the area. It was intoxicating.

At clusters of small tables, patrons perched on plastic stools eating, drinking, smoking, and gabbing. There were so many people, I wondered if anyone cooked or ate at home. I discreetly looked to see what others were eating. Except for the basics of *nasi goreng*, skewers of chicken satay, and rice curries, I didn't recognize anything. In the semidarkness I pointed to a pot and hoped for the best. After the proprietress ladled out a generous serving, I held out a handful of change and she picked out a few coins. I ate standing up: there wasn't a free stool available. The noodles with a mild peanut sauce were delicious and cost just a few cents. At another stall I bit into some blisteringly spicy food, repeating the shock of the meal I'd eaten with Budi.

On our way out of town the next morning, I noticed a Kentucky Fried Chicken outlet squeezed between a fabric store and a hardware store. Pointing it out to Paul, I said, "Well, Bandung is certainly going downhill." I grimaced and continued, "I can't believe Indonesians eat that junk."

"What are you talking about? KFC is great!" He said this so enthusiastically, I knew he was serious. I couldn't imagine how anyone could think the arrival of KFC was a good thing. At home I avoid KFC, McDonald's, Burger King, and all their clones. But instead of blurting out some sarcastic comment, I forced myself to calmly ask, "Really? What makes KFC great?"

"Look at it from our perspective," he said. "Here KFC is where you take your girlfriend if you really want to impress her. For us it's a fancy foreign restaurant."

I thought about what he'd said. KFC is brightly lit, spotless, and shiny. You can sit in padded chairs in air-conditioned comfort. The food resembles nothing sold or eaten locally. The prices are exorbitant in comparison to the food stalls, though still affordable as an occasional splurge. I could easily imagine a young couple dressed in their best clothes going there on a hot date. In Indonesia, KFC *is* a fancy foreign restaurant.

Now when I'm overseas and come upon that familiar red-and-white sign, it's a reminder that people in other countries don't see things as I do. It forces me to try to understand how local people experience their world.

TORAJA

I first learned about the Toraja while reading an article in National Geographic. *The Toraja are an ethnic group who live high in the mountains of Sulawesi, one of Indonesia's five main islands.*

Their funeral rituals are unique in the world. The dead are considered "sick." Rather than burying bodies immediately, family members live with the mummifying dead in their homes, sing and talk to them, even offer them meals. After about six months, they transport them to ancestral burial places. Photos in National Geographic *showed intricately carved figures adorned in local dress standing on ledges high on steep mountain cliffs.*

The flight from Bali into Ujung Padang was uneventful. But, for the first time since I began my journey through Indonesia a month before, I felt some trepidation. I was traveling to an isolated community with only the flimsiest notion of the culture or, more importantly, any practical knowledge of the area. I didn't know how to get to the

Torajan villages high in the mountains, where I might stay, or how I would get around once I arrived. And, despite my best efforts, I'd been unable to find a guidebook that gave more than rudimentary information.

I had a hotel reservation for the first night at the most luxurious, glamorous hotel in the city, all my bets being on the concierge being able to help. The rooms were dismal, but some staff spoke English, there were TVs that got CNN, and, most importantly, there was air-conditioning. I arranged for a car and driver to go to Toraja for four days.

The next morning dawned clear and sunny. After breakfast, the concierge introduced the hotel's chauffer and said he would take me on the two-hundred-mile drive to Toraja, the partially paved road being the sole way to get there. The concierge added, "The roads are pretty bad. On a good day, it's a nine-hour drive, but anything can slow it down."

"Oh? Like what?"

"After heavy rains, the roads collapse, or trees fall across and make them impassable. And there are many accidents."

I focused on the images in *National Geographic*, gulped, and agreed.

Initially we drove along the coast, dotted with fishing villages and houses built on stilts, with mountains looming in the distance.

As the taxi driver spoke no English, and my Indonesian was limited to the barest of pleasantries, we communicated by pointing at a map, hand signals, and a lot of smiling. We came to an understanding that if I patted him on the shoulder he would pull over, if possible, so I could take photos.

After a couple of hours, we began our ascent into the mountains. The driver stopped for lunch at a restaurant high on a hillside with a panoramic view of the harbor far below. The only other diners were a couple speaking Italian. They invited me to their table. Federico and Daniela, a couple from Milan about my age, spoke reasonable English and were also heading toward Toraja. We chatted about where we'd come from. When I said I didn't know where I'd be staying they gave me the name of their hotel, Rantepao. My relief must have been visible—that name kept me from worrying about where I'd sleep that night. I was certain, given the difficulty in getting to Toraja, a room would be available.

A few hours passed on a paved road before it degraded to a pothole-studded, narrow dirt lane that snaked around mountains. There were no guardrails, and I regularly had to turn away from steep drop-offs that looked deadly. The driver stopped often, even without my signal, sometimes for a great view, sometimes to make sure the tires were okay. *Well*, I thought, *he's conscientious.* That thought was immediately followed by, *Guess he doesn't want to die today either.*

About halfway through the journey, we passed a truck that had fallen into one of the many potholes and flipped. By the time we arrived, other drivers were surveying the scene and helping vehicles get past it without mishap. All those warnings and the driver's caution had clearly been warranted.

"Toraja!" the driver announced, waving his hand. I could see a pair of water buffalo slowly plodding through a field, a young boy sitting atop one of them. They were bathed in a golden glow from the setting sun. The boy waved and hooted. I guessed there weren't many visitors in these parts. I understood why. After nearly ten hours, my nerves were frayed. I was thankful we'd made it to flat terrain before sunset.

A few minutes later, we began passing some extraordinary

structures, but in the dimming light, all I could really see were the swooping rooflines of enormous buildings.

The driver sedately passed those buildings and proceeded into a very ordinary-looking small town. He pulled into a driveway, and I breathed a sigh of relief, observing a sign in several languages that announced "Hotel Rantepao." Before the taxi had come to a stop, a man emerged, flashing a broad smile. I could have kissed him.

The room and dinner were simple but better than I'd anticipated. I met up with Federico and Daniela for dinner but remember little about what we ate or what we said. Our beds beckoned, and sleepily we trundled off to sleep.

"Pardon me."

I looked up from breakfast to see a short man who, at first glance, appeared to be a doppelgänger for the Linda Hunt character in *The Year of Living Dangerously*. In that movie, she played Billy Kwan, the dwarf guide for an Australian reporter. Dare I hope this man would offer his services as a guide?

"I'm Yatim, missus." He bowed.

"Hi." I smiled.

"You are American?"

"Yes."

"I love Americans. Have guided many of them in Toraja."

"That's wonderful."

He took a deep breath as if to screw up his courage. "Do you need a guide? I am a very good one. I guided writer and photographer for the *National Geographic* magazine. Do you know that magazine?"

Oh my God, I thought. *How lucky could I possibly get?* "Yes, I know it. It's because of the article in *National Geographic* that I came here."

"Really?"

"Yes. In fact, I have it with me." I pulled out the somewhat tattered article and showed him.

He looked thrilled. "I must guide you!"

"Yes, you must!" With that, Yatim and I shook hands, negotiated a fee, and agreed to depart in an hour.

As the driver navigated the narrow roads, I stared out the window, and Yatim chattered. I understood about half of what he said. But it didn't matter; everything I saw mesmerized me.

Toraja is largely a farming area. Farmers start early and end late. They work in primitive conditions; many were slogging in mud up to their hips, hand weeding, planting, and sowing. Almost no one used machinery of any kind. Yatim told me water buffalo are revered but not used for labor. They are like huge family pets, pampered endlessly like cows in India.

Despite the poverty, Torajan architecture is distinctive and impressive. The large homes, shaped like swooping birds, are elaborately decorated and, to my Western eyes, unforgettable. *Tongkonan*, as they call the communal homes, shelter large family groups. The buildings stand on wooden piles, topped with a split-bamboo roof shaped in a sweeping curved arc. Yatim said the roofs often survive a hundred years or more. They decorate exterior walls with wood carvings and often have columns of water buffalo horns as additional ornamentation.

The first day we focused on burial customs. I didn't understand everything Yatim said and kept peeking at the *National Geographic* article as a reference. I wondered how they'd gotten their information, surely not from Yatim. I was grateful he didn't mind my asking, "Could you repeat that?" endlessly.

As depicted in the article, the cliffs are sheer and the burial caves high above ground level. Yatim explained that each cave be-

longed to a single family. They inter the dead from many generations in their family cave, stacking one corpse atop another. An
effigy of each ancestor, some life-sized and others a few feet tall, is
placed in front of the cave on a narrow ledge. Once a year, family
members dangle on ropes while they refresh the brightly colored
outfits of each effigy figure. I craned my neck and looked through
the telescopic camera lens to try to see the details of the hundreds
of figures standing in front of the caves.

"Use these." Yatim handed me a battered but very powerful pair
of binoculars. Peering through them, I could see intricately carved
figures. Some wore glasses or hats, others held pipes or handbags,
some smiled or seemed to laugh. Each was unique. Studying them, I
could see family characteristics: large noses or ears or unusually
shaped eyes.

"Only adult in caves. Babies in special place." We drove to a
grove of large trees with broad bases, each adorned with dozens of
miniature white flags. Yatim announced, "Baby trees."

I understood almost nothing of his explanation, except that
villagers wrap their dead infants in cloth and seal them inside the
tree. Later I read that the Toraja believe that over the years the
corpse is absorbed and returns to nature to be reborn. I never
learned the significance of the flags.

"Now we visit the carvers." When not creating effigies, the
carvers produce the decorations for the *tongkonan*. And for the few
tourists who come through the area, they carve trays, bowls, and
wall hangings. The carver was welcoming, as was every Torajan I
met. Working on a flat slab of wood, he demonstrated his tech-
nique. I asked Yatim if I might try carving. Yatim didn't seem to
understand my question, and it took some miming to get what I
wanted across. I guess no tourist had ever made that request before,

but I love working with my hands. When I confidently handled the tool and wood and began to make a design, the carver and Yatim both clapped in delight. I felt as though I'd done something for cross-cultural relations.

As we drove back to the hotel, Yatim announced, "Tomorrow we go to special ceremony."

"Oh? What kind of ceremony?"

"To celebrate new house. Big party."

"A *tongkonan*?"

He nodded his head. "Very, very special. Presentation of pigs."

I had no idea what he was talking about, but I was up for going to a party.

"Do I need to bring a gift?"

"Tomorrow morning we buy before we go."

Our first stop in the morning was to buy a carton of cigarettes, my gift to the new homeowners. I thought it a bit of an odd gift, but Yatim assured me it would be "best gift."

The house was more than a full year old, but this was the first time the family had enough money to spring for the festivities.

Driving to the even more remote location, Yatim explained that hundreds of people are invited—friends, relatives, and everyone from neighboring villages. The celebration lasts for four days, each with a unique program. The first day is dedicated to dancing and feasting on food prepared by family members. On the second day, chickens are ritually sacrificed and then eaten. The third day, which is when we were attending, is the parading of the pigs, followed by feasting, though not on pork. The final day is the sacrifice of the pigs and then cooking and eating them.

As we neared the *tongkonan*, we passed large crowds of people walking along the side of the road. Most women wore brightly colored head wraps, long loose skirts, and short blouses. They shaded themselves with paper umbrellas. The men could have been from anywhere in the world in their jeans and T-shirts. Young teenage boys carried sedan chair-like bamboo cages, decorated with flowers and greenery or carved and painted. "The pigs!" Yatim gleefully explained. His small body bounced with enthusiasm as we neared the party. I was intrigued, but as this was all new and very foreign to me, I mostly looked open-mouthed, trying to take it in.

The homeowners had transformed the area around the house into an arena with tiered rows of bleachers. Yatim scouted and found us "best place to see." Everyone was surprised to see a Westerner but cheerfully squeezed over to give us space to sit. The festivities had already begun, music blared through speakers, and the air was electric with excitement. I scanned the crowd of more than two hundred and saw only two other non-locals.

An ear-piercing screech directed my attention to a gently sloping path from the roadway to the front of the house. "The pigs! The pigs!" Yatim chanted as a team of four young men whooping and hollering charged down the path, the pig in its cage high above their heads.

When they arrived at the central area in front of the house they jumped and screamed with great glee and presented the pig to the homeowners. After bowing and a cursory inspection, the pig was moved to the side, where over a few hours it would be joined by many piggy companions. Each pig was presented the same way: teens holding the cage high above them, running down the slope, an enthusiastic screaming audience, and storage to the side of the area. The crowd laughed, chatted, and cheered each new arrival. I became bored with it after a half an hour or so, but the locals behaved as though each new pig presented was the first; no one seemed to lose interest. However, the sublime people watching entertained me, and I was endlessly amused by Yatim's enthusiasm.

Every so often, one of the pigs would break loose from its cage. Mayhem ensued while the young men tried to tackle the pig and wrestle it back into the cage. The audience alternately rooted for the pig or the teens.

In the middle of the proceedings, there was a long lull while the village elders met and conferred, as everywhere those in power must meet. During that break, Yatim suggested I present my housewarming gift to the owner. As instructed, I gave him the carton of cigarettes; it seemed to be much appreciated. I later learned that, while family members smoke some of the cigarettes, most will go to ancestors' graves. The dead don't worry about lung cancer.

We sat for another hour as the pig parade continued. I marveled at where I was and what I was seeing. This was an experience that few outsiders have, and it felt like a privilege to be there. I scribbled notes on everything I saw, vowing not to forget a single detail.

When I finally persuaded Yatim to leave, we returned to town to a small restaurant for a late lunch. The owner appeared to be a friend of Yatim's, but perhaps everyone in town simply knows everyone else. They chatted for a few minutes while I scoped out the decor, simple but spotless, with battered wooden tables and chairs. Yatim joined me at the table, telling me he'd ordered for us and I would have another special surprise. With that, speakers crackled, and Elvis launched into "All Shook Up." The owner returned from the kitchen laughing and chanting, "Elvis, Elvis, Elvis!" The other patrons launched into a rousing chorus; they knew all the words. Throughout our meal, the room reverberated with Elvis, the Beach Boys, and the self-appointed backup singers. Even in this isolated corner of the world, American pop culture is pervasive. I wasn't sure if I should be pleased or saddened.

Before we left, the owner poured a large shot of *tuak* (palm wine) for me. I knew I had to drink it, but thought, *This will either kill me or I'll be the happiest person around.* But neither came to pass. The somewhat acrid drink has a very low alcohol content, just 2.5 percent.

On the final morning, Yatim and I exchanged fond farewells. He gave me his address so I could send him photos. I couldn't read anything he wrote. I figured I could get someone in Ujung Padang to translate. I couldn't and felt terrible. When I returned to New York, I sent an envelope addressed to Yatim, Rantepao, Sulawesi, Indonesia. I have no idea if he received it.

HANDS ON

I was killing my last few hours in the city of Ujung Padang before a flight back to Bali. The dull city was a letdown after a week of exploring Toraja. When the concierge mentioned there were masseuses on staff, I scheduled a massage.

A pretty, petite woman led me into a cavernous room, divided by curtains into dozens of massage cubicles. She'd motioned for me to undress and to hang my clothes on pegs affixed to the poles. I was a bit surprised she didn't leave the cubicle as I began to disrobe. But she seemed far more interested in my clothes, particularly my lacy bra, than in looking at my body. After more than a month of travel, the bra was faded, the lace torn a bit, and one hook had gotten bent out of shape. When I'd put it on that morning I'd thought, *This isn't making the trip home; it's really getting tatty.* It was clear she'd never seen such a fancy bra, or one as large. In Indonesia, women are tiny, almost childlike in physique by American standards. To her, both my clothes and I must have been of Amazonian proportions. Just as I was about to take the bra off, she slipped out behind the curtain.

I'm an aficionado of massages—I've had them all over the globe—so I was willing to go along with whatever the local customs seemed to be. Massages help to relieve some of the stress of travel and are also a great way to learn about the culture. Almost every country has its own approach to hands-on therapy. In Thailand, I was dressed in silk pajamas and twisted into pretzel-like positions I didn't know my body was capable of assuming. The Turkish masseur slapped me with a towel and pounded me so fiercely I had black-and-blue marks as a souvenir. In India, my body couldn't quite shake the scent of rancid massage oil, even after two showers, though the therapeutic effects were blissful. The sounds of trickling water and soft gamelan music, a subtle floral scent, and the graceful decor in the spa in Bali were so soothing that I could have happily just soaked in the atmosphere for a while.

When I was out of my clothes, I climbed onto the table, carefully pulling up the sheet. The masseuse parted the curtains, entered, and with little fanfare tossed the sheet completely off me. With a somewhat less than gentle touch she began to rub my shoulders and stretch my arms. All the while she chatted cheerfully in a local language I could neither understand nor even identify. Every island in the country uses, in addition to Indonesian, its own indigenous languages. There are often six or seven different ones on a single island. Not sure how to respond to her, I uh-huh'd a couple of times, hoping I wasn't agreeing to some painful or expensive treatment.

After I was "warmed up," she climbed on the table and walked on my back and legs—up and down and up and down, all the while continuing to talk. I willed myself not to yowl after some of the more strenuous movements. Though it was painful, I hoped all that pressure would relax my knotted muscles.

Eventually, I realized the chatting wasn't with me but directed to her companions who were gathering outside the curtained area where I was being massaged. As their patter and laughter increased, I was certain they were talking about me and became self-conscious. In an effort not to get embarrassed, I convinced myself they were probably gossiping about boyfriends, coworkers, or the latest local celebrity.

After about thirty minutes, one of the masseuse's friends came in to assist. I became convinced they'd been talking about me, but of course I had no way of asking. The pain doubled as the two of them rubbed and stretched and pounded me. I silently prayed they wouldn't both walk on my back. A few minutes later, a third woman entered the now-crowded cubicle and joined the pummeling fest, giggling all the while.

The "treatment" ended with a playful slap from each of them. As soon as I slid off the table, the three women hopped onto it. They sat primly in a row and giggled some more as they watched me get dressed. "*Bagus, bagus*" they chanted like a Greek chorus as I lifted each item off the hook. It was one of the few words of Indonesian I had learned—I knew *bagus* meant "good" or "great." They were especially admiring of the bra. Each held it, gently caressing the lace and stretching the elastic. One latched and unlatched the hooks. Another ran her finger through the cup, as if measuring its depth, then balled up her fingers into a fist and demonstrated to her friends how much larger the cup was than her hand. The others had to do the same before the bra was carefully handed to me. I would have given this object of fascination to one of them as a gift, but what could they possibly have done with it?

On many levels, I was a novelty for them. They were not used to seeing a woman here; no self-respecting Indonesian woman, many of whom are Muslim, would ever have a massage in a public place. There were few Westerners; I'd only run into a handful during the week I'd been touring the area, and only one had been female.

Despite a few minutes of awkwardness and a few days of recuperation from their ministrations, it was as much of a peek into their culture as any touring I'd done. And I'd shared it with three women who, I was certain, had had an equally memorable experience.

THE PUPPET MASTER

I pressed myself against the wall, terrified the passing car would hit me. Yogyakarta, Indonesia, had been built long before automobiles were invented, but that didn't stop anyone from speeding through the narrow streets.

Jogja, as the city is known, is filled with master craftsmen. Shops abound stocked with exquisitely made handicrafts—fabrics in intricate patterns of jewel-like colors; silver pins, bracelets, and earrings in traditional and contemporary designs; clothing, carvings, masks, and more. With only a single day left in the city, I couldn't get enough.

I'd been walking aimlessly for a couple of hours, people watching, window-shopping, and stopping in teashops during several intense tropical showers. Though the downpours were brief, they saturated the hot air. My shirt stuck to me as though I'd showered fully dressed. My skin had changed from a healthy rosy pink to a

shade resembling raw steak. The wedding band on my swollen finger felt like a miniature noose, being tightened ever so slowly. My
head ached. Despite the discomfort, I kept exploring.

Peeling away from the wall, grateful once again I'd avoided
disaster, I looked into the tiny shop against which I'd been pressed.
"Ahhh," I gasped. The window was filled with puppets. I stood
transfixed, my mouth agape, peering at kings, musicians, soldiers,
Garuda birds, old men and women, and fantastical demonic creatures.

Dolls and puppets have fascinated me since I was very young.
My childhood collection started with my grandmother's battered
cloth doll, the only souvenir from her Russian childhood. Dressed
in a flowered wine-red skirt, embroidered shirt, and babushka
wrapped over long braids, it always made me wonder what my life
would have been like had my grandparents not emigrated. When a
neighbor traveled to Mexico and brought back a straw doll in a colorful serape strumming a teensy guitar, I could almost hear the music and feel the heat. After that, whenever anyone we knew traveled
overseas, I begged them to bring back a doll or puppet for me. I
loved examining the clothes, facial expressions, and hairstyles, so
different from my own. My growing collection was one way to experience exotic locales from afar.

Five, ten, perhaps fifteen minutes passed while I stood mesmerized by the puppets. Cars whizzed by; I barely noticed. I glanced up
only when the door to the shop creaked open. A slight man of inde-
terminate age smiled and beckoned me in with a gentle waving of
his delicate fingers. Entering with him into the enchanted land, I
felt like a giantess—Gulliver among the Lilliputians. Edging my
way through the narrow aisle, I was terrified that with a single false
move, I'd become Shiva, the Hindu god of destruction. In my

mind's eye I could see the wooden figures crashing to the floor, their heads smashed and limbs shattered. At the far end of the shop, the man pointed to a stool. I gratefully sat down, glad to be out of harm's way.

My host disappeared for a few moments. I sat motionless, afraid to touch anything on the crowded shelves. But my eyes feasted.

When he returned, he offered me a dainty porcelain cup from a carved wooden tray. Cinnamon perfumed the air. While I sipped sweet tea, he picked up a figure dressed in an elaborate headdress and a matching purple sarong flecked with silver threads and glittering beads. Her carved face was delicate and expressive. In his hands she came alive, exuberantly welcoming me to the shop—hugging me, kissing me, dancing with swaying hips and floating arms. Though the puppeteer stood only a couple of feet from me, it was as if he had disappeared. She and I were all that existed.

With a graceful wave of her arm she invited me to select another puppet. I chose a red ogre with a fierce expression and long fangs. She returned to wood and fabric while he bolted into life, moving so quickly and forcefully that, in my surprise, I almost crushed the teacup. The ogre's bandana and sash quivered with tense energy, suppressed power, and a hint of violence. When he returned to the table, a young boy jumped up. Though created from a solid block of wood, his apple-cheeked face seemed to laugh and smile as he scratched, skipped, and tumbled. The ogre reappeared briefly, followed by a queen in a glittering tiara and fur-trimmed robe, who delicately minced her way over to the boy. A story seemed to be unfolding as the action grew. The boy was clearly in trouble. He shrieked, twisted, and turned. But was the approaching queen good or evil? His savior, it appeared. I never quite understood the pair of old men clutching walking sticks, who squabbled with each other as they hobbled painfully across the room after they'd been banished by the queen. The full narrative of what had to be a local folktale remained a mystery. It was a story from a tradition I didn't know. But it didn't matter. I was enraptured by the aliveness of the puppets.

A small brochure, printed in multiple languages, explained that my host was a master puppeteer, and every week he gave public performances at the palace. He had crafted all the puppets himself. Though he spoke no English and I no Indonesian, we communicated easily. When I used gestures to ask how he made the puppets, he led me to a tiny, cramped workspace behind the shop. A row of carved, unpainted heads filled one shelf. Another shelf held arms and legs and bodies. The worktable was covered with tools, paints, glue pots, and a treadle sewing machine. Overflowing baskets held yarn, bits of metal, beads, wire, and scraps of the fabrics I'd been looking at all morning. I picked up an arm and body and motioned, asking how they were connected. He slotted a small peg into an elbow to demonstrate. Then he went on to show me how he painted, clothed, and decorated the puppets.

Back in the shop, he handed me puppets and taught me how to bring them to life. Hours passed. I began to feel guilty about how much of his time I was taking. Given my limited funds, I wouldn't be buying much. But I also understood money wasn't a concern. Big sale or small, it wouldn't have made any difference to our afternoon. He was a brilliant performer and I the perfect audience.

EXPAT WOES: 1992

My hiatus from the "real world" lasted for six months. The night before I flew home from Singapore, I had a clear vision. While my travel had been at a relaxed, slow pace, my subconscious had been working overtime. It decreed I should start a consulting practice with no partners or employees and work from home. That arrangement would provide the flexibility needed to take off whenever I chose.

A few months later I landed my first client, a major financial institution. They quickly assigned me to a project that required travel in Europe and Asia. My task was to help them understand why employees who had been transferred to another country rarely completed their assignments or, worse yet, left the company. The goal was to help them develop strategies to lessen the number of early departures.

This required interviewing European, Asian, and American expat employees and their families. It was the first time I'd had a close look at a very different type of traveler: those who don't voluntarily opt to travel overseas but find themselves living in an alien culture, often after an abrupt transition. The company expected employees to make the move quickly once they received their overseas assignment.

When they moved, everyone in an expat family made a major transition. Employees worked and children went to school, structuring their days; they were with other people and had opportunities to make friends. Their transition, while sometimes difficult, wasn't usually devastating. Spouses, usually wives, had a much tougher adjustment. Women from all over the world experienced similar difficulties, no matter their country of origin or country assignment.

Many had been employed before they moved but in their assigned country were unable to get work permits and forced to abandon careers. In new homes, on their own, they needed to navigate their way through a culture they didn't understand, in a language they didn't speak well, if at all. There was no regular schedule to fill their days and no easy way to meet people. Several women I spoke with broke down in tears during the interview.

"I've never been in such great shape in my life," an American woman living in Milan told me. "I work out at the gym every day for hours; it's a way to kill time." She did look great. "But I'm bored. My Italian isn't good enough to speak with anyone, not really." She shook her head sadly. "I miss teaching; I miss my mom and dad and my friends. I don't know how much more of this I can handle."

A British woman in Tokyo said, "The first month I was busy getting the kids settled in school and setting up our house." She laughed. "Well, that at least was an adventure. I couldn't read the labels on anything. One day I bleached out all the kids' sweatshirts instead of washing them." With a protracted sigh and a shrug of her shoulders, she went on, "Now I buy everything at the American shop. It costs a fortune, but at least I know what I'm getting. But that's just the practical problems. I can deal with those." There was a long pause before she continued, "I spend my days endlessly reading. I feel as though I've put my life on hold."

After these interviews I tried to imagine how I would negotiate for car insurance in France, use appliances labeled in German, or examine a grocery shelf in Japan to determine which bottle contained laundry detergent and which held bleach. Those issues just don't arise when you travel the world as a tourist but are unavoidable as an expat.

Many women spoke about their ongoing frustration and isolation. In the most extreme instances, the spouses sunk into a deep depression, scared by the new things and situations they needed to cope with while far from their normal support systems. Several marriages were on the brink of collapsing. A few had given their husbands ultimatums—return the family home or divorce. They were less concerned about the financial implications than their sanity.

But a few spouses wholeheartedly immersed themselves in some facet of their new life. They cooked local foods or learned to speak the language proficiently. They took classes or joined local craft guilds or expat clubs. Those activities helped them to cope with the strangeness of another culture and put them into situations where they could socialize. For the tiniest fraction of people, living in another country was an exciting adventure, fulfilling a life fantasy.

The discussions with these displaced women helped me to better understand my own relatives. Both of my grandmothers, at a young age, fled with their husbands from rural homes in Russia to escape the pogroms. When they arrived in New York, they didn't speak English. Neither had ever lived in a large city. Musiya, my paternal grandmother, became panicked by the speed and complexity of life in New York. The strangeness of everything around her caused her to behave like many of the expat women I'd interviewed: she retreated into her family, never learning more than a few words of English and rarely venturing outside apart from essential errands. By the time I knew her, she'd become agoraphobic. As a child, it was difficult to communicate with her, and I was put off by her foreignness. In contrast, my maternal grandmother, Bella, quickly learned English and how to get around New York City on the subway, where to buy fresh produce and get the best deals on clothes. Within a short time, she'd made many new friends and created a vibrant life far from her homeland.

At the end of the project, my client made numerous changes in the way they handled overseas assignments to ease the transition for families, including immersive language lessons, memberships in social clubs, and access to a service they could call for assistance with practical issues.

As I reflected on what I'd heard, I was glad I'd never gone through the wrenching experiences of either the expat spouses or my grandmothers. All my travel had been by choice. But I appreciated the window into the lives of people who'd done so, and I learned to value the qualities of bravery and resilience that helped some women to thrive.

Because of the success of that assignment, I worked on many more international projects that led me to facets of life I'd never been exposed to and sometimes had not even realized existed.

CONNECTIONS:
CIRCUMNAVIGATING THE GLOBE, 1996

D r. Quirid called very early morning, Monday, February 5. He spoke rapidly, with a hint of nervousness. "Your father was admitted last night. We didn't call you then because really, at that point, it was just a bit of difficulty breathing and a minor infection."

"How is he now?"

"He was much happier over the last couple of weeks. The antidepressants were working well."

"Good, glad to hear that. How is he doing now?"

"Well, the thing is . . ." Eventually the doctor got around to telling me my father had suffered a massive heart attack around two in the morning and had not survived.

Then he talked on and on about what good care my dad had received and described in detail what had happened right before the end. I couldn't really focus and wondered why he was going on at such great length. Finally it dawned on me—he thought there might be a lawsuit.

Since my father's separation from his second wife, my dad and I had spoken by phone once a week, a task I endured but never enjoyed. The calls were obligatory. I felt a responsibility to be certain his Parkinson's disease was under control and he was being taken care of. Once or twice a year, I visited him in Florida, making the trip as brief as possible. The news that he had died didn't cause me to shed a single tear. If I had cried, it would have been for what might have been, not what was.

Instead, I thought about logistics. I was scheduled to fly to London that night, the start of an eighteen-day business trip that would take me to six cities around the globe. Despite the enormous amount of work required and the prospect of extreme jet lag, I had been excited about circling the globe in a single journey—a first for me. The trip could not easily be delayed: I was supposed to run meetings in each city with dozens of people attending. Scheduling had taken months to arrange. So, after speaking with my brothers and uncle, the next call was to my client.

After assuring her I only needed a couple of days for the funeral, we came up with a plan. The itinerary would remain unchanged, except the meetings in London would be delayed. I'd combine London with a trip to Australia that had already been planned—allowing me a second global circumnavigation. My client's secretary promised to change my flights: West Palm Beach would become my first stop, and from there I'd fly to Paris and continue with the remainder of the original itinerary.

The funeral was perfunctory. All of us wanted it to be as short and simple as possible. We spent more time at the lawyer's office trying to unravel the legal morass my father had left behind than at the cemetery. Because he always felt he was being cheated, my father had changed lawyers every few months. There were numerous versions of the will. No final divorce papers from his estranged second wife could be found, but there was a signed prenuptial agreement. A confusing paper trail showed money being moved frequently between different banks and brokerage firms, and there were insurance policies with a defunct corporation as beneficiary. We found keys to more than a half-dozen safe-deposit boxes, for which my father had been the only signatory. Thinking about unraveling the mess gave us all headaches: he'd never told anyone exactly what he had or where to find it.

The one thing my dad had told me was his fear that at his death my brothers and I would swoop in like vultures and raid his possessions. Sad to say, but none of us wanted anything to "remember him by."

Richard, my father's accountant, had been the one person who'd spent a lot of time with him over the previous year. At one point, he and I were alone in his car, and I told him how sad and mean I thought my father's life had been.

"Yes, true," Richard said, "but he also did some very nice things."

"Please," I implored, "give me some examples. I'd like to be able to have some kind thoughts and memories about Dad."

And so he told me stories. Each one he related started out with promise. Like how he'd given a gift of $2,500 to Sophie, the woman who had taken care of him for eighteen months. "But," Richard said, "your dad refused to give her even one day off. She wanted to spend time with her own family and pleaded with him for a day, told him she had a friend who could come in her place. He blew up and said he couldn't do without her."

I sat listening, knowing what the outcome would be.

Richard continued, "He told Sophie if she didn't show up, she shouldn't come back again. Ever." He sighed. "She needed the job, so I don't think she took a day off for about two months." He sighed again. "Eventually she found another job and walked out on him."

There were several other stories—all with the same conclusion. Finally Richard admitted he could not come up with a single one without a "but . . ." in the middle.

I was relieved when I finally left Florida and started the business trip.

On the flight to Paris I sat next to a French scientist. We chatted about inconsequentials and then moved on to the impact of the Internet, which, in 1996, had just seen the debut of the World Wide Web.

"It's a great help," he said. "I can now communicate daily with colleagues halfway around the world. Before, I'd only see them once or twice a year at conferences."

"What kind of impact has that had on your work?" I asked.

"It's one of the reasons everything has speeded up." He chuckled. "It's also one of the reasons I'm always exhausted. I need to work when my colleagues are working . . . and they're in every time zone."

"I know the feeling. The pace has been picking up, and the world is getting smaller."

"True, but at the same time, my world is growing larger. I can be a real part of things happening thousands of miles away."

Our musings, while a welcome respite from discussions of

codicils and tax implications, brought me back to thoughts about my dad's life. I recalled the story Richard had told me about Joe, a mechanic he had recommended to my father. Joe and my dad had been getting along well; my father even took Joe and his girlfriend out to dinner several times. Then, for no clear reason Richard could discern, Dad took a dislike to the girlfriend, accused Joe of stealing from him, and they hadn't spoken again. It struck me that as the Internet expanded people's connections around the globe, my father's world had contracted as he'd pushed people away.

Once in Paris, my focus shifted to business, where I facilitated meetings with the survivors of recent staff cuts. It was tough to get them to concentrate on future directions for the company while their minds were occupied with concerns about how much longer they'd continue to have a job. It required concentration and a huge amount of effort for me to keep everyone engaged.

On my one free afternoon, I visited the Louvre, which, on a snowy day in the middle of winter, was blissfully free of tourists. On previous visits, I'd been entranced by the exquisite collection and spent time in as many galleries as possible, even though the museum had been crowded. This time I didn't look at much of the artwork. After being confined for days in a conference room, I just wanted to walk. Fortunately, the Louvre is enormous. I strode along the sweeping hallways, admiring the high arched ceilings and dramatic lighting, stopping a few times to admire the snow-covered landscape.

After Paris, I had a free weekend before the next set of meetings began in Milan. I spent it in Turin, Italy, with friends, a much-appreciated break after a grueling, difficult week. I didn't tell them about my father's death. Nando and Juliana are all about family: they wouldn't have been able to comprehend my being on a business trip, much less being cheerful, a few days after my father's funeral. But, surprisingly, I was cheerful.

Nando and Juliana's children lived nearby and joined us for dinner. It was a boisterous affair, complete with a young grand-daughter on whom everyone doted, lots of wine, a fabulous home-cooked meal, and much laughter. We lingered at the table for hours.

When I was a child, we sat down at a family dinner only on weekends, and then just long enough to consume our meal. At the dinner table, the slightest provocation from one of my brothers would set me off on a fit of giggles. My father would demand I calm down and continue to eat. But I couldn't control my laughter, so with each bite of food I'd begin to cough and choke, leading my father to send me away from the table.

Had it not been for his death, I doubt I would have been think-ing about my father or childhood at all. I had taught myself to be forward looking rather than dwell on unhappy memories. Still, I couldn't help wondering if and when it would start to bother me that I was now parentless and the "elder" generation to my niece and nephews. Mostly though, it felt as if a burden had been lifted from my shoulders.

Early Monday morning, Nando drove me to Principe di Savoia, the palatial, ultra-luxurious hotel in Milan. It was one of the perks of consulting for a financial services client who didn't worry about such expenses. For three days in Milan, I was so occupied with meetings I saw almost nothing of the city, apart from conference rooms and the opulent five-star restaurants where my hosts insisted I indulge in massive, gourmet meals. I concentrated only on work and the fear I'd gain ten pounds. In the odd free moments available, I fantasized about when I might tumble into bed and catch up on sleep.

I finally managed this on the long flight to Singapore. Leaving the airport, I soaked in the warmth and lavish greenery. When I departed Milan, it had been snowing fiercely; in Singapore it was a balmy eighty-one degrees. My body had no idea what time it was, or what day, but when I didn't dwell on it, I felt just fine.

The first afternoon, I needed to make some purchases before my next set of meetings. I asked the concierge, "Is there somewhere nearby that sells office supplies?"

"There's a mall connected to the hotel," he said, pointing me in the right direction.

"Any store in particular that's likely to have audio tapes?"

"I'd try Kmart; they'll have the best prices."

Kmart? I thought incredulously, *I can't believe I've come halfway around the globe to shop at Kmart.*

They were announcing a "blue-light special" as I walked into the store; another example of how "international" cities were becoming homogenized. Nearly all the shops and brands looked familiar, from Kmart and McDonald's to the Revlon, Clinique, Shiseido, and L'Oréal cosmetics in the department stores. As in the States, the electronics were mostly Japanese and Korean, the "fashionable" clothing French and Italian, and the fast food court interchangeable with ones in New York. The game arcade featured a salute to Hollywood, with machines named after American film stars.

Singapore, which I'd visited before, confirmed my opinion that in 1996 it was as sterile and dull as a city could be. I was glad to have almost no spare time. Deep within me, a precarious balancing act was taking place: trying to focus on work and deal with or, more accurately, avoid dealing with my father's death. It did occur to me that my father was indirectly responsible for my passion for travel leading to this trip. When I left for Europe at age seventeen, it was to escape his grasp on my life; I had wanted to put an ocean between us. Those years abroad left an indelible legacy—I had experienced my first taste of freedom and my lifelong addiction to travel had been born. I suppose I should have been thankful for this inadvertent gift, but I wasn't willing to acknowledge anything positive in our relationship.

My next stop, Hong Kong, buzzed with activity and excitement. In one year it would revert to Chinese rule, but at the moment, the city was British and proud of it.

Being there made me feel like a true world citizen. Hong Kong was halfway around the globe, but I'd been there often enough that I didn't need a map to get from place to place. The meetings were the best I'd had on the trip. Employees expressed both concern and excitement about the city's future and were deeply engaged when talking about it.

Over the weekend, I revisited some of my favorite parts of the city. I rode the tram up Victoria Peak for panoramic views of the area, crossed from Hong Kong to Kowloon on the Star Ferry a half-dozen times for the joy of feeling the breeze and for the great people watching, sampled mysterious foods in cavernous restaurants, and walked endlessly through boisterous, crowded streets.

Poking through some souvenir stands, I remembered, at age seven or eight, discovering a cigar box filled with colorful seashells and asking my mother about them. She told me that during the Second World War my father had worked as a propeller mechanic on an aircraft carrier cruising the Pacific, and he'd brought the shells back as a memento from the Philippines.

Fascinated that he'd traveled so far and intrigued by objects from the other side of the world, I pestered him with questions. I wanted to hear about the people, the scenery, and the food. Instead, he told me about the waste in the military, describing orders to drop used tools overboard when an inspection was scheduled. "The brass wanted to see clean tools," he'd say with a laugh. "How idiotic is that? Weren't we supposed to use them?" He never gave me a sense of the places he'd visited and never expressed interest in returning to Asia or visiting anywhere else. Once I was an adult and began to travel extensively, he never said a word of approval or disapproval about my obvious passion for seeing the world.

The final stop on my around-the-world trip would be Tokyo. On the Japan Airlines flight, I was the only female in business class. The other passengers ignored me, as did the cabin attendants. Even trying to get an extra bottle of water was a challenge. From the second I'd boarded the plane, there was an almost tangible sense of Japan being a male-oriented, hard-driving society.

A half-dozen flights were deplaning simultaneously when we arrived at Narita. Great crowds of very orderly people made their way through immigration and baggage claim. Then, calmly and quietly, they crammed onto the tram to the main terminal and queued up to buy tickets for the train into Tokyo. Though I was jet-lagged and couldn't read any of the signs, I managed to get a ticket and find the correct platform, train, and seat. For the thirty-five minutes into the city, I stared into space, too exhausted to process anything I was seeing.

At the central station, I somehow navigated my way through the swarms of commuters, the conflicting information signs, the moving walkways and escalators heading in different directions and made my way out of the station and to a taxi stand. I was quite proud of myself.

I handed the white-gloved driver a card with "Imperial Hotel" embossed on it. My client had given it to me when we'd been reviewing logistics, saying, "You'll need this."

As I always do when entering a new hotel room, I looked at the amenities. There was shaving lotion, a razor, a grooming kit containing shaving cream, aftershave, and hair tonic, but no bubble bath, no great smelling soap or moisturizer. The Imperial Hotel, one of the premier hotels in Japan, was clearly geared for male business travelers.

To make sure I didn't immediately succumb to jet lag, I went for coffee at the Old Imperial Bar, an imposing art deco space designed by Frank Lloyd Wright. There was only one other woman present. It felt like an old boys' club and wasn't a comfortable place to be alone, so I decided to head to the hotel's sushi bar. Sitting at the counter, I could watch the precision with which the chefs sliced fish, shaped rolls, and decorated plates. Each dish presented was unique and elegant. After determining I would eat almost anything, the chef showered me with small plates, each containing just a bite or two. When I questioned what some of them were, he told me in a firm voice, "Just eat. You like." And I did—salmon with garlic, daikon with some unidentified spicy crunchy substance, squid with ginger.

An elderly Japanese man, who'd been greeted by name by the staff and seemed to be well known to them, sat next to me. He asked for a variety of delicacies that elicited smiles from the other patrons and high yipping sounds from the chef. The middle-aged couple on my other side, also Japanese, seemed as tentative as I, receiving suggestions from the chefs and cautiously tasting each of the creations. The result from everyone was smiles: the food was sublime.

I was glad when the final meetings were over, knowing that I'd have a break before London and Melbourne. I was ready, *very* ready, to go home.

The day of my departure was freezing cold, snowy and raw, not conducive for walking. I thought about going to a museum or shopping area, but almost nothing opened until ten o'clock, and I needed to be back at the hotel by noon to check out and meet my friend Yuko for lunch.

Feeling trapped in the hotel with not enough to do, I realized that while on this trip, I'd thought about my father only when something specifically reminded me of how differently I lived my life from how he had lived his. I hadn't once broken into tears as I had often done after my mother died. I also didn't think about missing him. That, I decided, was a reflection of how small a role he'd played in my adult life. I tried but couldn't recall anything specific about the last conversation we'd had. Since he never had anything but complaints to share on our weekly calls, I usually tuned him out. I rarely volunteered anything about my life, and he never asked. Knowing I'd never speak with my father again didn't make me feel sad or happy or much of anything.

By noon I was in the lobby eagerly awaiting Yuko's arrival. I wasn't sure what we'd talk about after years apart. She and her family had lived near me for a few years while her husband worked in New York City. Our lives had been very different: she, the wife of a successful executive raising two small children, and I, focused on my career. I wondered if Yuko's desire to have an American friend and mine to have a Japanese friend was all we really had in common. Still, I was looking forward to seeing a familiar face and having a companion with whom to share a meal.

At Yuko's suggestion, we ate lunch at the "Western" restaurant in the hotel. At my local diner, I would have rejected the meal: vinegary wine, overcooked, rubbery swordfish, plain white rice, and soggy vegetables with no condiments of any kind. I chuckled inwardly, thinking my father would have preferred this food to the fresh, succulent sushi I'd eaten when I first arrived. He was a meat-and-potatoes man and suspicious of any unfamiliar food. If I'd followed in his pattern, rather than my mother's adventurous approach to dining, I'd never have survived traveling in other cultures.

Though I hadn't seen or written much to Yuko since I had been in Tokyo two years before, and despite my concern about what we would talk about, it was as if only a few weeks had elapsed. She shared photos of her two boys, and we talked about mutual friends.

I asked, "Now that you've been back in Tokyo for a while, what do you think about the time you lived in New York?"

She thought for a moment, then said, "I really miss the space. We had such a big house. Here, everything is small and cramped." I pictured the home her family had lived in, a typical suburban split-level, nothing fancy. But when she'd lived in New York, I'd had dinner at their home several times. In Tokyo we always ate out; she'd never suggested I come visit.

Yuko paused, as if considering whether she should continue, then went on, "What I really miss is the freedom."

"What do you mean?"

"In New York, I could do anything I wanted, dress any way I wanted, be friends with anyone I liked. Here, I need to be very careful. I could never go out of the house in jeans; it's just not acceptable for a woman my age." She carefully forked a small bite of food. "I even had a job. Here, a job would be bad for my husband's status."

She told me her husband was trying to get another assignment in the US, but it didn't look promising. After a leisurely lunch, she escorted me to the station for the train to the airport.

My forty-hour journey home took me from Tokyo to Dallas, then from Dallas to New York. I think I watched every movie on the plane, ate all I could eat, slept all I could sleep, read until my eyes were bleary, and played computer games until my arm hurt. At one point I noticed it was an hour earlier than when I had left Tokyo—the flight was wheels up at 7:05 p.m. on Saturday, and when I checked the monitor many hours later, it was 6:05 p.m. the same day. We'd crossed the international date line.

Back at home, I spent several days just hanging out as I adjusted to the Eastern time zone. I read the Sunday *New York Times*, caught up on mail, and slept a lot. And I had to call cousins and friends to tell them of my father's death. I was forced to think more about my father than I had the entire trip. Those who knew about my relationship with my father weren't at all sure what to say when I told them he'd died. As one commented, "With the kind of relationship you two had, this isn't exactly a Hallmark card moment." After uttering brief condolences, most friends shifted the focus to my trip. I was happy to answer their questions about what I'd seen, done, and experienced. Had my father still been alive, I suspected the only questions he'd have asked me would have been about how much everything had cost.

One friend asked, "What do you think about the world, now that you've gone around it in a single trip?"

"It seems to be shrinking. Physically, the planet remains huge. I'm still exhausted from the long flights and have horrible jet lag. But all of our connections are blurring the distinctions between nationalities and bringing us closer." I went on to describe what I'd observed on the flights and with my clients. "Many of us speak a common language, though there are loads of differences by country. Still, we seem to be moving closer together rather than further apart. Part of it, I think, is that with movies, TV, global brands, and the Internet, we have a lot of shared cultural references."

Speaking with another friend, I talked about the money I'd be inheriting. My father had been miserly during his life, so when we managed to untangle the legal issues, my brothers and I would all be getting something. Knowing about my strained relationship with my dad, and my fear that I in any way resembled him, she helped me cook up a plan to throw a huge blowout party to celebrate joy and friendship. I wasn't sure exactly when or what form the party would take, but I intended to "squander" a lot of money in a way my father would have hated.

I imagined a bright sunny day, a profusion of flowers, great food, and my yard filled with friends who'd flown in from all over the country, maybe even the world. I wanted to bring people in my life closer together, in the same way that, as I had traveled around the globe, I'd seen the world growing more connected.

The party, held in June, symbolically cemented my commitment never to live in the confining way my father had. I promised myself I'd do whatever it took to continue to expand my world. And I'd never stop traveling.

BRIGADOON REVISITED:
CRETE, 1996–2008

I have traveled to Greece six times, each visit separated by two years. A group of friends rented a house in the small hamlet of Moxlos on the island of Crete. Nowhere else on the globe holds quite the same place in my heart.

There's a small sign marking the turnoff for Moxlos. The first time I visited, I drove right past it, even though I had detailed instructions and had been looking carefully. The road is narrow and steep, one hairpin turn after another. Much of it is unpaved, and there's no guardrail in sight. On that first drive down to the coast, I held my breath, and my knuckles turned white. Over time I learned not to clutch the steering wheel quite so tightly but to remain wary—the view is so distracting. On most of the descent from the national highway to the coast, the village is hidden. Acres of silvery-green olive trees shimmer in the breeze, a sharp contrast to the intense blue of the ocean and sky. Down, down, down. Then, suddenly, a tiny village appears—one house jumbled upon the next, all whitewashed and looking like a Greek version of Brigadoon.

I was first invited there by Maggie, a woman I'd met in a class a few months before the trip. Maggie had lived on Crete in the 1970s and decided to return there to celebrate her fiftieth birthday. She rented the house for a month and issued an open invitation for friends to visit. Though I didn't know her well, the offer was too good to turn down. By the time that first trip was over, Maggie and I had become fast friends. For two weeks we bobbed in the warm, salty Mediterranean, drank retsina and ouzo, and ate fish caught just hours before. I tried to capture the view on sketch pads and with photos, but none did the scenery justice. We read books and talked for hours on end. That first trip felt like two months or two days, time there was so elastic. On subsequent trips, time was equally fluid, an ongoing party with a changing cast of characters, as we each invited friends to join our holiday. Sometimes there would be four or five people, sometimes as many as ten, squeezed into two adjacent homes.

The view from the front porch is etched into my memory—it's the image I conjure up in the dead of winter or when I'm feeling blue. I know that if I returned there this summer, I'd see the same blue water, string of islands, and distant mountains. In town I'd find the same men sitting nursing an ouzo in the taverna. The same *yayas* (grandmothers) would be hanging wash on the line to dry, and the same pink bougainvillea would be gaudily adorning the whitewashed homes. Going to Moxlos, or even thinking about it, means entering a world where time slows down and nothing changes.

In summer's heart, the light on Crete flattens three-dimensional objects during the heat of the day and puts everything in high relief at the periphery, sunrise and evenings. The water is a deep blue gray in the distance and pure, vivid aquamarine at the shore, with a spattering of lapis lazuli flecking it all. On days with a surf, flashes of light sparkle on the surface like a star-filled sky. The air has a hint of salt in it, mixed with wild thyme. There are few shadows on the landscape: there are no clouds to cast any. In Greece, it is good luck if it rains on your wedding day. But if you marry during the summer, the likelihood of that happening is slim. In six summers we experienced only a single day of overcast, drizzly skies.

Moxlos has a population of about five hundred. Because there isn't a single hotel or rooming house, there are almost no tourists. A few houses are for rent, like the one Maggie stumbled onto, but unless you can speak some Greek, they're difficult to locate. Our tiny rental is perched a few hundred feet above the coast, overlooking the sea, surrounded by an olive grove. In front of the house is a broad patio looking east. I'm sensitive to light, and the bedroom has sheer curtains. Most mornings, at about five thirty, I'd wake at the first hint of light. I'd patter out to the deck to absorb the grandeur of sunrise, from first paleness at the horizon until the sun, fully emerged across the water, blazed white-hot.

Looking off our deck to the left, a narrow plateau crisscrossed by goat paths hugs the shoreline. A steep drop-off keeps bathers away, but every morning and evening we hear bells tinkling as a herd of goats pass by.

In front of our patio and down the steep hill is a small rocky beach where we swim. The Mediterranean is salty and super buoyant. My body floats lightly on the surface of the salty water—there is a sensation of weightlessness. The sun warms me from above, while the water cools me from below. I listen to the waves lapping at the shore and piles of pebbles shifting with a soothing, skittering sound. Unlike what you might feel in a sensory deprivation tank, this is an experience of sensory stimulation. Once in the water, I would stay there endlessly, with nothing to disturb my solitude but a faint murmur in the depths of my brain that whispers, "No amount of sunscreen will help. Get out of the water now; you'll fry."

A small nameless island shaped like an olive pit lies to our right, about a quarter mile from the coast. Archeologists have found remains from a thousand years ago on the island, as happens almost anywhere a shovel is used on Crete. Behind the island and across an expanse of water, a hook of Crete's coastline stretches for miles. In the day, it turns nearly white in the sun's glare. At night, a few scattered lights twinkle in the clear air.

During the long, hot summer days, Moxlos is populated mainly by yayas, the Greek grandmothers. They dust and sweep, sew and cook, always busy but never so busy they won't flash a bright smile when I wave hello. Yayas dress in black to signify a death in the family. They've all seen death. You never see a yaya in midnight blue, green, brown, or, God forbid, pink. Most have shrunk significantly as they aged, or perhaps they started at five feet tall. Too much sun over too many years has given them a withered look. They sound like a pack of chickens, their high-pitched voices squawking and scrabbling their way through life. Beneath their black dresses lurk the elbows of Hercules. Despite their frail appearance, these women have a special skill in maneuvering their way through crowds. On line in the bank, they will magically appear in front of you. They may be seated at the back of a bus, but they're always the first ones off. At the Saturday produce market, an elbow will grind into your side, and the prized tomato on which you've had your eye will be firmly in their grasp.

In the evening, the yayas recede into their homes, and the men, who have been fishing or farming or doing construction all day, emerge. The sun that diminishes the women seems to strengthen the men, giving their faces a rugged, virile look. This is a village populated by Zorba the Greek look-alikes, right down to the T-shirts and caps. They congregate in the small cafés that line the dock. They sit for hours looking at each other, at any tourists who have found their way into town, at the dozens of cats that roam through the streets, and at the kids. Drinking beer, ouzo, and raki, smoking cigarettes, and playing cards, the men rarely move for hours on end.

Teenage girls latch onto any new male under the age of forty and flirt outrageously. With dark eyes framed by extra-long black lashes, wearing skintight jeans or skirts and cutoff tops exposing their navels, giggling and flouncing their hair, these girls give the impression of Lolita wannabes. But that veneer is thin. Below it, firmly anchored, is a good little girl who goes to church every Sunday and obeys her parents. The minute Mom or Dad or Yaya calls, she stops whatever she's doing and does what she's been asked.

There's a minuscule pier in town where a pack of small boys practice cannonballs, each trying for the largest possible splash. A fusillade of high-pitched laughter accompanies each attempt. In the evening, the younger children, the prize of every Greek family, transform the center of town into their personal playground. The elders keep a watchful eye on impromptu games of soccer, tag, and the Greek version of statues played until late at night.

Dinner, stretched out over many hours and lubricated with many bottles of wine, occupies us every evening. We stroll down the dirt road to the village and make our way to one of the small cafes lining the shore. One of our favorites is Manoli's restaurant. The couple who own it speak excellent English and over the years have become our friends. They often host loud, raucous parties in our honor, complete with *bouzouki* music and dancing.

Food in the village is simple and unvarying. No dinner is complete without a salad made with tomatoes still warm from the vine, crunchy cucumbers, olives, and grape leaves, splashed with local olive oil and sprinkled with salt and pepper. There is a menu, but looking through it is useless—they rarely have any of the listed items. Instead, we hand ourselves over to the proprietor, who knows what we like and brings out plate after plate of food that was in the sea or still growing earlier in the day. We sometimes have the same meal two or three nights in a row. No matter—each bite is a joy.

In the dead of winter, I still dream of the view and the mountains and sunrise over the Mediterranean. But we had to give up Moxlos after it became part of the EU. Airfares doubled, and prices for the rental of house and car more than tripled. People who'd been part of our group for years could no longer afford to go. Since then, we've rented houses in Maine, Oregon, Michigan, and Tobago, looking to capture that Moxlos magic. We haven't found it yet but continue our search. We fantasize about returning to Moxlos and look for any excuse to make that fantasy a reality.

THE TRANSLATOR: SINGAPORE, 1997

Though I have never learned to
speak any other language
proficiently, I became a
wunderkind at understanding
people who spoke English with
heavy accents. I never thought of
this as a special skill until . . .

"We're bringing all the Asian branch managing directors into Singapore for a meeting, and we'd like you to facilitate a session on improving regional communications."

It was the type of assignment I loved. My client was a US-based company with offices around the globe. Their employees all spoke English, though most had a heavy accent. The issues were straightforward, and I knew what approaches would work well to get people to open up, dig deep into the root causes of the poor communications, and create workable solutions. Working with people from a variety of countries would elicit cultural differences that usually led to heightened creativity.

In advance of the meeting, I interviewed several of the managing directors by phone. They spoke about time differences, poorly written English that led to misunderstandings, and the lack of an easy-to-use intranet to share information.

On the first morning of the two-day meeting, there was a happy commotion as the sixteen participants filtered into the conference room, greeted colleagues, grabbed cups of coffee or tea, found their name badges, and got seated.

"Good morning, everyone." The room quieted down as I introduced myself and laid out the day's agenda and a few ground rules, like no cell phones or side conversations.

"To start, I'd like each of you to introduce yourself. Tell us your name, office location, how long you've been with the company, and your top issue for today—what's the communication concern you'd most like to have addressed and resolved." Their faces reassured me they understood what I was saying and would cooperate. I continued, "Mr. Singh, I always start on my right, so you're up first."

"I'm Darsh Singh from the Delhi office. Six years, two as managing director for India." Everyone in the room nodded; they all knew him—the introductions were more for my sake than theirs. We listened as he explained, at length, the problem his office was facing. I had to concentrate to understand his heavy accent. When he finished, about half the faces turned expectantly toward me, but no one said anything. So I summarized his concerns and wrote *Who to contact in other offices and need for a detailed directory* on the flip chart and proceeded.

"Thanks, that was great. Mr. Kim?"

"Jung-hoon Kim, Seoul. Twelve years. Is problem about client data. Different file formats. We can't read. Makes no sense."

Again, the participants turned toward me. This time I saw confusion on their faces; they were clearly perplexed. "Everyone get that?" I asked. Most shook their heads no. "Mr. Kim suggested there are different file formats being used across the region. That's causing problems accessing data."

Participants smiled and nodded in agreement. *Different file formats* went up on the flip chart.

We proceeded around the table. After each person spoke I paraphrased the concern cited. One major communication problem, articulated by not a single person, was the different accents used by personnel in each office. Even when the words and grammar were correct, they just couldn't understand each other.

I imagined phone calls between offices in different countries being like the game of telephone I played as a child. Each kid would whisper a message into the ear of the next person in line. After four or five whisperings the last player would announce what they heard to the group. The message always became garbled along the way, so what the last player heard differed significantly from what was originally said. As a child this was hilarious; in business it was disastrous.

After years of watching Hollywood movies, everyone in the room understood my American accent. So, in addition to facilitating, I spent eight hours repeating what each person said, translating English into English. I felt like a parrot. I would never have imagined, with command of only a single language, I would be called upon to be a translator.

Trying to adapt to this new reality, I changed many of the exercises to written rather than spoken tasks. This helped, but only a bit. There was always the need for further explanations, and that necessitated my translation.

By day's end, I was exhausted. I ate dinner and collapsed into bed, my head aching, every muscle tense, knowing I'd have to do it again the next day. Worse yet, I had no easy solution to solving their biggest obstacle to effective communications.

On the second morning, I addressed the issue head-on. Forcing people to acknowledge the problem made the remainder of our time together easier. Instead of nodding and proceeding without truly understanding what had been said or looking to me to translate, participants would ask the speaker to repeat, use other words, or write the main thought on the flip chart. This led to the realization that they'd been avoiding a major obstacle because they wanted to be polite.

This lesson was important to them, and to me. I began every multinational meeting with a preface about language, accents, and the need to admit when they didn't understand something that had been said. My first exercise with multinational groups became a skill "test" to determine if they could really understand each other. We played "telephone."

CHAOS IN CAIRO: EGYPT, 1997

Linda and I had first planned to go to Sicily. She would be returning from a business trip to Ethiopia, I would be coming directly from New York, and Sicily seemed to be a good midway point. But the trip from Addis Ababa would have taken her

three days, connections being what they were in that part of the world. So we settled on another midway point, Cairo. I was elated with the realization that I'd arrived at a stage of life where Egypt was a convenient meeting place.

I was a bit wary about traveling in Egypt. About six months before our planned arrival, a bus filled with German tourists had been bombed in the middle of Cairo, targeted by Islamic fundamentalists. Still, I'd never been in Egypt and wanted to see the ancient and well-preserved antiquities for which the country is famous. I figured that because tourism is such an important part of the Egyptian economy, and with such a recent incident, security would surely be tight. And I rationalized that with just two of us traveling together we wouldn't be much of a target.

We met at the Cairo Marriott, a hub of international activity in the city, situated on a small island in the middle of the Nile. The hotel lobby is opulent, befitting the building's history. Originally, it was the Gezirah Palace, designed to resemble the palace at Versailles. It was used to house European royalty for the Suez Canal inauguration celebrations in 1869. When it was converted into a hotel, two huge towers were built, flanking the original structure. Every room features a terrace with a view of the river and a glimpse of the smoggy city beyond.

It's a playground for anyone with a bit of money, either their own or their employer's. Saudi sheikhs, Italian and Japanese tourists, foreign workers from across the globe, Jordanian families, European and American aid workers, African businessmen, and other guests all rub elbows in the elegant surroundings. Seeing such a hive of activity in the hotel lobby reactivated my security concerns, alleviated only slightly by the presence of metal detectors and security guards. But as we were already there, I shoved thoughts of terrorists into a deep corner of my brain.

The hotel provided only a partial refuge from the chaos and cacophony of the city. Wherever we went, our ears were assaulted by honking, drivers pressing down on their horn incessantly, perhaps to express frustration or maybe to just let others know they were coming through. Five times a day the honking was accompanied by blaring muezzins announcing the start of prayers, the amplified calls emanating from hundreds of mosque loudspeakers. That distinctive sound defines Cairo. It was so loud I took to inserting earplugs as soon as each call to prayer began. Even from our room on the twenty-sixth floor, we could hear both the horns and muezzins clearly.

Cairo's noise pollution was equaled by the air pollution. Emissions from excessive traffic and unregulated factories produced a thick, dirty haze. In the hotel, with the terrace door firmly closed, dirt and gritty sand would sneak into the room. Despite the diligence of the housekeeping staff, our room always felt faintly dirty. After my first walk through the city, I came back with a desperate desire to shower. It took several minutes of intense scrubbing before I began to feel clean. I started to think of washing as an archeology dig—each layer of grime removed represented artifacts from the ancient city.

Linda said that public transportation in Cairo was unreliable and dangerous, so we relied on taxis to get around the city. I'd thought motorists in Turkey were aggressive, but drivers here made the Turks seem like church ladies on a Sunday morning. Three-lane highways always had a minimum of four cars abreast, and often five, jockeying for position. On my initial ride from the airport to the hotel, I held onto the seat as firmly as possible. After the first five minutes, I closed my eyes, unwilling to watch as we weaved at top speed through a sea of buses, trucks, and cars with mere millimeters between us. Fears about terrorists melted away, replaced by fears of a horrific car accident—I was convinced death was more plausible than safe arrival at the hotel.

In this country of maniacal drivers, there wasn't a seat belt to be had. Most cars looked decrepit, and many were held together, literally, with wire and duct tape. They usually sported an array of dents and dings, and some didn't have bumpers. Egyptians, who were otherwise polite and friendly, all seemed to transform into Type A personalities the second they hit the road.

Thankfully, Linda, who had often worked in Cairo, knew how to negotiate with cab drivers. On the first morning, she walked down the line of taxis in front of the hotel. At the newest, cleanest car she talked with the driver, offering him five days of work at a good rate. Then she promised a bonus if he didn't drive like a maniac. It must have killed him to drive so slowly and conservatively, but the lure of the bonus was enough to keep him from truly outrageous vehicular behavior.

One morning we headed off to Giza, site of the pyramids. It is now a suburb of Cairo and a tourist trap of spectacular proportions, as befits the spectacular setting. Rising out of a sand sea, the antiquity, size, and scope of the pyramids and sphinx are truly awe-inspiring. But the surrounding area was a hive of hustlers and thieves. Tourist brochures, the concierge at the hotel, and even our driver warned us to be very, very careful. They said pickpockets were rampant and devious, the scams numerous. We heard stories of foreigners being "kidnapped" while on short camel rides and having their wallets stolen. People would offer to take photos of tourists with a backdrop of the pyramids and then sprint away with expensive cameras. The mounted police, on camels rather than horses, stood ready to chase after hustlers.

Another morning, we arrived at the Museum of Egyptian Antiquities a few minutes after it opened, hoping to avoid the crowds regularly attracted by the world-renowned collection. The museum was one of the places where I was most concerned about security, it being a prime tourist attraction in Cairo and the destination of the bus of German tourists that had been blown up. I was reassured when we had to pass through metal detectors to enter.

I'd studied Egyptian art in college and seen the collections at the Metropolitan Museum of Art in New York and the British Museum in London. But Egyptian art up close and in situ was a different and profoundly moving experience. The collection was stunning. I spent a lot of time staring open-jawed at the delicacy and grace of lines and shapes crafted thousands of years ago. Colors remained vivid on mosaics, furniture, and frescoes. Stylized sculpture ranged from perfect miniatures to larger-than-life kings and queens, who now regally observed the crowds of tourists who'd come to pay tribute. There was artwork that looked so contemporary it could easily have been created within the previous ten years. Jeweled neckpieces and rings and bracelets wouldn't have looked out of place on a runway during Fashion Week.

As we were leaving, I was glad we had arrived so early. Crowds had gathered in the courtyard, pushing their way into the front entrance. The guards had moved the metal detectors aside to get as many people through the doors as quickly as possible, expediency trumping security. Later that day I noticed that the metal detectors at the side entrances of the Marriott had also been abandoned. The large machines were decorative rather than functional. This seemed to me to be symbolic of much of the Egyptian approach to security.

Between excursions, Linda and I spent hours sipping mango juice and observing the other guests on the Marriott's garden terrace, one of the great people-watching meccas of the world. African couples strolled by, dressed in fabulous, brightly colored print outfits, with elaborate hairdos and makeup, resembling kings and queens. Packs of raucous Italian tourists decked out in *galabeyas* (the local version of the loose-fitting cover-up gown worn in many Islamic countries) looked as if they were going to a third-rate costume party. Americans could be identified by their Nikes, jeans, and baseball caps. Japanese tourists, cameras dangling around their necks, clustered together tightly—as they seem to do wherever they travel.

Not surprisingly, the majority of guests were Middle Easterners. Packs of men sat huddled together, smoking water pipes and holding whispered conversations. I imagined a lot of their wheeling and dealing was about oil, or maybe buying expensive new toys with their oil money. Each of these groups wore different head coverings. There were bright blue squares simply secured with a headband, and crisp white scarves folded elaborately into something I thought of as the "flying nun look." Some had on the checkerboard pattern scarves made famous by Yasser Arafat, a style that always seemed to be linked with a scruffy chin and whiskers looking a few days old. It was as if the wearers were perpetually trying to grow a beard but not succeeding. I wished I had access to a Middle Eastern expert who could teach me about the variations and identify which country or religious group was associated with each style.

After almost a week in Cairo, we flew to Aswan. It was a relief to be in a sleepy, lazy town after the bustle and anxiety of Cairo. Once again, our hotel sat on an island in the middle of the Nile. I appreciated that we could get around without taxis. We spent our days browsing through the market and visiting local archeological sites, but mostly lolling on the river in a felucca (small sailboat). The boats, with crew, were for hire for next to nothing. We lazed on the river, gliding silently across the water, taking in a landscape that was sometimes expansive green fields, in other places golden desert. For the first time in days, it felt as though I could really breathe.

For the next five days, we cruised up the Nile, ending in Luxor, home of the Valley of the Kings—one of the most important archeological sites in Egypt. History came alive as we explored the collection of tombs, most of them more than three thousand years old. Because of the arid conditions, the opulently decorated tombs are well preserved, the colors of the painted decorations still bright. The Temple of Queen Hatshepsut, a massive, almost contemporary-looking edifice ringed by bare rocks of an identical hue, was elegant. In Luxor, engrossed by the magic of the art, architecture, and history, and far away from Cairo's maniacal drivers and potential for terrorism, death became a celebration, not an imminent danger.

Before returning home, we needed to spend one final night in Cairo; neither of us was looking forward to it. On leaving the airport, we were hustled into a taxi by the dispatcher, not one either

Linda or I would have chosen—its exterior festooned with scrapes and dents, the front headlight dangling loose. The driver took off with a lurch before I had the door fully closed. Rather than heading onto the airport road, he sped into a large parking lot, swerving around parked cars. I was sure we were about to be robbed.

Then I saw where he was headed—a narrow opening in a chain-link fence that led directly out to the highway. This shortcut could, perhaps, shave three minutes off the journey. As the taxi neared the opening, I saw the headlights of a large vehicle rapidly approaching the gap from the opposite direction. I screamed. This did not deter the driver: he hunched his shoulders and stomped even harder on the gas, determined to get through the opening before the oncoming bus. The bus didn't appear to be slowing either. At the last possible second, our driver slammed on the brakes. I closed my eyes and mumbled a hurried prayer. The sound of shattering glass punctuated our abrupt stop.

When I opened my eyes, we were literally inches from the nose of the bus. That driver had braked as hard as our own had, and the front windshield of the bus had popped out. I could hear people screaming and crying inside the bus. The two drivers got out, examined their vehicles, and swore at each other. Though shaken, neither Linda nor I was hurt—our luck had held.

One month after we returned home, fifty-eight tourists were killed by terrorist gunfire in the courtyard in front of the Temple of Queen Hatshepsut in Luxor. I remembered that we had lingered there for a long while, oblivious to the dangerous layout of the site —an open horseshoe, surrounded on all sides by hills, with only a single point of egress. Only when reading about the incident did I realize just how lucky we'd been.

TRADITIONS: SOUTH OF FRANCE, 1998

During the year I worked on a project in Brussels, I became friends with Pascale, one of my main contacts at the firm. After completion of the project, she and I remained close while she moved to Japan and then London with her Danish boyfriend, Morten. When I was invited to their wedding in the South of France, I was thrilled. This would be the kind of weekend I had fantasized about when I first grasped hold of the idea that people jet-set abroad for just a few days. What could be more romantic than a wedding in the South of France?

But I was also a bit nervous, certain I didn't have the right wardrobe. Before leaving home, I spent excessive time and money hunting for what might be appropriate.

L ate afternoon, I walked through the town of Beaulieu-sur-Mer. Sandwiched between water and mountains, with palm trees dotting the shore, the views were dramatic. Pastel-tinted concrete buildings topped by red-tiled roofs resembled an artist's vision of the perfect village. Squinting slightly, I could imagine what a water-color rendition would look like. I understood why the rich and famous gravitated here. Before I'd spoken to or seen anyone in the wedding party, feelings of inadequacy bubbled up.

To ward off this nervousness, I headed toward Villa Kerylos, the location for the wedding reception, for a sneak preview. The Greek-style mansion juts out on a promontory looking into the sea, with a sweeping view to the east of Saint-Jean-Cap-Ferrat and west to Monaco. The panorama was breathtaking—I shot a full roll of film.

As I was readying to leave, I ran into Morten, the nervous groom, doing a last-minute check.

He did a double take, as if surprised to see me. "Hey, Karen. Great to see you." I gave him a quick hug.

"This place is amazing," I enthused.

"Only the best for Pascale." He waved an arm as if demonstrating that he'd personally designed this magnificent space. He looked back at me quizzically. "When did you arrive?"

Pascale is the one I'm closer to, so I wondered if he even realized I'd been invited. Or he might have been overwhelmed with wedding details, and his mind was in a fog. I chose to believe the latter.

After a few minutes of idle chatter, I said, "See you at dinner."

"Right. Dinner." He kissed my cheek and wandered off. Yeah, he was in a fog.

Leaving him, I walked on a path along the sea to Saint-Jean-Cap-Ferrat. Surrounded by small cafés and bars, the harbor was crammed with expensive-looking yachts. The setting sun cast a buttery glow that could have made a slum look jewel-like. Shining on the sea, mountains, and pristine pastel homes, the golden light transformed them into a Shangri-La, romantic beyond cliché. I regretted being alone; why hadn't I brought my boyfriend? Then I remembered the expense and simply fantasized.

In town, I ambled over to the church. Just as I arrived, Pascale came out. She and the best man, also named Morten, were practicing walking down the church steps—uneven, ancient stone. In shorts and spike heels, her concentration was on keeping herself from tumbling, even with Morten's iron grip on her arm. I feared for a sprained ankle and wondered how she'd manage in a wedding gown with a train. After the fourth successful attempt, she looked up.

"Karen, you're here!" She ran over and engulfed me in her arms. Pascale reminds me of Audrey Hepburn, with wide eyes, pronounced jaw and cheekbones, and a long, elegant neck. She also has that Audrey Hepburn quality of simultaneously appearing gawky and elegant. Always fragile looking, she seemed thinner and more translucent than ever. She couldn't have been more than a size two, which was suprising given the number of meals I'd shared with her when she ate like a farm hand. Unlike her husband-to-be, she seemed both calm and excited for the festivities to begin.

After chatting about flights and wedding plans, she slipped on a pair of flats, and we strolled over to the restaurant for cocktails and dinner. Although I don't generally like cocktail parties, this one intrigued me. Guests chatted in a dozen languages, slipping back and forth from Danish to French, German to English, English to French. Apart from several British guests and me, English was a second language for everyone. I had worried that as an English-only speaker, the others would have to accommodate me or I'd miss a lot of the conversation. It quickly became clear that the Danes don't speak French well, and no one but the Danes speak Danish. The Italian, Flemish, and Germans all preferred English, so the problem was averted.

Morten (the groom) was a bond trader, and about half the group worked in international finance. The male guests looked like they were ready for a fashion shoot in a trendy magazine. Model thin, most women were fashionably dressed and artfully made up. As the only American, and not an especially fashionable one, I knew I stood out in minimal makeup, wearing a simple skirt, blouse, and sandals. Spotting a few less-than-model-perfect women wearing understated slacks and T-shirts or simple cotton dresses made me feel less conspicuous. One even had the look of a leftover hippie, in a long flowered skirt, a neon T-shirt, and a long strand of beads.

All the Danish men seemed to be named Henrik or Morten. Had I called out "Morten," six of them would have looked up. The champagne was divine, but surprisingly the food wasn't—bland and boring, so boring I can't recall what we ate. I didn't eat much. With a Henrik or Morten constantly refilling my glass, I became giddy. By the end of the evening, a group of strangers from different cultures, with different languages, customs, and lifestyles, bound only by friendship with Pascale and Morten, had coalesced into a group of friends.

As the party wound down, Pascale gave us strict warnings to be at the church promptly at 4:45 the following afternoon. Over the years working with Pascale, I knew her to be punctual and precise. It seemed we all knew to obey her edict.

The next afternoon, I took great care dressing and applying makeup, but I suspected despite my efforts, I would appear the poor relation in this well-heeled, elegant crowd. My prediction was correct. The men wore morning coats or tuxedos or perfectly tailored, stylish suits with crisp shirts and silk ties. Most women wore long dresses, in luxurious silks, satins, and brocades, with bold matching hats. I wore a silk pantsuit and hadn't thought to wear a hat.

The harbor was the backdrop for the courtyard where the wedding party gathered, surrounded by ancient buildings. Church bells tolled as ushers shepherded us into the church. The small church featured a graceful, arching roof, weathered wood pews and altar, and exquisite stained glass casting jewel-toned light on the congregants. Decorated in masses of white roses and lilies, the scent was heavenly.

In her wedding gown with satin bodice, full flowing tulle skirt, veil trimmed in satin, a bouquet of red roses, red roses in her coiffed auburn hair, and perfectly applied makeup, Pascale looked like she had stepped onto a movie set. On the arm of the best man, she walked down the aisle beaming. With a broad smile and sparkling eyes, she was enjoying the event as much as the guests. After four years of living with Morten, she seemed certain of her intent. Morten met her at the front of the church dressed as meticulously as she. With his curly blond hair and striking looks, he cut quite a figure. The two together were stunning.

I didn't understand a word of the ceremony, spoken in French. After they had exchanged vows, seven different people—the priest, Pascale, Morten, and four witnesses—had to sign a sheaf of papers. The signing took longer than the vows.

The wedding party followed the newlyweds into the courtyard where we toasted them with champagne. Then the photography began, again taking longer than the ceremony. They posed on the steps of the church, near the harbor, and in front of Morten's blue Aston Martin.

The reception, in the splendid Villa Kerylos, was unlike any wedding reception I'd ever attended. After cocktails and canapés, we were led into the formal dining room: eight tables laid with starched white linen, sparkling crystal, silver, porcelain, and large bouquets of white roses. It would have done a royal family proud. Dinner included multiple courses of luscious food, accompanied by copious amounts of French wine punctuated by endless speeches. Speeches at weddings are a Danish tradition and went on for a couple of hours. They tended to be funny and were meant to mildly embarrass the newly-wed couple. A toastmaster stage-managed the speakers. We heard a lot about Morten's foibles: his torturing of the English language, his love of expensive cars, his playing cards instead of studying while at university, and his eye for beautiful women.

The long, rambling, slightly drunken speeches were delivered in a mixture of English and Danish from Morten's childhood friends, his relatives and business associates. But no one said a word about Pascale, and no woman had spoken at all. Later I was told Danish and Belgian women are too shy. I didn't buy that; it seemed an unspoken facet of sexism. I couldn't allow that to pass. Adding to my discomfort was that at every wedding I'd been to in the States, the focus was largely on the bride; here she seemed a sup-porting cast member rather than the star.

I screwed up my courage, told myself that after years of making presentations to clients, including boards of directors, this shouldn't be difficult. But I hadn't prepared anything, so I had to think on my feet after consuming a lot of alcohol. I willed myself to be brave, approached the toastmaster, and told him I'd like to speak. He introduced me as Pascale's American friend and mo-tioned me to the front of the hall.

"I met Pascale about eight years ago when I was, as Pascale used to describe it, a 'corporate shrink' at her firm in Brussels." (I'd been working on a communication plan for them.) "We hit it off immediately, and thanks to Pascale and an expense account, I got to eat at some of the best restaurants in Brussels. I must have gained ten pounds working on that project." I heard chuckles and apprecia-tive murmurs from the guests.

"She told me about Morten, but I didn't meet him for several years. When they were living and working in Tokyo, Pascale regularly called me, and I became her personal shrink." I went on to tell the story of their horror at receiving an exorbitant electric bill. Morten had Pascale plug and unplug every appliance in their apartment while he watched the electric meter and pronounced what they could and could not use. I'd both sympathized and laughed at her predicament.

"After they'd returned to Europe and had been living in London for a while, Pascale thought she'd like to move to New York. Morten wasn't terribly interested in this idea. So she enlisted me to drive Morten around Westchester and show him there are lots of trees, beautiful homes, lakes, and gardens—that is, New York isn't all skyscrapers." I ended my brief speech by offering a toast to Pascale and Morten, to their health, happiness, and wishing that they should always be surrounded by friends.

The speech was a hit. Pascale's friends, both female and male, thanked me profusely for the rest of the evening and well into Sunday. They appreciated my "evening out" the speeches. Morten's Danish female friends thanked me for speaking "as a woman." I've no idea what the Danish men thought, though I suspect they wrote me off as a brash, feisty American. Fueled by champagne and wine and the success of my speech, all worries about my appearance vanished.

Speeches concluded, the party moved to the courtyard for dancing and yet more booze—champagne, wine, brandies, and cognacs. They distributed cigars, with only a few wisecracks about Bill Clinton. Even in the South of France, at a wedding, I couldn't escape the Clinton jokes.

Toward the end of their first dance, a Viennese waltz, Morten's friends put him on a chair, lifted him up, removed his shoes, and snipped off the toes of his socks, a Danish tradition. There appeared to be several versions of the origin of this tradition. One of the Henriks told me it was because he would have to limp without complete socks so other women would know to stay away. A different Henrik explained it was because no woman would want a man with hole-y socks. Whatever the reason, they laughed and laughed and laughed.

I laughed along with them, grateful to feel comfortable and accepted and part of this magical evening.

TRAVELING IN FEAR: BRAZIL, 1998

After many years of traveling for work,
most business trips became routine. The
hotel and meeting rooms
felt interchangeable. But occasionally I'd
spend time in a city or country new to
me. My time in Brazil, both before and
during my meetings, was unlike any
other business trip I've experienced.

One week before my scheduled business trip to Brazil, my client was briefing me, not about the upcoming project but about security. He had started by telling me not to wear expensive jewelry, which as an experienced traveler was obvious to me. His more urgent and less expected advice was, "Never, ever get into a taxi we haven't arranged for you."

Taxis in New York City routinely rip off tourists, but I'd never even considered warning any of my many out-of-town visitors about that as a potential danger. I jokingly said, "How much more can they overcharge than New York cabbies?"

His face turned stony. "Take what I'm telling you seriously. Every day foreign visitors are picked up by what they think are legitimate taxis and then driven into the worst of the favelas—the slums." He sighed. "We had that happen to one of our executives a while back. After robbing him of everything, they left him there to fend for himself."

I was genuinely shocked. "How awful. What happened?"

"It ended okay, but it was very frightening for him." He shook his head. "And scary for the rest of us too. We really ramped up all our security precautions." He looked me right in the eye and continued, "Businesspeople are particularly vulnerable; thieves target them. You *must* be careful when you're there."

Then he explained other trip logistics, which I only half heard. I was mentally questioning the necessity of this trip—maybe we could conduct our business via teleconferencing?

But they had scheduled the meetings, made hotel reservations, and bought airline tickets—I'd be leaving in a week.

A few days later, I met a colleague for dinner. Gina speaks fluent Portuguese and travels to Brazil often, for both business and pleasure. I'd hoped that she could give me some tips on fun offbeat things to do, as well as calm my simmering fears. Instead, she said, "Think of Rio as a poisoned flower, beautiful and enticing but very dangerous."

Her lurid stories of rampant thievery and murdered tourists emphasized my client's point—I was heading into danger.

Travel junkie that I am, since my client was paying for a business class ticket, I would take advantage of it, despite all the warnings. I kept reassuring myself I was savvy and street smart and had never been robbed in New York City. For years I'd been poo-pooing all the nonsense about the dangers lurking on every street corner in Manhattan. I knew with just a little common sense I'd be fine. Still . . .

I'd planned a long weekend in Rio de Janeiro before my business meetings in São Paulo. Once in Rio, assuming there was safety in numbers, I joined a Gray Line tour. In the company of a busload of tourists, I walked near the statue of Christ atop Corcovado Mountain (the quintessential symbol of the city), drove through the business center of Rio, and saw the favelas—from a distance. The tour was efficient and safe, but not very satisfying. I'm more of a wander-around-and-explore traveler.

Nevertheless, I got a sense of the city. Its spectacular beauty bedazzled me, with water views from nearly everywhere and a backbeat of pounding surf against sugar-white beaches. It's a place of all-day, all-night, in-your-face partying and erotica.

During the day, gorgeous bronzed bodies, in the most minimal of attire, crowded the beaches. At night at a samba show, the dancers wore costumes that made Las Vegas showgirls seem prudish. Bright orange wings sprouted from a hot pink dress; neon yellow fringe swung from a skimpy white bikini top that had small gilt cages to hold in ample bosoms, with nipples peeking through. Glittered headdresses that looked heavy and unwieldy were strapped on the tops of heads that bounced, swayed, and dipped to a frantic rhythm. Men wore skin-tight neon green pants that didn't hide a thing. There was such thick makeup on both men and women—inch-long eyelashes, golden eyelids, juicy red lipstick—that their faces appeared surreal. Anywhere else, the elaborate structures and gaudy colors would have looked garish, even ridiculous. In Rio, on perfectly fit, curvaceous bodies that wore the costumes proudly, they looked festive and fun.

I loved the show but couldn't erase the thought that all of this took place in a carefully sheltered environment. The theater was an escape from the reality of poverty, desperation, and constant crime. Scenes from the show *Cabaret* came to mind, debauchery as an escape from mounting horrors in Nazi Germany, and I wondered if samba didn't have the same societal function in Brazil. I also thought of busloads of tourists in New York viewing Times Square through a window and then ducking from the bus right into a theater to see a show. It was the first time I'd had even a smidgen of empathy for them.

After two days, I'd had enough of seeing the city in the company of a crowd and went for a long walk. I happened upon a parade of samba school students shimmying along the beachfront. The dancers, all small kids in elaborate costumes, boogied their way accompanied by a marching band resplendent in sky-blue satin uniforms. It was nearly impossible to keep from joining in, and many of the beach crowd leapt up from their towels as the music approached. Despite their scanty coverings, they had no inhibitions about shaking their hips and bopping along. The joy and energy were palpable and infectious. I followed along snapping photos, a dopey smile pasted on my face. But I also couldn't help tightly clutching my handbag and wondering where everyone stowed their keys and cash.

Then it was time for work. "São Paulo is a lot less beautiful and a lot more dangerous." Gina's words echoed in my thoughts during the long, dull taxi ride from the airport into the center of the city. Here there were no water views. The city is flat and seemed to go on forever—an endless, featureless landscape of buildings, billboards, and highways crammed with pollution-belching traffic. The sun hid behind choking thick smog. High walls and gates surrounded even the most modest of homes. Any wall that could be climbed over was topped with barbed wire or broken glass.

My client had arranged for me to stay in one of the most exclusive hotels in São Paulo (company policy to keep me safe). Registration took longer than usual as the desk clerk thoroughly inspected my documents and explained the hotel's extensive security measures. Going to my room would require showing photo ID twice. The elevator would only stop at my floor and floors with public facilities—the pool, health club, and restaurant.

In the room, in addition to information about room service and tourist attractions, there were multiple messages instructing guests to lock all valuables at all times. A large sign warned guests to only open the door to people who showed proper credentials. How guests were supposed to distinguish between legitimate and falsified documents was, however, not explained.

The next morning, leaving the hotel for the office, both the taxi driver and I had to show our IDs to exit the hotel parking area. It surprised me that the drive was only ten blocks, a distance I would have walked in any other city. But walking from the hotel in business attire with a briefcase would have set me up as a target. I wished they'd booked me into less conspicuous lodgings.

At the top of the drive leading to my client's office tower, and yet again at a security booth before we entered an underground parking area, both the driver and I had to show our IDs. Inside, a security officer grilled me. He took my passport and photocopied it, snapped a photo of me, and then phoned for permission for me to proceed upstairs. At any of the offices I'd worked at around the globe, including major Wall Street firms, those measures would have been more than sufficient to speed me up to my meeting. But in São Paulo, before I met with my client, there was still another escort, additional security codes, and a glassed and locked reception area. This procedure was scrupulously followed each of the three days I worked there.

Even in the post-9/11 era of security tightening, I have not experienced such precautions anywhere else. Yet, despite all the vigilance, I never felt safe in São Paulo, unless one considers being in prison a form of safety. Guidebooks described wonderful museums, galleries, and shops, but that's as close as I got to any of them. I was too scared to walk by myself in the city. I ate all my meals in the company of my clients or in the hotel.

But I struggled then, and still do, over how real the danger was. In Rio I'd had the most fun when I had ventured out on my own. Using common sense about where to go and what to wear, I had never felt threatened. But in São Paulo, the stories told to me and the security measures I experienced had paralyzed me, and I never mustered the courage to test the reality.

Since that trip, I've refused to listen to scare stories. After having had several close brushes with disaster, I've become a fatalist. Crime and tragedy happen all the time, all over the world, and I'll die whenever I die. However, I am no longer scornful of tourists in New York City who are terrified to ride the subway or take a walk on their own down Fifth Avenue. I hope I never experience that fear again in any part of the world. But I understand it.

MUSIC UNDER THE STARS:
MOROCCO, 1999

I'd visited Morocco in the 1980s and had been enchanted with the fairytale-like casbahs, the stark desert landscapes, the exotic crafts in the markets, and the warmth of the people.

So I was happy to join my friend Maggie when she traveled to a sacred music festival in Fes, which had been my favorite city on my first visit.

In my experience, sacred music was limited to hymns, gospel, carols, and the cantor at synagogue. This festival exposed me to a broad swath of spiritual music from across the globe. But more than that, it immersed me in Moroccan culture in a way no tourist trek could have done.

T he crowd pulsed with excitement as it made its way into Bab Makina, the central gateway to the royal palace in Fes and the venue for the final night of the international sacred music festival. From the moment we entered through the massive stone gate, I knew the concert would be memorable. Armed guards stood crisply along the edge of a red carpet awaiting the arrival of the Moroccan crown prince. Their dress uniforms glittered with braids and gold buttons that reflected flashes of light from searchlights scanning the area.

Keeping carefully off the carpet, Maggie and I followed the usher to our seats. We'd seen Bab Makina from outside a few days before, and it had been impressive. Now, it was breathtaking. Floodlit, the stone walls blazed white against a black sky. The massive open-air structure held more than one thousand people, and it was quickly filling to capacity. The stage, draped with rich red velvet, sat in front of a massive keyhole gate.

King Hassan stared solemnly at the audience from three huge photos that dominated center stage. I wondered what he, had he been present, would have thought of the rich stew of Moroccans, Arabs, Africans, Europeans, and Americans filling the seats.

This was a very different Fes than I'd experienced on my previous trip to Morocco. Then I'd been impressed by the city's timelessness. A stroll through the thousand-year-old medina (walled city) was like walking back in time. Instead of cars, donkeys navigated the narrow twisting paths, transporting copperware, tiles, leather, and other goods made the same way they were when the city was first built. Tucked behind bland walls were lush gardens and homes that brought to mind tales of Aladdin and Ali Baba. Women baked bread in communal ovens, and men congregated at tea shops, smoking water pipes. Chickens squawked in wooden cages. Shops sold tantalizing crafts. The streets smelled of tanning leather, potent floral perfumes, donkey droppings, baking bread, and a thousand other scents that seemed to have accumulated over decades and clung to the walls. It felt magical, far removed from the globalized and homogenized world.

When we walked through the medina on this trip, it remained a world apart from modern Fes and the festival we were attending. But the festival showed a different face of the city.

This concert, like so many other things in Morocco, followed a schedule far different from the printed program. While the organizers hurried about doing last-minute sound checks, the food stalls did a brisk business selling soft drinks and sacks of salted nuts. A screen was set up showing a video extolling the virtues of doing business in Morocco. One little boy, perhaps five years old, seated behind us burbled in a thick Moroccan accent, "Five Blind Boys, Five Blind Boys." He'd been well prepared for what was coming.

While waiting for the music to begin, people jumped in place and flapped their arms hoping to generate warmth—no one had come prepared for the cold or the wind. It whistled through the amplification system, creating an eerie moaning sound, wailing as if in agony.

The delay allowed me to carefully observe the audience. People wore an astonishing mix of clothing: sacred and profane, old and new, East and West. There were women in halter tops and jeans and others in full coverings, with only their eyes peering out of the black. Many women dressed in head-to-toe djellabas (a caftan-like covering with a long, peaked hood hanging down the back, dangling a silken tassel) in blacks and browns, with only their faces visible. But there were also djellabas in pale pink and lime green and a rainbow of other colors—often with slits going well up the legs or high-heeled shoes peeping out beneath. The men uniformly wore Western dress—mostly jeans and casual shirts.

Forty minutes late, the concert began. The opening act was a Senegalese group, the Gnawas, who drummed and monotonously chanted. Audience members ignored them completely and continued to party, talking, eating, smoking, and making calls on cell phones. Their music became background to the festivities. Had I wanted to listen, it wouldn't have been possible; the group of twenty-something Moroccans around me were far too distracting. A few spoke a little English and wanted to practice with us, ensuring we couldn't hear a thing. After about half an hour, the Gnawas abruptly stopped and exited, to a smattering of applause.

After a lengthy pause, Liz McComb came onstage. Although she's an American-born gospel singer, McComb is far more famous in Europe than in the US. Backed up by piano and drums, her voice was clear and filled with emotion, her range and depth electrifying. Her rendition of "Joshua Fought the Battle of Jericho," rocking and raucous, riveted the audience—this is what they'd been waiting for. Everyone who had shivered their way through the endless chanting was drawn into toe-tapping, hand-clapping participation. People shouted and swayed. They shrieked their approval at earsplitting volume. Despite the still-present wind, the place felt warmer.

The young Moroccan women were the most enthusiastic. The pack seated next to and behind us literally danced with joy. After a few minutes, they climbed onto their chairs, yelling and singing along. They knew all the words. Some of the loudest and most animated women were covered head-to-toe in shapeless black djellabas. It had never occurred to me that someone looking so traditional would, in the right circumstances, behave exactly as a "westernized" woman.

Liz remained onstage for well over ninety minutes and didn't seem to want to get off. We could see the festival organizers motioning for her to stop, but, fueled by the energy of the crowd, she eased out of one song and into another with the smoothest of transitions. I figured the only way they would get her off the stage would be to get a hook. It was quite a sight, this Black woman dominating an ancient Arab site with American gospel music. At last, she finished to wild cheering, whistling, hooting, and hollering.

After a short break (while the stagehands hustled like mad), the Five Blind Boys of Alabama began their set. If the atmosphere had been charged before, within minutes the whole place exploded with even more potent energy. The portraits of King Hassan presided over a nearly ecstatic audience.

On stage a group of Black gospel singers wearing sunglasses, dressed in shimmering red shirts and black tuxedos, exuberantly sang American gospel. Their spirited harmonies celebrating Jesus got everyone, Moroccan and foreign, dancing in the aisles and on chairs—clapping, stamping, swaying, screaming. As I stood on my chair, it felt as if I had joined a swarming hive, all movement and crackling electricity. I wondered if the group received the same passionate response from American audiences and whether American crowds were this diverse.

For the finale, the Five Blind Boys invited Liz McComb and the Gnawas to join them onstage. There, in one of the most ancient cities on the globe, American gospel singers and Sufi chanters made exuberant music to an international crowd that went wild. As music, I wouldn't rush off to buy the CD. As evidence that the world is shrinking, it was extraordinary.

Later, as I replayed the concert in my mind, I realized that nothing in my experience or anything I'd read about the Middle East and Muslim countries had prepared me for it.

I'd seen Morocco as a country rooted in ancient traditions. On my prior trip, I'd spent much of my time wandering in the thousand-year-old walled medina, unaware that modernity had touched Fes at all. Now, I was seeing another side of the city and country, one that has in many ways politically separated Morocco from its more conservative neighbors.

I'd always envisioned Middle Eastern Muslims as tribal and closed to outsiders. The diversity of the audience and the wild, gleeful response at the concert was both a joy and an eye-opener.

THE CAMEL TREK: MOROCCO, 1999

After the music festival, Maggie and I traveled to the far edge of the Atlas Mountains for a camel trek in the Sahara Desert. It would be a counterpoint to the crowds at the music festival and a chance to process all we'd experienced.

O n the first morning, I walked at the front of two parallel lines of camels. A gentle Moroccan led each line, singing and chanting, as our group of eight headed into a sea of sand. The soothing rhythm of the camel tenders' voices calmed the animals, and me too. At regular intervals, one or the other would turn and ask me, "*Ca va?*" ("How are you?") At my hearty "*Bien,*" they would smile and return to their song. None of the rest of our little band uttered a single syllable. In the intense heat, speaking would have required effort and energy.

Two hours later, wiping stinging beads of sweat from my eyes and blinking in the blinding white rays of the sun, I wondered why I'd agreed to this trip. Weak-willed, I thought. A pushover. Maggie's suggestion of a trek in Morocco had sounded exciting. But then I'd agreed to it on a frosty February day in New York.

The one condition I'd set was that I wouldn't ride a camel. I'm terrified of heights and of falling. I'd been on a camel once, for about twenty minutes; the movement both scared me and got me queasy. After I dismounted, I'd kissed the ground.

We set off on the five-day trek from Zagora, a small village at the edge of the Atlas Mountains. The guide insisted on bringing a camel along for me, "In case you decide to ride. It is very hot this time of year." He'd been certain that at some point during the five-day trek, I'd change my mind. I knew that no matter how hot it became, riding a camel wasn't an option.

By the second day, I had become impatient with the frequent stops to stretch legs or rewrap head coverings and by the complaints of my fellow trekkers: "It's so uncomfortable." "My stomach is heaving." "I feel like I'm seasick." "I'm getting leg cramps." I decided to walk ahead a bit, then wait for the group to catch up. The camel tenders pointed out the direction and a landmark—a stand of palm trees—where they'd meet me. In the desert's emptiness there wasn't much chance of getting lost. That became the pattern for the remainder of the trek.

Others in the group would sometimes walk a little way with me, but they had a tough time maintaining my pace. I was a woman on a mission. My goal: to escape the heat as quickly as possible. I strode briskly, fantasizing about blizzards, the Swiss Alps, the over-air-conditioned office in which I used to work, walk-in freezers. I cursed Maggie for suggesting this adventure. I cursed myself.

By the third day, I didn't bother waiting for the group. I just took off, knowing that the faster I walked, the sooner I'd get to shade and water.

Despite my grousing, the desert captivated me. I tried to identify tracks in the sand: camels' huge cloverleafs, barefoot human, don-

key, Land Rover, Nike and Reebok, fox, iguana, dog, and a long
slithery snake trail. The texture beneath my feet changed as I strode
along. In places the sand was hard-packed, almost concrete-like,
and scattered with small pebbles which made it the best surface for
walking. More challenging were little tuffets formed by a mixture of
salt and sand that crunched and collapsed when stepped on. The
soft, powdery sand was the prettiest to look at but tough terrain to
negotiate. My feet would sink deep into it; each step required effort
and deliberation. Pull out right foot, raise it up, put it down, pull
out left foot, repeat, repeat, repeat. Trickier yet were the areas
thickly strewn with large rocks. In those areas, each step was a battle against a sprained ankle. Even the camels slipped and slid. The
guide quipped, "We call the country 'Morocco' because there are
'more rocks' in Morocco."

Mid-morning on the third day, I turned, looked back, and
peered into the blinding light, wondering where the group might
be. In the featureless, flat expanse of desert, I couldn't see a hint of
camels. Even in the shade, it was well over a hundred degrees. But
what was I thinking? There was no shade. I panicked, convinced I'd
strayed far off the trail and my bones would never be found. I wondered if I was in the early stages of heatstroke. Why hadn't I bought
the medevac insurance when I'd had the chance? Like an overheated
pooch, I panted; then after a few deep breaths, I calmed down. I
drank a swig of water and turned back toward the stand of palms,
our meeting point, then put one foot in front of the other and
plodded forward.

Like a mirage, a hand-woven Berber tent loomed ahead of me.
Left foot, right foot, left, right, faster, faster—blessed shade was
near. At high noon, hot fingers of sunlight poked through the
weave of the tent, but any shade was welcome. I nearly dove inside,

much to the cook's amusement. The staff thought my walking peculiar and were, I think, amazed I'd stayed with it. The cook handed
me a bottle of almost-cool water. It was like a gift from Allah. I
chugged it down, tossed it aside, grabbed another, and downed that
one too. Although I'd come only six kilometers from our starting
point that morning, it felt as though I'd traversed the whole country. The rest of the group arrived on their camels forty-five minutes
later.

My hands became dark and parched. Had they been detached
from my body, I wouldn't have recognized them as my own. In the
sun I wore large dark sunglasses and a white scarf they had taught
me to wrap like a turban to protect my head and neck. I probably
had a raccoon tan, but my face was so red from the heat it would
have been hard to tell. The rest of my body was pale white, covered
by a film of sand sweat-plastered to my skin.

If the heat and sun weren't enough, as we set out again, the
misery of a sirocco, a sandstorm, engulfed us. Within seconds, the
only sound audible over the roaring wind was coughing. The wind
yanked the ends of our turbans loose, and we swathed our mouths
with the snapping fabric. The camel tenders stopped, and the guide
motioned for us to stay still, to not fight the wind. As quickly as it
started, the storm stopped. When we peeled off layers to shake out
the sand, gritty yelps of laughter erupted. We'd become a new and
odd species; sand had flowed under our cuffs and collars, coating
every surface and crevice with fine particles. The sand combined
with sweat to cover each of us in a full body mudpack.

On the fourth morning, I woke at dawn from a deathlike slum-
ber. As I slipped out of the tent and watched the day begin, sunrise
reflected on a cliff passed from deep rust, through rose and peach,
to dusty white when the sun was fully up. The camels wandered in

from who knows where for breakfast. In the brilliant early light, their hides looked gold, flecked with deep brown. Some had eyelashes an inch, maybe even two inches, long. They arranged themselves in a circle and began munching, chomping, chewing oats, and burping. The sounds were sharp, with no background noises to dampen their clarity. My fellow travelers moaned as they emerged from tents and stretched sore muscles.

On the trail, a few hours and several kilometers later, the heat reached a new intensity. It was baking, boiling, broiling, frying-eggs-on-the-sand hot. Water became precious beyond gold, and the shade of an occasional palm the best gift ever. I tried to think cool thoughts but failed. When I removed my sunglasses to wipe the sweat from my eyes, the glare was like a piercing scalpel.

At the top of a dune of powdery sand, I looked down upon a ribbon of brilliant green. I thought the heat had finally gotten to me. This had to be a hallucination: it was so cool and inviting. I looked back. The white sand glittered, and I could make out two lines of camels. I turned forward, expecting to see more white. But no, there really was green—an oasis, not a mirage. Ahead a narrow band of vegetation seemed to stretch for miles. I ran down the dune laughing, headed toward a stream snaking through palm trees. Just the look of the flowing blue water framed by greenery made me feel cooler. There were even a few red-and-pink flowers, colors I hadn't seen in days. But the look was deceiving. Even in the shade, the wind blew hot. I sat under a towering date palm as close to the water as I could get and waited for the group. I heard a TV in the distance and the high-pitched voices of children playing. People passed by and waved hello. A jeep drove down a narrow road.

When the group caught up, a few people decided to walk with me. After the emptiness of the desert, the tiny village was teeming with life. We savored every palm tree and human interaction. Later, as we sat outside a shop sipping warm Cokes, I wondered if the rest of the group had discovered an air-conditioned shop and decided to stay the night. They were taking much longer than usual to catch up. But no, the guide met up with us and explained that a speeding motorbike had spooked a camel. My worst fear had been realized: the camel had thrown the rider. Our fellow traveler was at the local clinic. Fortunately, she sustained no serious injuries.

That night, our last, we camped on the far side of the oasis just beside a high dune. By the light of the moon, Maggie and I climbed to the top. Below, the sand was silver. Above, endless stars sparkled. We lay down on the soft surface, sunk in slightly, and stared at the sky. Every now and again a shooting star streaked by. We didn't speak. My mind filled with vivid images of the beauty I'd seen— dunes that looked as though they'd been sculpted by Brâncuşi. Vast blue skies. Smiling camels. Sunsets that turned the sky blood red. I wanted to fix those images in my mind.

I finally broke the silence. "Thank you for inviting me."

DEVILS TOWER: WYOMING, 2001

On my fiftieth-birthday journey through the US, I visited several must-see locations I'd never managed to get to because of their remoteness.

Those iconic places, like Mono Lake in California, the Okefenokee Swamp in Georgia, and the Upper Peninsula in Michigan, require dedication and time to visit. One place I absolutely had to see was the Devils Tower in Wyoming. The dramatic ending of one of my all-time favorite films, *Close Encounters of the Third Kind*, had been filmed there.

I sat alone watching the young man in a National Park Service uniform snap a match against the box and carefully, reverently light a tightly wrapped bundle of sage. Behind him, in the distance, was the dramatic profile of the Devils Tower, a sacred site for many Native Americans. As children ran about the edges of the amphitheater and the sun dimmed, the sweet scent from the smudge stick permeated the air.

A weathered man wearing a fringed and elaborately beaded

leather shirt and slacks sat silently, his head bowed, in a chair facing the audience. As he slowly unfolded his long legs and stood, the chattering diminished, his presence powerful enough to make even the youngest of the children somehow know to lower their shrieks. The young ranger welcomed the audience and introduced the speaker they'd invited to the park, a Cherokee elder visiting from Oklahoma. In the growing stillness, the elder walked to center stage. His trailing feathered headdress rustled like an animal padding quietly behind him.

Here was the great tribal chief I had imagined as a child. Here was a man of wisdom and faith. A man of tradition. Of morals. Of history. A teller of great tales.

For a few minutes, he stood silently, his eyes closed. Then softly, in a solemn voice, he chanted what sounded to my untutored ears like a Cherokee prayer. Opening his eyes, he looked up at the sky and paused for a long while. When he spoke again, his eyes still raised, it was in an only slightly louder voice. I leaned forward and strained to hear what the National Park Service had described as a sacred origin tale.

Thwack. Someone slapped at a mosquito. *Thwack, thwack.*

A squadron of kamikaze mosquitoes had invaded. I tried to ignore them and to focus all my attention on the chief. *Is he still speaking Cherokee?* I wondered. But then I heard, "The water beetle . . . mumble, mumble, mumble . . . and plants . . . mumble, mumble." I leaned closer, determined to hear. *Psst, psst, psst.* Bug repellent sprays hissed in the audience.

" . . . trees and forests . . . mumble, mumble."

Long minutes passed. Children fidgeted, giggled, then parents shooed them off to play in the dimming light.

Bug repellent did nothing. The rhythmic *thwack, thwack* of

slapping was now accompanied by a few choice swear words, muttered just slightly louder than the sacred recitation.

The chief stood ramrod straight, seemingly oblivious to everyone's discomfort, and rambled on. " . . . streams . . . mumble . . . horse ran like . . . mumble, mumble . . . and. . . ."

Near me, a woman in an outfit similar to the storyteller's, the chief's wife I assumed, joined the slapping fest. *Thwack, thwack.*

As the slapping continued, people began quietly slipping away. I glanced at my watch and sank deeper onto the bench. How long a story would this be? My choice of the front row had been a mistake. I was eager to get back to the campground so I wouldn't miss the start of the screening of *Close Encounters.* It was the reason I'd come to this difficult to reach park. For me, the movie is a compelling tale about passion and obsession, curiosity and the search for truth. I wanted to see the location of the central action of the film for myself, to experience the mystery and power of the place.

". . . and then beetle . . . mumble, mumble."

An insect landed on my arm. *Thwack. Thwack.* In the dim light, I could see a bump rising where the mosquito had bitten me.

I tuned out the chief's story. In the distance, I could see the Devils Tower and fantasized about spaceships and aliens. I imagined twinkling lights that were too bright and moving too fast to be stars. I thought about the origin questions that have intrigued humankind for millennia. Then I scolded myself. In front of me was living history, in a sacred space, under a canopy of stars.

I'd wanted the chief's tales to be spirit lifting, profound, and prophetic, but the sound of mosquito warfare was louder and more dramatic than his Cherokee creation myth. I heard no perspective-shifting truths.

Given my impatience and discomfort, I couldn't wait for the

chief to finish so I could leave to see *Close Encounters,* for the eighteenth or nineteenth time, this showing with the real Devils Tower as a backdrop.

As soon as I could, I fled the amphitheater and rushed to the screening. I understood that the tales with real meaning for me haven't come from my ethnic heritage, and can't be borrowed from other traditions. My sacred stories come from the movies. Thank you, Steven Spielberg.

HOMEGROWN ART: MISSISSIPPI, 2001

Outsider artists don't follow anyone's traditions; they invent their own. These artists are untrained, unschooled individuals who draw on their own unique understanding of their culture and experiences. The art they create is raw, expressive, bizarre, outlandish, unconventional, nonconforming, genuine, and truly original. After seeing a friend's collection, I became hooked and started to collect too. I've traveled to many out-of-the-way neighborhoods to track down artists and visit them.

The woman behind the desk at Kosciusko's tourist office greeted me with a cheery smile. In a soft drawl she said, "Welcome to Oprah's hometown." Before I said anything, she held out a leaflet and continued, "Here's a map of all the important sites. You should start with her birthplace."

It wasn't surprising that she was determined to send me on a pilgrimage of Oprah sites. But I shook my head no and smiled. I explained that while I'm a fan of Oprah's, I'd come to town to meet

L.V. Hull. "The article I read about her mentioned that she loves to have visitors. Is that true?"

"Well, yes," she said reluctantly, "but you really should see Oprah's church. That's where she had her first audience."

Once again, I shook my head no.

"All right then, but at least drive up Oprah Winfrey Road."

"Is it on the way to L.V.'s?"

"No," she responded with a sigh, and grudgingly gave me the directions I wanted. Rolling her eyes, she continued, "You can't possibly miss her house."

I'd become interested in outsider art (also known as primitive or visionary art) thirty years before, when a friend who was a collector told me about his visits with outsider artists. He had explained that their art isn't the same as folk art, which is based on tradition and passed from generation to generation. Outsider artists haven't been formally trained and don't work from anyone else's traditions—they invent their own. Some live their lives on the brink of reality, in fantasy worlds or religious fanaticism.

The artwork in my friend's collection made me smile. It was sometimes bizarre, often constructed from unconventional materials, but made with a lot of heart and absolutely original. What intrigued me most were his stories of these eccentric, driven artists and photos of their often weird, art-filled homes and studios.

For decades I'd been attending art fairs in the Deep South, collecting outsider artwork and meeting the creators. Through those contacts I'd learned about other artists and mapped out road trips to visit them.

As I turned onto L.V.'s street, I instantly understood about not missing the house. Tucked into a row of modest, well-tended suburban homes, L.V.'s yard was a blaze of color. A forest of painted objects and signs extended from property line to property line. Shoes and dolls and bottles adorned with stripes and plaids and polka dots in startling color combinations sprouted from sticks, like psychedelic flowers. Piles of wildly decorated cans, buckets, baskets, and tubs had been transformed into rock formations scattered about the "garden." Several washing machines and dishwashers, every inch covered by words and swirls and yet more polka dots, looked like hills growing out of the landscape.

I'd barely gotten out of the car when the head of a rotund woman with shining dark skin popped out of the front door. Waving, she welcomed me with a thick drawl, "Come in. Come in."

I edged my way through the narrow path across the phantasmagoric garden and into the house. Following the bright red of L.V.'s dress, I snaked through mountains of completed projects and the raw materials for new ones. Paintings and polka-dotted hubcaps covered the walls. Plaques painted with pithy sayings in vivid colors were stacked against the walls twenty deep.

The three R's of Life:

At 25 Romonce.
At 45 Rent.
At 65 Rhumatic.

~

Being brave is the art of making sure
no one knows your scared to death.

L.V. picked up a purple-and-green boater, a sombrero festooned with orange, pink, and blue swirls, and a fedora polka-dotted in fanciful yellows and greens and dumped them from one chair onto another already half-buried chair. She motioned for me to sit.

With a broad sweep of her arm, a jumble of unpainted plastic jugs clattered onto the floor as she perched on a chair beside me.

She chattered as if she hadn't spoken to anyone in months, though I suspected this was her normal speech pattern. Distracted by the riotous colors surrounding me, I only half heard what she said. My eyes darted from one wildly adorned object to another. It felt as though I had wandered into someone's dream, or maybe their hallucination. After several minutes of gaping open-mouthed at the art, I focused on what she was saying.

"See, people from all over town, they bring trash, and I make it art. I got a talent."

"You must work all day and night to create this much," I said.

"Well, I don't sleep much. Sometimes in the middle of the night, it's like God is waking me up and saying, 'L.V., go paint.' So I do. Course, I also paint during the day. I paint whenever I inspired. Sometimes there's just no stopping. My friend will come by and say, 'L.V., how long you been up? You gotta eat. You don't, you gonna get sick.' So then I remember to stop, cause I don't like the doctor. Seen too much of him lately."

She paused to catch her breath, before her stream-of-consciousness monologue continued. "And it ain't just me thinks I'm a artist. I been written up in a couple of those fancy magazines."

Dozens of questions raced through my head. What had gotten her started painting? How did she find anything in the clutter? Where did she get the paint? What did her neighbors think? But I realized I wasn't going to be able to break into L.V.'s river of words. Once L.V. got started talking, it was like her painting—there was just no stopping her. So I settled back, focused on her face instead of the surroundings, and let her stories wash over me.

L.V.'s face was a dark rich brown and smooth. Her eyes were

deep and ancient looking. I couldn't guess her age. It might have been anywhere between forty and seventy.

She held up a watering can. "This got a little hole in it, so it ain't good for much. Least that's what Mable said when she brought it. She used to throw stuff out. But now, she knows I gonna take it and make it art. I recycle, ain't that the word? People all over town, they bring me stuff. I've become the dump. But I don't mind. I need things to make my art. See this boot, it got a hole too." She pointed to a Wellington boot, now painted electric blue, dotted with red, white, and pink. "Don't it look fine?" She flashed a pleased smile. "Used to be just plain, but I got an eye. It's like things talk to me. They say, 'L.V., make me pretty.'" The boot surely didn't look plain anymore.

"Some people, they jealous. They say they could do it too, if they wanted. I say, 'So go do it.' They don't. Or if they do, it don't look like much. See, God gave me this talent; he didn't give it to them."

Her eyes fixed on a half-painted picture frame; she picked it up and rambled on. Each object had a history. I finally squeezed in a question. "L.V., what do your neighbors think about your art?"

"Some of them, they don't like it. They just don't understand art. They want me to have a boring yard like theirs. Some of them, I guess they think I'm a fool. Then one of them tour buses shows up, and out come all these fancy people to see L.V. I know they peeking out behind the blinds to see. When those rich people leave, holding my artwork, well, I guess they think maybe L.V. ain't such a fool. Course, maybe they think those rich people are fools. But those people sure do buy. They know I'm a artist. They understand. And *Southern Living*, they wrote about me. Bunch of other magazines too. Want to see?"

This went on for a couple of hours, with no prompting from me. As it was getting late in the afternoon, I asked her if she'd be willing to pose for a photo. Without hesitation, she extracted a painted hat from the jumble behind her and popped it onto her head. In the photo, she looks like she's dressed for church, in a red print dress and straw hat polka-dotted in a dozen colors. She's framed by a near-solid wall of painted baskets, shoes, and toys.

Other than asking me where I live, she had no questions. I guessed that her interior life is so overwhelming that she can't take in any more information. I pondered the age-old question: Do all great artists teeter on a line between insanity and genius? I wondered how one knew the difference—or if it mattered.

"So, L.V., I'd really like to buy some of your artwork." She rooted around and handed me a small cherub seated on a twig bench, painted and polka-dotted in a rainbow of color. "First, a gift. Everyone needs an angel."

THE WILD WEST: WYOMING, 2001

Roy Rogers and Dale Evans, the Lone Ranger, and the Cartwrights, those long-ago TV characters, were glamorous figures to me.

When I think of them, I see rugged individualists crouched low on glistening horses thundering across vast plains and mighty mountains fighting for truth and justice. Or they're swinging a lasso that rises and falls in slow motion, neatly roping a calf. I always knew who to root for; I just looked for the white hat. My one experience on horseback, at age seven, consisted of a half hour of whimpering, then wailing and pleading to get off. At that moment it was clear I'd never be a cowgirl; I'd have to love them from afar.

When I arrived in Cody, Wyoming, and heard there was a nightly rodeo, I had to see it. Locals advised me to sit in the Buzzard's Roost. "You won't be looking into the sun at the beginning, it's got the best view of the action, and you'll get to see some good-looking butts."

The Cody rodeo is a bona fide competition, with prize money at stake. It is held nightly each summer and provides steady work for young cowboys. They get experience, and many go on to major national competitions.

It was something of a letdown that seated to my left was a couple from Tenafly, New Jersey, and to my right a guy from Westport, Connecticut. Directly behind me was a family from France, a middle-aged couple with a young daughter and son.

As we waited for the rodeo to begin, crowds filed in until the Buzzard's Roost bleachers were full. Only a few foolish souls sat on the sunny side, in full heat with glare in their eyes. Guess they hadn't thought to ask where to sit.

In the ring, a few riders and horses worked out, but the real action was immediately in front of me as cowboys prepared for the first event. The term cow*boy* is exactly right. Most riders didn't appear to have started shaving yet. My eyes were riveted on them as, a few feet in front of me, they dropped their jeans, padded their butts and inner thighs, then pulled up their jeans and attached chaps and spurs. When fully dressed, they loosened up their muscles by elaborate stretching routines and/or doing a modified St. Vitus's dance.

At precisely eight thirty, the announcer's voice boomed, "Welcome to the Cody Rodeo, best damned rodeo in the West! Let's all stand for 'The Star Spangled Banner.'"

As the final crackling notes trailed off, a pack of horses galloped into and around the ring. The kicked-up dust transformed the scene into an impressionist painting, pure color and light and shadow. A roar rose up from the crowd. The rodeo had begun.

Unbroken horses for the bareback riding event were packed into small individual holding pens perhaps twenty feet in front of me. In close quarters, the horses whinnied and stamped, making it clear they were not happy. "*Mon dieu,*" yelped the woman behind me.

Young boys, some swaggering, some fidgeting, and a few looking just short of terrified despite frozen grins on their faces, climbed over the barrier and onto the horses. "Holy Christ," muttered the guy next to me. "Who in their right mind would do that?"

"Ya gotta be young and brave."

"Or young and stupid."

A team of older experienced men fussed over each boy for the two or three minutes before his ride, pushing and prodding their charge into perfect position. They whispered advice and put a comforting hand on a shoulder or punched it, doing whatever they could to instill confidence.

The booming voice announced, "Here comes our youngest rider. Let's give a hand for Jesse, age sixteen, from Whitesboro, Texas, riding Pepperpot." With that, the gate opened, and Pepperpot and Jesse stormed into the ring. His ride and the applause for him were much shorter than the preparations.

I flipped through the program while there was a pause in the action. There were ads for two local orthopedic surgeons; setting up shop close to a rodeo is no doubt a wise business decision. There were a lot of knee braces, a cowboy with a heavily taped nose, and several guys walking with decided limps. Rodeo looked scary: at all times, cowboys were a single kicking hoof away from disaster.

During the bull-riding event, a cowboy got thrown—one second, the rider was on the bull; the next, he lay immobile in the dust. The audience collectively gasped, certain he'd broken bones and couldn't move; we were terrified he'd get trampled by the bull. There was a loudly muttered "*Merde,*" and then complete silence. Transfixed by impending disaster, everyone held their breath while clowns maneuvered the bull from the ring. Even the deafening voice of the announcer stopped for a minute. The guy from Connecticut with whom I'd been chatting grabbed my wrist and clung to it.

A medical team burst into the arena and hovered over the thrown rider. A few long minutes later, the cowboy slowly got up and, with several people supporting him, gingerly limped off. The entire arena burst into applause. Actually, *all* of the cowboys walked a little bowlegged, stiff, and sore looking, immediately after getting off the bull, regardless of how successful their ride had been.

Some events, like calf roping, felt oddly familiar to me, as if I'd watched cowboys lasso calves a thousand times. Why this should seem familiar to a woman who's spent most of her life in New York City, I've no idea—it isn't a typical evening's entertainment in the Big Apple. I guess rodeo has simply seeped into my consciousness; it's part of being an American.

Wondering if the French family was experiencing the same sense of déjà vu, I asked and heard a long rambling answer of which I only understood "*Magnifique, oui?*" and "*Tres dangereux, non?*" I never did find out. But it brought to mind an experience I'd had years ago while visiting Paris. The TV flicked on, and there was John Wayne in boots and a ten-gallon hat swaggering about and twittering in a high squeaky dubbed voice. I laughed so hard my sides ached. So, perhaps like me, the French family watching the rodeo was familiar with the basics and astonished by the details.

The only folks participating in the ring who looked to have much life experience were the clowns. They didn't get much glory, but they worked hard and seemed to love their job. The clowns became my heroes, the ones figuratively wearing the white hats.

While most cowboys participated in only a single event, the clowns were in the ring for nearly the whole evening. Using nothing more than a small prod and their own smarts and agility, they protected the cowboys from the bulls and unbroken horses. At the same time, they entertained the crowd, managed the movement of animals out of the ring, and bantered with the announcer.

One ornery bull made sudden, sharp, threatening moves, first toward the cowboy and then the clown. As deft as a toreador, the clown maneuvered the bull away from the cowboy. Then he took a running leap and landed behind a fence microseconds before the bull could butt him.

At evening's end, after the crowd had considerably thinned, the sun had burned orange in the sky and been replaced by blazing megawatt lights, the contestants galloped once again around the arena.

"*Magnifique!*"

"*Extraordinaire!*"

"Wow."

Zozobra is a Santa Fe, New Mexico, celebration that has been held annually for more than seventy-five years. It's a ritual burning of a sixty-foot effigy of "Old Man Gloom." The idea is to dispel the problems and pain of the previous year and start fresh. When I'd first read about and seen photos of the enormous flaming effigy, it had promptly gone onto my must-see list. I wanted to experience Zozobra in person. Years later, an exhibit about the event at Santa Fe's folk art museum further piqued my interest.

But then I read that the almost fifty thousand revelers celebrate in a relatively small, confined area. After the serenity of the blaze, a huge party erupts. The revelers get drunker and drunker as the night progresses, and the festivities continue until dawn. Despite my desire to see Zozobra's flames and join in the celebration, I knew I'd never do it. I also know that, except on TV, I'll never see the ball drop on New Year's Eve in Times Square. Joining a dense, celebratory, drunken mass of humanity is just not my thing. In fact, it terrifies me.

So I was delighted when my friend Kim forwarded an invitation to a smaller version of the Santa Fe event held by a friend of hers in Albuquerque. This more intimate burning of Old Man Gloom was referred to by the organizer as NotZozobra.

"NotZozobra," twelve feet high with a menacing expression, stood at the end of the cul-de-sac. Made from a base of chicken wire and papier-mâché, he had paper skin, outstretched arms, and a bulky body sporting a button-down shirt and flowing skirt. A small group gathered around the imposing effigy was busily writing and drawing on his paper skin. He was still mostly white, with only a few colorful phrases inscribed.

"Have a marker." An open box of rainbow colors was thrust at me. "If you want space to write, you should start now."

I reached in and selected blue, green, and neon pink. That was the easy part. Deciding what to write would be more difficult.

Putting off the moment when we'd need to put pen to paper, Kim and I went into the house to greet our host and down a couple of stiff margaritas.

By the time we returned, NotZozobra was a lot more colorful. I read what other people had written. ""Breast cancer." "Temperamental car." "Mother with Alzheimer's." "Alimony payments." "Cheating husband." Some guests were initially hesitant to be engaged in this "pagan" ritual; they'd come for the booze and camaraderie. Markers in hand, they urged others to write. But within a short time, encouraged by a little prodding and those high-octane margaritas, everyone joined in. "Horrible boss." "Allergies." "Plumbing problems."

It was tough for me to write anything. It wasn't that this ritual made me feel silly or shy. I loved the idea, and the added alcoholic lubricant should have made the words flow easily. But no one I knew was ill or having serious problems, and in the middle of a seven-month road trip around the US, there wasn't much gloom for me to shed. I felt very blessed. Eventually, feeling pressure from other guests to write something, anything, I added a couple of perennial personal demons—chronic pain stemming from an accident and my inability to lose weight. Newly arrived guests added more woes as the sky grew dark. To my eyes, NotZozobra began to resemble a NYC subway car from the eighties. He was more of a merry hodgepodge of color, words, and symbols than something dark and ominous.

Despite drought conditions in Albuquerque that made fire a serious and constant danger, no one in the neighborhood objected to the burning of NotZozobra. In fact, they joined in. Neighborhood kids shinnied up the nearby lamppost and masked the glare of the streetlight with a dark cloth. All the surrounding houses turned off their lights. As the sun set, we were submerged in darkness. Anticipation grew. There's a little pyromania in all of us.

The host had written in his invitation, "The person who comes from furthest away gets to light up the sucker." In years past, firelighters have come from as far as Japan. That year they had to settle for someone from New York . . . me. I'm a nonsmoker and not used to lighters. I was also drunk. In the darkness, I fumbled with the lighter—every time I flicked it, the flame blew out. A rising chorus of suggestions and jeers sent the host running into the house for a box of matches.

A single flick of match against pavement and a quick but surprisingly steady trip to the figure's white skirt transformed NotZozobra into a small inferno. For several minutes, the only sounds were the crackle and hiss of the fire, the occasional stomp of a foot landing on a flyaway bit of burning paper, and the sizzle from water poured onto a spark. As we silently watched, the towering figure was reduced to a middling campfire. Guests joined hands and danced around the remaining flickers, singing and laughing. Perhaps Old Man Gloom had done his job and lightened their burdens, or the spirits the revelers had imbibed made them light-headed and lighthearted.

This event took place on September 7, 2001. Four days later, the Twin Towers fell. My elation became anguish. Had we written our problems and pain then, a twelve-foot-high NotZozobra, or even a sixty-foot one, could not have diminished the gloom.

IN FRONT OF THE SALAD BAR:
TENNESSEE, 2001

My friends Maggie and Penny joined me
on a two-week leg of my cross-country
journey. Maggie shares my passion for
outsider art, and Penny is an avid
music enthusiast. The three of us have
traveled together many times, sharing
a love of exploring and a willingness to
go almost anywhere and try almost
anything. We love the new and
unexpected and have often wandered
into the "authentic" heart of a place.

A guitar player sprawled on a hand-carved wooden chair. Crammed onto his scraggly gray hair was a black squishy felt hat. He was a large, meaty man, with timber-like legs planted firmly on the floor, a moon face, and fingers like sausages. But oh, how those fingers flew. The fiddle player seated next to him simply couldn't remain still. First he tapped his toes, then he got up and paced. Then he broke into a jig, playing all the while. A tall, stately woman with perfectly coifed white curls played banjo and sang with a soft twang. Although there were only three of us in their audience, they played as if they were at the Grand Ole Opry.

My friends Maggie and Penny and I had come upon this impromptu performance while strolling through the grounds of the Museum of Appalachia in Norris, Tennessee. Buildings had been moved to the site from all over the region. The museum displayed many thousands of artifacts depicting life in Appalachia.

At the end of each song, we applauded enthusiastically. The fiddle player tipped his hat in appreciation and said, "You gals should go over to the Lake View Inn tonight."

Penny, who'd been hoping to find some local music, asked, "What's there?"

"Every Monday they have a pickin' session. It's great fun. Just make sure you get there *real* early; it fills up pretty good."

Heeding his advice, we arrived at the inn more than an hour before the music was set to begin. A nondescript motel in a strip of other nondescript motels, the Lake View's parking lot was the only one that was full. So full, we could hardly find a spot among the pickup trucks and muddied station wagons. Despite all the vehicles, there weren't many people to be seen and not a note of music to be heard. There also wasn't a restaurant or store of any description, a sight that dismayed us because we hadn't eaten dinner.

Inside the motel, we saw where the people were. Within seconds of our arrival, we were welcomed like old friends, not by the musicians who'd sent us there but by Pat, the self-appointed greeter. A petite woman with startlingly red hair and a megawatt smile, she led us into the large banquet room used for the "pickin." Pat schmoozed with us, learning our names, hometowns, and how we'd found out about the concert. Then she led us to the front of the room and squeezed us into a group of people surrounding a table in what was obviously a prime location.

"These here ladies came from all over the country jest to hear us tonight." Pointing at me, she chortled, "She's from New York—ain't that something?"

Everyone stopped their chattering, turned, and looked at us with what seemed to me to be a mix of openhearted welcoming tinged with a bit of suspicion. The suspicion didn't last long; they were happy to welcome visitors and have someone new to appreciate their stories and jokes.

"Who do we pay for admission?" Maggie asked.

"Pay? Don't need to pay no one. This here is free."

"That's great. Can we give a donation?"

"Hell, no. This here is *free.*"

Pat explained, "The motel contributes the room, and the musicians play because they love it." Then, in a voice just above a whisper, she added, "Lots of folks couldn't afford to come if they had to pay anything at all."

Most of the crowd looked to be senior citizens, though there was a sprinkling of twenty- and thirty-year-olds. The regulars came armed with huge Tupperware containers of candy and crackers, popcorn and pretzels. There may have been lots of junk food, but there was a strict policy of no alcohol or smoking in the room. Though everyone obeyed the rule, I saw people regularly squeezing their way through the ever-growing crowd and slipping out a side door. Then, a few minutes later, I'd catch them sneaking back in. I never did determine whether these furtive trips were for smokes or booze—or both.

As we waited for the performance, a stream of people stopped by the table, curious about the "foreigners." They'd hold out their Tupperware container and offer us whatever was in it. I snagged a handful of Hershey's kisses, Maggie grabbed some peanuts, and Penny went for the pretzels. Not the healthiest of dinners, but we appreciated the generosity, and at least our rumbling stomachs wouldn't compete with the music.

We were asked over and over again where we were from. Our table companions, all of whom lived within a few miles of the motel, couldn't believe we'd come so far to hear local "pickin'." I began to feel exotic—a real foreigner in my own country. Even if Pat hadn't advertised our origins, our clothes were a giveaway. We wore earth-toned cotton in a sea of pastel polyester and bright reds, blues, and greens.

Pat returned several times to make sure we were okay and to hawk "genuine handcrafted" miniature wind chimes. We noticed no one else was buying, but we each bought one anyhow. On the bottom were "Made in Hong Kong" stickers.

A woman who'd been hovering near us for a while gathered her courage, came over, and asked, "Know what happens when you sing country music backwards?"

"You get confused?"

"It becomes rock and roll?"

"It becomes gospel?"

She guffawed at all of our terrible stabs at an answer. "Naw. You get your wife and job back."

Several people made it a point to explain the punch line, afraid we wouldn't understand. Eventually, Pat stood at the front of the room and made a string of announcements: a musician in the hospital, the birth of a grandson to a woman in the audience, someone looking for work, a woman who needed a lift home. By the time she finished and the music started, a fire marshal would have been horrified—there wasn't even standing room.

The first three musicians twanged a few chords and swaggered onto the "stage"—a few square feet in front of the empty salad bar.

The crowd went wild—hooting, stamping their feet, clapping. After a few fancy licks from the fiddle player, everyone quieted down just a bit so they could listen to the music. These guys could play! It didn't take long for their up-tempo tunes to rev up the audience. The room vibrated from music and foot tapping. After two songs, the musicians loped offstage, back behind the salad bar.

The next group received an equally warm reception. "Red," an older gentleman who now had pure white hair, seemed to be the emcee. He didn't do much to introduce the acts; we learned about the musicians from folks who sat near us. In a stage whisper, they would tell us the players' background and the local opinion about their abilities. Dozens of groups played, two songs apiece. There were soulful ballads, banjo solos, bluegrass, dueling fiddles, and genres of music I couldn't begin to identify. There was no hook, but there might just as well have been. Red was there as a traffic director, making sure everyone who wanted to perform got the opportunity. If someone tried to sneak in a third tune, one scowl from Red sent the players scurrying away.

The musicians ranged from folks with more enthusiasm than talent to musicians as good as any major recording star. A core group of pickers and strummers played backup as needed.

Unlike the audience, many of the musicians were young. Most were professionals, some from Nashville, some from Branson, Missouri, others on the country circuit. One "visiting" musician was a local celebrity. He'd grown up in the area and made a name for himself in Nashville. He played a mean bass and Dobro (slide bar guitar). His fingers plucked and strummed at jet speed, his sound complex and pure. The crowd screamed for him to come back and play another tune, but Red made sure he got his allotted two songs and no more.

After more than three hours, Maggie, Penny, and I said farewell to our new friends and snuck out—the music was still going strong, the room still crammed past capacity.

RUSSIAN TALES: 2004

My heritage is Russian, or maybe Polish or Ukrainian, depending on the year. My grandmother Bella told stories of growing up there under the tsar and then fleeing the country to escape persecution. While I was always curious about seeing the land of my ancestors, the political environment during the Cold War didn't encourage tourism.

Then, post-perestroika, my brother Mike visited Russia on business and came back marveling about the experience of seeing a population where many people looked as if they could be relatives

I decided it was time for a visit. None of my friends were interested in going there with me, so I traveled solo. First to Moscow, where I spent a week. Then I joined a tour that cruised the Volga River from Moscow to St. Petersburg, where I spent another few days exploring on my own.

"Need a taxi, lady?" the man asked for the eighth time since I'd emerged from immigration. It was August, and I'd just arrived in Moscow for a three-week vacation. I restrained the urge to swat him away like a mosquito. Instead, I picked up the pace heading toward the "Official Information Booth." When I asked the best way to get into central Moscow, the woman pointed to a bright yellow stand topped by a large "Official Taxi" sign. As I turned in that direction, the man who'd been following me slipped inside the booth. He smirked a bit and whipped out a price sheet. The printed fare was 124 euros (about $150). I laughed.

"Wait, I make discount."

"How much?" I asked.

"One hundred dollars, US." I turned away.

"How much you want to pay?" he asked, raising his voice.

I thought about the information in the guidebook and said, "Forty dollars."

"Sixty," he countered.

When I asked for fare info at a different "Official Information Booth," the woman picked up the phone. Within seconds my buddy from the "Official Taxi Booth" trotted over. Our dickering over the price picked up right where we'd left off. He finally agreed to the forty dollars I'd originally offered.

In many parts of the world, negotiating a price for *anything* is expected. Merchants like bargaining, but I hadn't expected to be confronted with this in Russia. My impression was that everything was tightly controlled, and the populace strictly adhered to the rules. Clearly, this wasn't the case.

At the hotel, the desk clerk told me to always carry a copy of my passport. She warned that if I was stopped by the police and was without proper identification, there'd be big trouble. I never found out what "big trouble" might ensue, but I sensed her concern and made sure to always carry the copy of my passport she'd made for me.

On my first walk, in the underpass below Pushkin Park, I saw a young couple look around nervously as a police officer approached them and demanded to see their documents. While he examined their tattered papers, tears welled up in the woman's eyes. Non-Muscovites must prove they have a legitimate reason for being in the city. It's the most desirable place to live in Russia, and people from less prosperous areas try to sneak in, find work, and make a life there. I guessed this couple would be sent home.

Minutes later I watched a different policeman stop a stylishly dressed woman. She reached into her designer handbag, pulled out something, handed it over quickly, and kept walking. It took me a few minutes to figure out that the woman had given the cop a bribe to prevent him from hassling her. As I walked further down Tverskaya Street, the "Fifth Avenue" of Moscow, the scene was repeated several times, always with especially well-dressed individuals or people emerging from expensive vehicles. The transactions were quick. Once I was close enough to see the ruble notes change hands but couldn't catch the amount.

I'd never seen such a blatant demonstration of police corruption anywhere on the globe. It seemed the stuff of TV cop shows, not the real world. I know corruption exists in New York City, but it surely doesn't happen so overtly.

No police approached me at any time during my Russian travels; I must have stood out as a foreigner. Once my radar had been activated, I saw many similar furtive transactions across the country. What would it be like to live in a place where the society seemed to accept public servants who are always on the take? I tried to imagine transit or beat cops approaching me for a bribe and how I might respond. I couldn't even imagine it; it isn't part of my reality. But watching it happen over and over both chilled me and made me feel grateful for our imperfect but better system.

Thank God it was a quiet Sunday morning when I took my first ride on the subway. It is the most efficient, least expensive way to travel around Moscow. It took a couple of tries to get my nerve up to step onto the escalator headed down to the trains. Mayakovskaya station is about three or four stories below ground, reached by one long, steep, *very* fast-moving escalator. I held my breath, quickly stepped onto it, grabbed the handrail, and tried not to look down or to think about what would transpire if something happened and a crush of people needed to get out.

Two days after leaving Moscow, I read that the Mayakovskaya station had been bombed by Chechens. My fears hadn't been unwarranted; several people died, and many were injured in the stampede to exit.

When the train pulled into the station, the doors opened before the car stopped completely. I made a mental note to never lean against the car doors, as I often do in NYC. As the train clattered through the tunnel, I looked at my fellow passengers. My brother's description of the population had been accurate. My face blended in with the riders, though my clothes marked me as a foreigner. A man seated across from me could have been my uncle Kal. Another was a near clone of a close family friend, also of Russian descent. Many others could have been distant relatives. All looked pale and a bit drawn.

My maternal grandmother left Russia as a young bride to escape pogroms or the possibility that her new husband would be conscripted into the army. Over the years, she'd had intermittent contact with her siblings and cousins, though many had not survived the World Wars. When she was seventy, she traveled to what was then the Ukraine, to visit a brother and cousins living near her childhood home in a village close to Kiev.

I remembered the blurry photo she'd brought back of a second cousin who looked very much like me. It was a window into an alternate universe, the life I might be living if my grandparents hadn't come to America. That knowledge shadowed me the entire time I was in Russia and made this trip more personal than most of my travels. I wished I had a way to locate my second cousin, but with my grandmother's passing, all contact information had vanished. And, while I knew my second cousin most likely lived in Ukraine, I kept expecting, or at least hoping, to run into my doppelgänger.

On that first subway ride, I headed to Arbat, the old art and literary quarter of the city. Miraculously, I didn't get lost as I changed onto three different subway lines. Each station is unique, with wide platforms and connecting corridors. Many have high vaulted ceilings; all are spotlessly clean, well lit, and filled with sculpture, mosaics, chandeliers, paintings, marble inlays, and frescoes. Several stations have a theme related to their location. The one near the largest gymnasium in town has sports figures; the one named Belorusskaya features mosaic floor tiles based on a traditional Belorusian carpet design. The contrast to New York's often dark, dingy, and filthy stations was startling.

I had assumed that the sumptuous architecture and decoration had been constructed before the Communist revolution, but no, they were Stalin's idea. The subways and grand government office buildings had been constructed in the 1930s for use by workers. Stalin formulated a plan to rebuild the city and personally supervised construction of the most ambitious and opulent structures.

While he was creating beautiful monuments to leave a lasting mark, Stalin was decimating the population. Under his reign, during World War II, sixty-five million people perished from deprivation and from his ruthless elimination of anyone who opposed him or his policies. That number represents half the present-day population of Russia. Every tour guide found a way to bring up his atrocities; he left an enduring legacy of suffering. I was told by several people that March 5 is considered a national holiday—it's the day Stalin died.

In contrast to Stalin's grand edifices, more recent Soviet archi-

tecture, especially from the Khrushchev era, was soul deadening—
square gray, cheap-looking boxes with no ornamentation that had
weathered badly and reminded me of cellblocks. Most Muscovites
lived in dingy walk-up apartment blocks far from the glitter of Red
Square and the tourist areas. I saw them only because I got out at
random subway stations and walked around.

Later in the trip when visiting St. Petersburg, the city center
had been repaired and freshly painted. They were sprucing up in
anticipation of celebrations of its three-hundredth year. Hermitage
and Peter's Palace were opulent and displayed treasures that took
my breath away. But, walking just a few blocks away, I came upon
rain-stained buildings with crumbling facades covered in graffiti,
downspouts separated from buildings blowing in the wind, cracked
windows, and sidewalks in serious disrepair. Wires for the trolley
system dangled precariously over streets. At night, lighting was
dim, and the streets took on a menacing quality. Center city St. Petersburg looked worse than New York City's slums.

Thinking about an endless, cold winter and these dismal
neighborhoods, I could understand the reason for Russians' love of
vodka, the high rates of alcoholism and suicides. I hoped my relatives fared better in their small town.

Compounding the poor housing were food shortages. I'd had
them vividly demonstrated to me several years prior to this trip
when Russian cousins of family friends visited New York. Their two
favorite subjects for photos were their relatives and the local Stop &
Shop. They couldn't get over the supermarket. They explained that
no one at home would believe them without proof. They weren't
interested in museums, architecture, or parks; they just wanted a
daily visit to the supermarket so they could stroll the aisles. Dinner
at my aunt's home nearly had them in tears—they couldn't com-

prehend that the quality, variety, and quantity of food served represented a normal weekend family meal. For them, the abundance of food was the greatest demonstration of American wealth and power.

Given that experience, I was interested in walking through markets, especially ones outside of Moscow. In the central market in Yaroslavl, a midsize city a few hundred miles from Moscow, apples, oranges, and pears sat between bunches of carrots and a heap of green beans. There was fresh meat, fish, honey, dairy, sweets, and canned goods. But despite the selection of items, there wasn't much of each—a couple dozen well-weathered apples, a few cans of this or that, and a small number of eggs. By first world, or really any market standard, it was a meager display. But for Russians, it was luxurious. I took photos of the displays to show my relatives the scarcity of food, even now, years after the introduction of a loosened market economy.

My guide for a tour of the city, Tatiana, explained that during the Soviet era, almost nothing was available in Yaroslavl. Most people spent a full day each weekend going to Moscow to stock up.

She told a joke demonstrating Russians' dark sense of humor: "The Russian definition of dementia: a man standing in front of a grocery store with an empty bag, who doesn't remember if he was going to the store or coming back."

At the end of the tour, Tatiana approached me and hesitantly asked, "Do you have any large denomination dollar bills?" When I said yes, she asked, "Would you be willing to exchange some small bills I got as tips for larger ones?"

"Sure, but why?" I imagined it might be easier to stash a few large bills than a stack of ones and fives. But no. Tatiana explained that banks won't take any foreign bills that aren't perfect. The slightest rip or mark will cause a bill to be rejected or discounted.

She went on to say, "If I go to the bank with fifty one-dollar bills, I might get forty dollars' worth of rubles. Or thirty. Or whatever amount the teller feels like giving me that day." It was yet another example of rampant corruption. When Tatiana took my crisp fifty-dollar bill in exchange for her pile of well-used singles, she beamed, the first real smile I'd seen from her. Then her smile faded, and she anxiously asked, "You will be able to use these bills in America, won't you?"

Having established a friendship of sorts, Tatiana and I went for tea, and she told me about her life. Her mother is an English teacher who insisted that from a very early age Tatiana learn English. In college, Tatiana studied languages and now speaks several fluently. She was very lucky, and thrilled, to get a job as a guide. "All my friends try to get jobs where they have contact with foreigners. We think those are the best in Russia." For four months a year, she works long hours, seven days a week. In that time, she earns significantly more than would be possible working in a conventional job for a full year. Almost all the money comes from tips, not salary.

During the 1980s and 1990s, the media often reported that Gorbachev, Brezhnev, and other high-ranking Soviets were spending the weekend at their dachas. I'd always thought of a dacha along the lines of Camp David, a luxurious retreat in the country, a rustic home nestled in a thick stand of fir trees, or perhaps an apple orchard. Dachas were where rich folk went for the weekend. I was right about one thing—they are the Russians' weekend retreat in the country. But, apart from that, I had it all wrong. *Every* city dweller, no matter how poor, has a dacha.

During the Khrushchev era, food shortages were rampant. To help alleviate the problem, the government gave everyone who lived in a city a plot of land on which they could grow food. Each weekend workers left city jobs to work their land. Though shortages were less acute when I visited, city dwellers still maintained their dachas and gardens.

The plots of land are small. A half dozen or so could probably fit into a suburban American half-acre backyard. Surrounding Moscow are rows of new dachas, looking a little bit like a Lilliputian Levittown. I saw many fronting onto major highways, not exactly a peaceful retreat. Each miniscule plot had a look-alike, square, one-room cement structure plus an apple tree, cherry tree, tiny vegetable garden, and, very occasionally, flowers.

A few older dachas still exist, more in line with what I had imagined: small cottages in faded blues and greens with gingerbread around peaked roofs and windows decorated with lacy curtains. A profusion of hollyhocks and daisies often framed the scene. They reminded me of Hansel and Gretel.

As I traveled around the country, Russians' fascination with all things American could not be missed, even by the most casual tourist. While cruising on the Volga, each time the boat arrived at a new destination we were serenaded by street musicians. The music selections included "Do You Know the Way to San Jose?," "Hello, Dolly," "Chattanooga Choo Choo," "New York, New York," and, most frequently, a rousing version of "The Star-Spangled Banner." Though we often arrived at the same time as German tour groups, there was never their national anthem or any oompah music. Nor was there ever any Russian music. I asked several guides about this, but no one had a good explanation. I chalked it up to a vision of America as a land of plenty.

McDonald's had opened their first branch in Moscow a few months before I visited, and I happened to walk past it one day. While I wasn't interested in eating a Big Mac, I went in to look

around. The restaurant was packed, with a long line of people waiting to order and others holding trays of food hovering to find a table. Most patrons wore business attire—office workers, I guessed,
anxious to sample real American burgers and fries. After trying fast
food at a local establishment, I understood the appeal. Though far
less expensive, the local burgers were soggy, mealy, gray, and tasteless.

Across Moscow and St. Petersburg, dozens of teenagers with
insulated backpacks walked through downtown areas selling Pepsi
and Coke, mainly to tourists. The cost was too high for an average
Russian. On one walk, I was lured over to a truck blaring music
with a crowd gathered around it. A group of teens were urging people to try Russian cola. Judging from the tasters' expressions, Russian cola didn't pose a threat to Pepsi or Coke.

On the cruise down the Volga, we had a guest lecturer, Irina,
who was a professor at Moscow University and a former translator
for Gorbachev. She told us that during the privatization that occurred after the breakup of the Soviet Union in the early 1990s,
government-owned companies and their assets were sold for six
billion rubles to a few select individuals. These assets were independently estimated to be worth six *hundred* billion rubles. When I
visited, 7 percent of Moscow's population owned 73 percent of the
country's assets. Prior to privatization, there were no Russians on
the Forbes' list of the hundred richest people on the globe; in the
Forbes' 2004 annual report, there were twenty-five.

As wealth grew for Russia's 1 percent, the average Russian's life
was as bad or worse than ever. Irina explained that when the country went through privatization in 1991, stock was issued to all citizens. The certificates were valued at ten thousand rubles. After six
months, they were worth four bottles of vodka. After twelve
months, they weren't worth the paper they were printed on. Most

people's pensions were wiped out in 1998 when currency was devalued overnight with no warning. Her mother's entire life savings ultimately bought a single bottle of cooking oil. In 2004, forty million Russians lived below the country's poverty level. Irina was not at all hopeful. "It's déjà vu," she commented about current policies, "I've seen this before, and the outcome wasn't good." Irina mourned the loss of great minds to emigration, alcoholism, cynicism, and suicide. She believed most Russians were in a constant state of despair.

As an American, I was saddened by these statistics and by her message of gloom and doom. Americans, even when faced by horrible events, are generally optimistic—we believe in a better future. In Russia they saw the worst. The entire country could have benefitted from a heavy dose of antidepressants.

Then again, Russians have vodka. Their vodka was better than any I've ever had, anywhere. It goes down smoothly, leaves a warm feeling, and washes away troubles. It is one of the few readily available, cheap staples. Given the political and economic state, I understood why Russians love it.

Had my ancestors remained in Russia and survived, I'm certain I'd be drinking vast quantities. Even as a tourist, I felt the need to drink it often; it was the best way to soften the depressing environment I encountered and the dark visions of my alternate life.

ARRIVALS: VIETNAM, 2004

My generation cannot think of
Vietnam without remembering the
war—the draft, protests, napalm,
nightly body counts and horrific
images on TV, and the scenes of
the final days before the US
departed in defeat from Saigon.
But as the years passed and daily
reminders of the war faded, new
images of a thriving country began
to take their place. The new
Vietnam beckoned.

SAIGON—YOU UP. YOU DOWN. YOU FUN.

In the back of the taxi, I struggled to understand what Han was say-ing. Twisting in his seat, a grin stretched across his thin face, he re-peated the cryptic message. "You come. You up. You down. You fun."

Maybe it was the jet lag, I thought. After twenty-four hours of traveling from New York to Saigon, my brain wasn't performing up to par. I smiled wanly at Han, the hotel representative who'd been sent to fetch me, hoping that would satisfy him. All I wanted was to wash my face and go to bed. The tough parts of arriving were over. I'd gotten through passport control in record time. It was a little odd that my bags had been X-rayed before I was permitted to leave customs, but that had been quick. For a few seconds, not more, I tried to understand the purpose of doing a security check once passengers were off the plane. I decided to think about it later.

Walking into the steaming night had been a shock. The sight of hundreds of people rimming the exit, all chattering and waving banners nearly did me in. I looked for a sign with my name on it. None in sight. I exhaustedly paced back and forth until the police shooed me from the area. Too tired to come up with even the simplest of plans, I stood waiting for something to happen. After a long fifteen minutes, a slight man rushed toward me brandishing a hotel placard with "Karon Gorsbowatz" neatly printed on it. I nearly took him into a bear hug, but sweaty, smelly, and nearly twice his size, I restrained myself. He introduced himself as Han, then apologized, "So late, so late." He grabbed my bag and ushered me into a waiting car.

Though I wanted to capture first impressions of the city, it was impossible to keep my eyes open. I came out of my reverie to the repeated refrain, "You come. You up. You down. You fun." My savior from the airport so wanted me to share in his happiness that I fought the urge to close my eyes again and ignore him.

"Up? Down? Fun?" I asked stupidly.

Han nodded enthusiastically. "Fun, Fun. You up. You down and fun. Fun!"

Speeding through the night, I silently prayed that the hotel was nearby. Though it was nearly eleven, the taxi was engulfed in a river of bicycles, mopeds, and cars. Masses of people filled outdoor cafés. It was New Year's Eve, or at least I thought so, and I assumed they were celebrating. The scene was definitely festive. But isn't the big Vietnamese celebration Tet?

My questions to Han brought another round of "Up. Down. Fun." That didn't help at all.

When we arrived at the hotel, Han took my elbow and led me through glass doors held open by two gorgeous young women. With perfectly coiffed hair, expert makeup, and dressed in pastel, ankle-length gowns and white gloves to their elbows, they looked like they were leaving for a prom circa 1957. I felt a bit like Alice down the rabbit hole—nothing made any sense at all. But then, I'd expected to be surprised by many things in Vietnam; my knowledge of the country had been formed by images of war that were more than forty years old.

The lobby was jammed, but by this point I didn't pay too much attention to what was going on—the prospect of a washcloth and pillow trumped all else. At the front desk, the clerk handed me a key and said, "Your friend is waiting for you." Then he added, "Be sure to come back at midnight; we're having a party."

Maggie had arrived earlier that day, after a week in Thailand. I was happy to be with someone I could understand, trusted, and was past the fogginess of jet lag.

Exhausted or not, Maggie insisted I return to the lobby with her; the New Year's Eve celebration wouldn't wait until tomorrow. I splashed water on my face, and we headed downstairs. All decorum of the public space was lost in the ton of tinsel heaped in piles on tables, chairs, sills. Dozens of sparkly "Happy New Year" signs hung crazily from the chandelier. In the center of the room stood a large artificial Christmas tree in a shade of green never found in nature. Decorating it were china plates sporting photos of staff members. It was amazing that I hadn't noticed any of this on my first pass through the lobby.

"Maggie, please tell me what's onstage. It can't be what I think it is."

With a mostly straight face she said, "If you think you see a guy playing a garden hose, you're not hallucinating." She couldn't re-strain herself from snorting. "Actually, he sounds pretty good."

Spotlit, a tuxedoed musician had a length of green garden hose looped around his arm. He blew in one end and fingered a set of holes drilled into it. The sound was high-pitched, a cross between a trumpet and a kazoo. Was that "The Stars and Stripes Forever" he was playing?

A waiter held out a tray; I plucked off a frothy pink drink and downed it. After a couple more sweet drinks that may or may not have contained booze, I moved beyond fatigue and arrived in a party mood. At midnight, I joined in singing "Auld Lang Syne" with the crowd drunkenly belting it out in English, French, and Vietnamese. That painful rendition was followed by what must have been toasts to the New Year. After each person pronounced their wishes, we all clinked glasses and swigged. This went on for a very long time. Then flashes of scenes from the movie *Good Morning, Vietnam* swam through my mind. I woozily worried that a bomb might ex-plode in the lobby. But the war was in the distant past, and prom queens don't throw grenades. By two in the morning, the party had petered out.

I'd arrived, gone up to the room, come back down, and definitely had fun. You up. You down. You fun. That much I now understood. By morning I hoped I'd be ready for whatever other surprises Viet-nam had waiting for me.

MR. DRIVER—HANOI

They must put new drivers on the late-night airport run to save lives—the drivers' and the passengers'. That was the only possible explanation.

It was well past eleven when Maggie and I arrived in Hanoi. We'd had a very long day. We collected our bags and headed out into the night. After a few minutes of squabbling and confusion between the dispatcher, passengers, and drivers about who got which taxi, we were directed to one of the cars.

Our driver seemed very young, maybe seventeen or eighteen. In New York he probably would have just received his adult driver's license. As we climbed into the back seat Maggie told him our destination, the Asia Hotel. The driver sat rigidly upright staring out the windshield, in no way acknowledging our presence. I repeated the hotel name, hoping for some reaction. Dead silence. Instead of an answer, he slowly put the car in gear. We took off at a stately twenty miles per hour, a speed he maintained for the full distance into central Hanoi—about twelve miles.

By this time Maggie and I had become accustomed to the bedlam of Vietnamese traffic. It's a rich brew of motorcycles, bicycles, cars, trucks, and mopeds all playing a constant game of chicken. They go at top speed when they can, cut each other off regularly, and seem to obey no communal rules of the road. To add to the chaos, there are almost no traffic lights and absolutely no stop signs. Despite this, traffic does flow quickly with a minimum of fuss —no swearing, no road rage, no horns.

Except, that is, for our Hanoi driver—he used the horn constantly, though at the late hour we were traveling, there was almost no one else on the road. He beeped at cars in the right lane to signal that we were on the left. He tooted pedestrians to make sure they didn't wander into the road while we were in the area. He warned cyclists that we were about to go past them. Sometimes he honked the horn for no apparent reason at all. When he wasn't pounding on the horn, he gripped the steering wheel as if it might otherwise fly off. With eyes straight ahead, he sat ramrod stiff and exuded fear. I kept thinking the guy would have heart failure if he had to drive during rush hour.

After about twenty minutes, he turned off the main road and drove through a poorly lit residential area. "Asia Hotel?" we asked, becoming concerned about where we might be headed. Instead of replying, he began to make what appeared to be random turns. Maggie and I sat in the back seat, willing ourselves to neither burst out laughing or crying, nor to fling open the door and leap out of the car.

After twisting and turning through a maze of streets, we entered a brighter area that might have been the start of the city. Another twenty minutes passed. Maggie and I became increasingly giddy—mild hysteria, I think. Our bodies shook with laughter. We put our fists into our mouths to keep from giggling out loud. Anything unusual we did might have pushed "Mr. Driver," as we now began to refer to him, over the edge. At last we arrived in central Hanoi. Mr. Driver meandered past all the large hotels and dozens of smaller ones, finally stopping at a small, seedy-looking one. It wasn't ours. The front-desk clerk came out, looked at our reservation, and explained to the driver that he'd brought us to the wrong hotel. Then, in perfect English, the clerk said to us, "You could stay here tonight." We told him that we'd already paid for the room. With a sigh of resignation he gave lengthy instructions to Mr. Driver and told us, "Driver will take you there."

But Mr. Driver didn't seem to know where to take us. For the next fifteen minutes, we continued our sedate twenty-mile-per-hour night tour of Hanoi. We looped around the same few streets over and over again. Maggie and I vigilantly looked for the Asia Hotel; it was nowhere in sight. Unfortunately, we didn't see another taxi or patrol car, or we would have leapt out of the car. More than an hour had now passed since we'd left the airport. Maggie and I were both exhausted and frustrated. Since I don't speak a word of Vietnamese, I pulled out my phrase book and tried to find something useful to say. In the dim light I struggled with sentences like "I would like to go to the hotel now please." By this point I'm sure he knew that was what we wanted; in fact, he probably wanted it even more desperately than we did. I read and reread the name of the hotel and the street. I showed him the paper, which meant nothing to him.

At long last the taxi stopped, and like a mirage, there was the Asia Hotel. We handed Mr. Driver the 150,000 dong we owed him, plus a generous tip. We figured he deserved something for his suffering. He didn't smile, just shook his head sadly, and with a loud honk, eased away at twenty miles per hour.

We found out later that Asia is pronounced "Ah-see-a," so that every time we asked for Asia, the man hadn't a clue. Inside the Ah-see-a Hotel, reception had no record of our reservation.

The front desk clerk took pity on us and located an available room. We decided we'd be able to sort it out in the morning. At least we wouldn't have to get back into a taxi.

THE BOAT RIDE: CAMBODIA, 2004

While we were in Vietnam, Maggie and I decided to take a short hop over to Cambodia to see Angkor Wat, the world-renowned archeological site. It had recently become a safe destination, after years of isolation during and after the Khmer Rouge reign of terror.

We reasoned that we should see it before it became overrun by tourists. The vastness of the ruins, their beauty and intricacy, and, in some remote areas, spookily vine-enshrouded structures delighted us. But before we left the country we wanted to see some of modern-day Cambodia.

M r. Thy (pronounced "Tea"), our Cambodian taxi driver, skill-fully sped through the busy streets of Siem Reap. The route to the "scenic boat ride" headed away from Angkor Wat and other archeological sites that Maggie and I had been exploring for the past few days. A few miles out of town, he made a sharp turn, and the car bounced from asphalt onto dirt. The narrow road, really an overgrown path, led from the mainland to the pier. Arrow straight, it was lined on both sides with shacks and beyond them murky water. Craterlike potholes forced Mr. Thy to weave his way cautiously. Even creeping along, the car created clouds of dust that settled onto the flimsy structures. Mr. Thy closed the car windows and blasted the air-conditioning to ward off the scorching heat. Looking through the window was a bit like watching a movie; nothing seemed quite real.

To protect against rising lake tides, shacks were propped on narrow poles a foot or two above the ground. They were the size of small garden sheds, but each seemed to be a family home. Women crouched next to cooking fires. Men clad only in briefs or shorts lounged in the sun on rickety benches. Small naked children kicked up puffs of dust as they chased each other. Scraggly dogs with prominent ribs sniffed around looking for scraps. Though there wasn't an obvious source of electricity, in a few shacks groups of people clustered around TVs. A stench from rancid oil, cooking fish, dust, and decay seeped into our refrigerated air. It must have been overwhelming in the huts. For twenty minutes we drove along this road. The further we went, the shabbier the houses became, until some appeared to be nothing but a shell with a few scraps of clothing hanging on a line outside.

As in the rest of Cambodia, the aftermath of the Khmer Rouge regime in the 1970s was evident. Most people were young; executions, forced labor, and starvation had killed the greater part of several generations during the reign of terror. In every cluster of people at least one person was missing a limb—the result of land mines that, forty years later, still hadn't been totally cleared.

Mr. Thy stopped the car beside a gleaming glass and steel structure that prominently displayed a sign in Cambodian and English, "Official Government Office." A local gendarme, resplendent in a tan uniform with epaulets, braids, and sharply creased trousers, approached the car. Silently, Mr. Thy turned over our ten-dollar-per-person boat fare—"payable only in US cash," a sign announced—and the gendarme wrote out a receipt. The transaction was completed in under a minute. We pulled away to drive past more dusty shacks and lethargic people. Maggie and I didn't say a word. We were both thinking that twenty dollars would have been a fortune to anyone here.

Eventually we came to an area of greater activity. The shacks were a bit larger; some had stools and signs and stacked cases of bottled water and beer. The kids seemed noisier. Men bustled about small boats tied to the shore. Mr. Thy stopped the car and pointed to a young man standing on a covered boat. "He'll take you. I'll meet you back here." The guide smiled and hurried over to greet us. I took one look at the plank he'd run down and panicked. It was about eight inches wide and was propped at a thirty-degree angle from the muddy shore to the boat deck. Below it swirled fetid water in which pools of oil, bits of plastic, and other trash floated. Though the span was no more than ten feet, to me, it seemed as long as the Brooklyn Bridge.

I've been phobic of heights and falling since childhood. My breathing got ragged and my palms clammy. In mute panic, I watched as our guide ran back up the plank. He turned toward us, waiting for us to follow. "No way," I rasped. "I can't do that."

The guide scampered back down the board with the grace of a gymnast. Well aware of my fear, Maggie tried to explain, but he didn't understand her. Thinking that I was concerned about its sturdiness, he went to the middle of the plank and jumped up and down a few times. "No problem," he said in perfect English. People began to gather to see what was going on. I looked frantically for any other way to get on the boat. There was none. Finally, with the crowd drawing closer I took a few tentative steps onto the plank. My heart beat like a tom-tom. I couldn't do it. I backed down.

The crowd grew and began to chant, "No problem, no problem." Two teenagers ran up and down the plank, jumping on it together to demonstrate its strength. I wished a large hole would open up and swallow me. The Cambodians were the ones living their lives in constant danger, yet I was the one who was afraid. I desperately wanted my fear to evaporate and allow me to calmly walk those ten feet.

From the boat, the guide leaned over and offered me a hand. On shore, a young man held out his hand to steady me. I still couldn't do it.

Peals of laughter rang out from the spectators, a group that had grown large. It wasn't mean-spirited; this was probably the most entertainment they'd had in a while. Even I started to laugh—there was no way not to. I was embarrassed, but in some odd way, it felt as though I was bringing some joy to these people—who looked as though they could use some. Later, when I was past my panic, I wondered—what terrifies them? Or have they been so ground down by poverty, war, a repressive government, and an unforgiving climate that they're numb to whatever befalls them?

Finally realizing that I wasn't going to walk up the plank, the guide came up with Plan B. He borrowed an ancient rattan chair from a nearby house and submerged it in the mud next to a shabby boat closer to shore. He demonstrated climbing on the chair and onto the boat. I should have been mortified; instead, I felt only relief. It didn't matter how much of an idiot I looked, I clambered up the chair and onto the deck. The crowd applauded.

Unlike the other tourist boats, Maggie commented that this one had no life jackets. But they wouldn't have made much difference. Drowning wasn't the issue. Two minutes in that water would have killed anyone from the developed world. After we were settled on the splintered, graying benches, the guide started the motor, and we sputtered up a long canal and into the lake. Faded buildings anchored in the shallow water formed a floating village. Anything you could imagine on land was available there: shops, clinics, a Catholic church, mechanics, fuel stations, a school, fish farms, pigs in cages. Dogs patrolled most floating docks.

The young man piloting the boat told us, using gestures and the few English words he knew, that the village moves according to the season. In the wet season, it moves closer to Siem Reap, and the road we drove in on becomes completely submerged. In the dry season, the village moves further into the lake, where the fishing is better.

Small children in blue-and-white uniforms paddling home from school waved a greeting. Young women with floating convenience shops darted between homes and boats. Laden with beer, cigarettes, tins of food, and other necessities, the tops of their boats cleared the water by inches. A couple of other tour boats puttered by, passengers staring open-mouthed at serene lake vistas shoved up against extreme poverty.

I was so engaged and appalled and guilty at being a spectator that I almost forgot my fear of getting off the boat. As we neared the dock, the crowd surrounding it had multiplied. So had my heart rate. Accompanied by a whistling, applauding, enthusiastic audience, I tentatively stepped onto the chair and back to shore.

AT THE ROOF OF THE WORLD:
TIBET, 2007

I'd been thinking about traveling to China for decades; I had just never managed to get there. I missed the era of Mao suits and an economy held together by a force of will. When my friend Maggie and I finally did visit China, it had been transformed. New airports, roads, and bridges, as well as towering skyscrapers, factories, and massive housing blocks were being built at an astounding pace.

The popular joke was that the national bird of China is the construction crane. One day in Beijing I did a slow 360-degree turn and counted thirty-eight of them.

Two weeks of a whirlwind tour of the tourist highlights—the Great Wall; Xi'an, home of the Terracotta Army; Chengdu, home to the largest panda preserve; and a cruise on the Yangtze; among many other sites—left me happy to be going to what I thought would be a slower paced, more laid-back environment: Lhasa, Tibet.

B efore we arrived at the airport to depart for Lhasa, we were told that any news, photos, or information about the current Dalai Lama were strictly forbidden in Tibet. Warnings were repeated that there would be fines and could be jail sentences if the authorities determined that we possessed any information about him. Though

Tibet is considered by the Chinese government to be part of their country, a separate visa and immigration check were required for entry. After passing the internal Chinese scrutiny, we boarded a brand-new CAAC Airbus. In keeping with the local joke about it, that "CAAC" stands for "China Airways Always Cancels," our departure was delayed by more than an hour, no explanation given.

As the flight passed over the Himalayas, I got my first glimpse; they didn't look much different from the Rockies—snow-covered peaks with deep valleys and the occasional river gorge. Then the mountains sharpened. The peaks became jagged, knife blades slicing the sky, a series of lethal weapons, tightly packed. New mountains, I thought. They have none of the softness or gentle curves of North American or European mountains, even the highest of them. The Himalayas looked fresh, unweathered, untouched. They are also very high; Lhasa, cradled in a valley between peaks, is at twelve thousand feet.

Ninety-five percent of Tibetans are Buddhists, and religion is deeply ingrained in their lives. Tibetan Buddhism combines traditional Buddhism with local beliefs of the Bom, the indigenous people. We saw our first evidence of the extent of the religion while on the ride from the airport to Lhasa. Hundreds of banners of multicolored prayer flags were draped across the river, on mountains, on homes. Ne Ma, our local guide, explained that monks direct exactly where and when to place the flags. Some are placed on specific holy days and celebrations, some for personal occasions, and all for good luck.

The driver pulled over so we could take pictures of a pair of yak wandering on the side of the road. For the locals, it would be like tourists to Wisconsin stopping to photograph every cow. Still, this time of year, most yaks were high in the mountains where it's cooler.

Massive animals, far larger than cows, with long horns and very shaggy fur, they are a mainstay of Tibetan life. When alive, they provide milk, butter, and cheese and are used as transportation. Slaughtered, they provide meat, fur, and leather. The bones are used for jewelry and tools. Most wild yaks are extinct, but large herds of domesticated yaks survive. If I got the numbers right, the human population of Tibet is two million; the yak population is five million.

Coming into Lhasa, the contrast between it and even the smallest Chinese town we'd seen was immediately obvious. The largest city in Tibet, Lhasa's population was about two hundred thousand. In contrast, in cities we'd visited in China, people would casually say, "Oh, this is a small town; it's only got three million." In Lhasa, there are no skyscrapers and few construction cranes. The traffic was sparse, and the air was cool and unpolluted. On the way to the hotel, we passed the Potala Palace, the spiritual home of Tibetan Buddhism. Perched high on a hill above the city, it's where the Dalai Lama would reside if he were in Tibet. It dominated the view everywhere in Lhasa.

At the hotel, we were greeted with a cup of yak butter tea, the most common beverage in Tibet. The greasy, mild drink, served at room temperature and offered at all ceremonial occasions, is not my favorite. This was followed by a lunch of yak cheeseburgers—yak meat, yak cheese. It was our first of many local specialties we tasted: yak lung, yak blood, yak blood sausage, yak and onion stew, yak meat stuffed spicy peppers. Yak definitely doesn't taste like chicken; it has a gamy but tasty flavor.

Wandering through Barkhor Bazaar, we explored stall after stall, shop after shop filled with tantalizing goods. While some offered typical tourist fare, T-shirts and baseball caps emblazoned with yaks, most of the goods for sale were uniquely Tibetan. Religious items predominated—prayer wheels, *thangkas* (religious paintings), strings of prayer beads, prayer flags, cups and wicks for burning oil, and other items I couldn't even begin to identify. Elaborate silver and semiprecious stone jewelry was in abundance, so much so we were nearly overwhelmed. There were stalls displaying locally useful items: pots, pans, and hundreds of blenders. Around the edges of the bazaar were enormous advertisements for blenders, and I wondered why they were so important. Turns out that you need a blender to make yak butter tea.

All around us swirled humanity, mostly Tibetan, some Han Chinese, some Western tourists. Most interesting to me were the monks, recognizable immediately by their burgundy-and-saffron robes. If not for the robes, however, they would have been indistinguishable from the rest of the crowd. For spiritual people, they seemed to have adopted the ways of the modern world. They wore sneakers and sunglasses, chatted on cell phones, bargained with vendors, and were friendly when we asked to take photos.

In the center of the bazaar is the most famous temple in Lhasa and, perhaps of the Tibetan faith, the Jokhang Temple. We had arrived at an auspicious time, the middle of the holiest festival on the Tibetan calendar, the celebration of the birthday of the Shakyamuni (Buddha). For ten days leading up to this event, people from all over the country poured into Lhasa.

I spent hours observing the scene. The worshippers' clothing reflected local preferences and customs from around the country, and the variety was enormous. Many wore brightly colored garments decorated in intricate embroidery. Others wore neutral colors, punctuated by bright belts or scarves. Several large groups all wore similar-colored clothing, which I assumed was to distinguish one town or social group from another. Nearly everyone wore woven hats with wide brims to protect themselves from the sun, which at Lhasa's high elevation was intense. I found Tibetans, young and old, to be very attractive, with high cheekbones, broad faces, glossy black hair, large white teeth, and café-au-lait-colored skin.

Worshippers threw herbs, barley flour, and beer into the flames of large, open ovens in front of the temple. So many people were throwing in herbs that in one oven, flames shot several feet up from the flue on the top, causing many to stop and stare. In another oven, the fire was nearly smothered by large piles of herbs until a monk raked it out. Smoke bellowed out from the ovens, creating a haze, and the scent of basil, mint, and lavender blanketed the area.

Huge crowds of Tibetans ritualistically circled the temple, roughly a quarter of a mile. By doing this ritual walk, giving donations, and burning herbs during the holy period they are "ten times blessed." To be meaningful, worshippers circled an odd number of times: one, three, five, seven. While most walked, dozens of people prostrated their way around the building while they murmured prayers in a low voice. Prostration is an act of extreme faith and was painful to watch. Worshippers stood up, then dropped to their knees, extended their arms in front of them, raised their chests in prayer, then got up, walked to where the tips of their fingers had reached, and started the whole process again. It took some people many hours to circle the temple. Most of those prostrating themselves were older—some appeared to be in their seventies or eighties, with few below age forty. Walking in the mass of people, I feared that someone would get stepped on, but that didn't seem to happen. Everyone was mindful of the diving bodies and gave them space.

In the bright outer courtyard of the temple, about a hundred monks sat in rows on the ground chanting. Our Chinese guide, Lisa, told us that this happens only during the festival period, and she'd never seen it before, despite many trips to Lhasa. The monks were of all sizes, shapes, and ages. Worshippers surrounded the monks and prayed intently, their lips moving silently as they chanted.

Movement into the smaller inner sanctum of the temple was slow but orderly. People chanted and spun prayer wheels as they inched their way forward. The main room of the temple, once we'd squeezed our way in, was dark, lit only by yak butter lamps. The lamps shrouded the room in smoke, darkened every surface with an oily patina, and permeated the space with a slightly rancid odor. For me, the whole scene was exhausting, exhilarating, slightly claustrophobic, and very nearly sensory overload—in fact, most everything but peaceful or spiritual.

Outside the temple area, Lhasa felt like a different city, far more practical and business focused. All the newest buildings were home to Chinese companies. The signs on all shops were in three languages: Tibetan, Chinese, and English. Written Tibetan is flowing and beautiful. However, I would have been happy not to read the English translation. The beauty of the script lost some of its charm when I understood the signs to mean accounting service, computer repair, or cars for hire. When I asked our guide about the prevalence of the three languages, I learned the Chinese government had decreed all public signage must be in Tibetan and Chinese. English was there for tourists.

Potala Palace, traditionally the summer home for the Dalai Lama, is a highlight of all trips to Lhasa. Because the current Dalai Lama, the fourteenth, is in exile, the palace had become a museum rather than a functioning residence. Still, it is considered holy and is revered by Tibetans.

The palace sits high on a hill, accessible only by climbing nearly four hundred steps. Normally, that wouldn't be too difficult, but at the high altitude it was a tough journey. The steps were of uneven heights and required concentration so I wouldn't trip. My breathing grew ragged as I silently plodded upwards.

To control crowds, every group was assigned a time to visit. We got three thirty, the height of intense sun. In addition to start time, there is a strict limit of one hour to visit the interior. If you don't get out on time, the tour leader is fined one thousand yuan, a hefty sum. So we were strictly warned not to wander off or to linger, no matter how interesting or photogenic something appeared to be.

The palace was divided into two large sections: the white building, containing the offices, administration, and living quarters for the Dalai Lama, and the red building, the spiritual, holy place. In the white building, we viewed the official meeting rooms, the Dalai Lama's personal study, meditation room, and sleeping quarters, as well as a large assembly room. More interesting, the red building contained prayer rooms, gold and jewel-encrusted Buddhas, sacred texts, and the tombs of previous Dalai Lamas—that is, all but one of them, who turned out to be a playboy and eventually disappeared. The Tibetans don't know where or when he died. I guess the process of finding the reincarnation of the Dalai Lama isn't infallible. We rushed through dozens of rooms, each filled with sacred and priceless relics.

It was during the visit to the palace that I became most uneasy about the dominance of the Chinese. A living, breathing sacred place had become an historic relic of a slowly dying culture. The Chinese describe their takeover of Tibet between 1951 and 1959 as the "Peaceful Liberation." Thousands upon thousands of monks and nuns were slaughtered by the invading Chinese. The Dalai Lama escaped through the mountains. Some peaceful liberation.

After our visit to Potala, my fellow travelers and I began to ask more pointed questions about the political and social situation. When I asked what language was most often used, our Tibetan guide answered, "It depends where you are. At home most everyone speaks Tibetan, especially outside of Lhasa."

That didn't seem like a complete explanation, so I pressed further. "What about other places?"

He explained that radio and TV were broadcast, and all public information was distributed, only in Mandarin. Children studied in Mandarin only; no Tibetan textbooks were allowed to be printed. In effect, Tibetan was being relegated to a fringe language. Ne Ma, usually smiling and cheerful, grew somber as he told us that to be a high school instructor or university professor you needed a degree from a Chinese university. This forced educated Tibetans, like one of his brothers, to live in China for an extended period and absorb the culture. "He returned to Lhasa more Chinese than Tibetan."

From what I gleaned, modern-day Chinese no longer get what they want by mass killings; instead they are undermining traditions and language. And what they want in Tibet are its rich deposits of chromite, iron ore, lithium, and other minerals.

But despite the Chinese desire to eradicate their culture, Tibetans remain devout Buddhists. That's one piece that will be tough for the Chinese to eradicate. Most Chinese are totally secular, and the few temples we visited there appeared to be more museum than active sites for worship. I suspect the Chinese don't fully grasp the intensity of belief, tradition, and devotion held by Tibetans.

On the morning of the Buddha's birthday, *the* holy day, the crowds near Jokhang Temple were even denser than they'd been when we'd first arrived. I was swept into the stream of worshippers circling the temple. On this circumnavigation of the temple, I discovered a small outbuilding with a massive prayer wheel, maybe twelve feet high, and eight or nine feet in diameter. Around the edge of the building were dozens of three-foot-high prayer wheels. An endless flow of people walked along, slowly spinning the wheels. Each prayer wheel, from the smallest to the largest, contains scripture. Most pilgrims haven't read the scripture, but by spinning the wheel, they get "karma credit" for having "studied" it.

After five days, nearly everyone in the group was ready to leave. Though wonderfully exotic and intellectually captivating, Lhasa was a difficult place to visit, physically and emotionally. The air was dry—desert dry. For the whole stay, my eyes had constantly itched and felt as though small pebbles were scratching them. I hadn't slept well and had woken up every morning with a bloody nose. My skin soaked up moisturizer like a sponge and still felt parched and papery. Despite taking a low dose of Diamox, a drug that helps to alleviate symptoms of altitude sickness, I still had an occasional stab of pain slicing through my scalp and eyes. The Diamox also had a strange side effect of causing extremities—toes and fingers—to tingle at odd times with no warning. Some of the group had felt nauseated for days.

The physical pain was an annoyance. Far more upsetting was the understanding that Tibet was getting swallowed by the Chinese. All the Tibetans we spoke with were circumspect about politics. What was said seemed to bear little resemblance to what was in their hearts. On the last day, after yet another barrage of questions, Ne Ma finally revealed his fears: "In the future, there will be a Tibet but no Tibetans."

INDIA AT LAST: 2011

At least a dozen friends had traveled to India and came back with vivid tales of their journeys. Roughly half had loved the country: they enthused about the brilliant colors, the magnificent sights, and how exotic and stimulating the experience had been. The others had come back ill, upset, or frazzled, describing the overcrowding, poverty, stench, and being surrounded by mobs of begging children. One friend had holed up in her hotel after two days of touring, unable to deal with the mass of humanity and chaos.

While I've traveled to many impoverished areas of the globe, I've learned to deal with my dismay about it. However, I'm never comfortable in crowds. My idea of hell is New Year's Eve in Times Square—India sounded like a perpetual night in Times Square. But when a group of friends wanted to go, I gave in and decided I needed to experience the country for myself.

THE RICKSHAW RIDE

"Hold on at all times," our guide cautioned. "It can be a rough ride." He told us to brace ourselves with our feet firmly against the front support bar of the three-wheeled bicycle rickshaw. I tried to figure out a way to simultaneously maintain secure seating and hold onto a camera. It seemed impossible.

This was my first afternoon in India. I was still jet-lagged and reeling from the unfamiliar and extraordinary sights, smells, and sounds I'd experienced in just a few short hours. With a bump off the curb, we lurched into traffic heading for Delhi's Chandni Chowk bazaar. My driver, with his cell phone pressed to one ear, turned around and smiled encouragingly at me, while at the same time plowing into the middle of the road. I wanted to scream, "Get off the phone!" but couldn't. My voice had deserted me. Instead, I instinctively held even tighter onto the rickety metal frame.

My tour group formed a parade of ten rickshaws immediately swallowed by a sea of people preoccupied with their own errands and the competition for space in the narrow alleys.

Potholes, both wide and deep, and piles of rubbish turned the route into something of an obstacle course. I watched as the rickshaw in front of me went into an especially large crater. It tipped at an alarming angle before righting itself. The passengers went pale and frantically clawed for a more effective way to hang on.

Overhead a twisted spaghetti of power wires appeared to have been installed by a deranged electrician. It would have caused any building inspector in the US to go into apoplexy. Lines dangled, often low enough that I could have reached up, grabbed a wire, and yanked if I'd had the desire to bring the whole thing crashing down. That, however, would have meant unclenching my fingers.

As humanity swarmed around us, we slowed down; the throng made it impossible to maintain forward motion at anything but molasses speed. Rickshaws, bicycles, and overly laden carts of wire or fabric or crates filled with who knows what gently jostled into each other every couple of minutes. No one seemed to notice or care about these collisions. Traffic frequently came to a total standstill, the soup of people and vehicles congealing and making it impossible to go forward or back. Everyone shoved, twisted, and turned in an attempt to unblock the knot, then squeezed their way forward for a few dozen yards before it happened again. It was during one of those stops that I had the courage to pry my fingers from their death grip on the support bars and snap a few photos.

Sitting in the rickshaw, I was high enough up that, despite the crush of bodies, I could look into the shops. Hundreds of narrow stalls, perhaps ten or twelve feet wide, lined the alleys. On one street, everyone sold decorations for weddings—every tiny storefront a dazzling display of color, glitter, and shapes. The bright hues and sparkling goods made up for the fact that almost no daylight filtered through from above. It was a bit like traveling through a high-walled labyrinth. If I were claustrophobic, it would have taken only a couple of minutes before I'd have been hyperventilating. Though I don't suffer from panic attacks, it took some effort to concentrate on anything other than what might happen if there was a fire or any kind of emergency. I would have liked to photograph the lovely displays, but with every lurch and crash, I was reminded to simply absorb the sights—mental snapshots would be safest.

At the edge of one road, barbers gave haircuts, tailors sewed clothing, and vendors fried dough in huge vats of bubbling oil. I shuddered to think what would happen if a serious collision occurred near one of those vats. We went past booksellers, stationery shops, and jewelers. Near the very end of our ride was a street of used car parts. The guide later said that if you drove into the area to buy a part for your car and left your vehicle for more than a moment, you might well end up needing to buy parts from your own car back from the same seller. This was a whole new twist on chop shops.

Interestingly, I can recall the sights but not a single smell or sound from that ride. It is as if I had been only able to mentally record the visuals; anything more would have pushed me into total overload.

Three weeks and many cities later, we arrived in Varanasi. Given its reputation as a holy city and the spiritual center of Hinduism, I had hoped for some respite from the crowds, filth, and noise I'd grown to detest.

Our first evening in Varanasi, I went on my second rickshaw ride in India—it being the only possible way to travel to the banks of the Ganges River. The traffic getting there surpassed anything I'd experienced in the rest of the country, something I hadn't thought possible.

For this ride, no one needed to remind me to brace myself and hold on tightly. I had white knuckles and a massive adrenalin surge before we even pulled into traffic. Our roughly one-mile ride began on a wide boulevard. Here the rickshaws looked even more fragile in comparison to the trucks and cars rumbling along the road.

As if possessed, my driver raced around other rickshaws, people, and anything else in his way. He'd pedal furiously, then lean back and coast for as long as possible, working again only when necessary. We pulled out of the way of larger vehicles with only millimeters to spare. Apparently it requires less manpower to get a rickshaw up to speed and coast than to move at a steady pace. A couple of times, I was convinced as we hit yet another pothole that the whole contraption would flip. Within minutes, my hands ached from gripping the side of the rickshaw, yet I wouldn't, couldn't relax my grasp for even a second to stretch my fingers.

The population density was stupefying. In Delhi we'd been traveling in narrow alleys. Here the streets were wide but equally packed. Pedestrians and vehicles competed not only with each other but with strolling cows. In India cows always have right-of-way, and they amble at their own pace on a path only they can discern. As we cycled by a row of shops, a cow wandered into one and stood there, looking over the wares. No one seemed to take much notice.

Cross traffic and people making turns played chicken with oncoming vehicles; they'd edge into traffic seemingly without looking, as if daring other drivers to run into them. Conveyances came within inches of each other at relatively fast speeds before someone would give way. A man on a motorcycle piled with boxes higher than he was blithely yakked on a cell phone as he wove through traffic, appearing unaware that he nearly caused several collisions. A rickshaw delivery van sped past us carrying four refrigerators, wobbling unsteadily as the vehicle dipped into potholes. On another rickshaw, a family of seven, including elderly parents plus a mound of parcels, plodded along. The driver struggled to maintain any speed at all, while cars and motorcycles raced around them, belching exhaust fumes.

I was grateful, if only momentarily, to be in a rickshaw rather than on foot as I watched pedestrians walk into the flow of vehicles. Locals seemed calm as they proceeded at a steady pace while the ongoing traffic parted to create a narrow slot around them. Tourists were the ones with terrified expressions who froze mid-step, unable to move forward or backward. Some became immovable islands, with traffic a rushing river flowing past them.

Unlike my ride in Delhi, I have a vivid recollection of both sounds and smells from the ride in Varanasi. The noise level was nearly unbearable despite the fact that, by that point in the trip, I'd learned to wear earplugs whenever I was out and about. Throughout India, drivers lean on their horns as a way of announcing their location; the horns are a never-ending chorus. Here they were used so frequently by so many cars that the honking merged into a deafening cacophony, totally useless as a way of attracting the attention of other drivers.

With all of the cows, there was a lot of excrement. That smell, combined with the press of sweating humanity, burning incense, rotting trash, exhaust fumes, a tang from the river, and wafting smoke from the two riverside crematoria created a thick and inescapable stench. This was on a relatively cool evening in February; I cannot conjure up what that smell might be like in midsummer.

All the members of my tour group seemed dazed as we walked the final short distance to the river. This, we were told, wasn't an important or especially crowded evening in the old city of Varanasi. During holy periods, there can be three or four times the number of people vying for space to make their way riverside to enjoy the blessings of "Mother Ganges."

IN THE JUNGLE

We left early for our drive to Ranthambhore, site of a famous tiger sanctuary. For five hours, we shared roads in a free-for-all with pollution-belching trucks, honking cars, overcrowded buses, mopeds, cows, pedestrians, bicyclists, rickshaws, pigs, camel carts, monkeys, and a lot of excrement. After ten days in India, I was no longer astonished by the congestion; it was, in fact, almost exactly what I'd expected when I'd first imagined traveling here.

India was the one major country on the globe that I'd resisted visiting for decades. I felt I *should* visit it but didn't really want to. What I'd read and heard about the hordes of people terrified me. Surely such a mass of humanity would unleash my latent agoraphobia. But finally, after years of fierce resistance, friends had convinced me to travel with them to tour the country for three weeks.

I'd assumed that in their company, I'd manage to deal with the crowds while taking in what have been described as some of the most magnificent sights anywhere.

Now, here I was in Northern India, coming face-to-face with everything I'd hoped to avoid. It was turning out to be even more difficult to appreciate the beauty than I had anticipated. Through the dust-streaked bus window, I observed a huge crowd that had amassed in one village for no observable reason. We came to a standstill for several minutes, then moved at tortoise speed through a sea of pedestrians, animals, and vehicles. Our guide was at a loss to explain the unusual density in what appeared to be a typical small town. No weddings, no funerals, no accidents, no officials mucking up the normal chaotic flow of traffic—just lots and lots of people. India's population problem was impossible to miss.

Regulations must exist in India, but they certainly aren't enforced. I spent a lot of time, when we were able to move, staring at the continual and terrifying game of vehicular chicken that swirled around the bus. I marveled at the crumbling streets, more pothole than pavement, and the rats' nests of wiring that dangled precariously above them. Mostly, I wondered how anything productive happened within this chaos. The seeming randomness of everything around me challenged my professional and personal philosophy of process and clarity.

We were en route to the tiger sanctuary in Ranthambhore National Park. For centuries, this area has been famous as a tiger habitat. The Mughals had come here to kill them; we were coming to shoot them with cameras.

I was glad we were headed to a more serene area for a few days. After two weeks of nonstop sensory bombardment, I didn't just want a break, I needed one. Scenes of elegant women in shimmer-

ing silk saris and white horses with pink toenails that were bedecked in silks and feathers for a wedding delighted me. But every
day, almost every hour, was filled with fresh sights that challenged
and distressed me even more. Since the moment of my arrival, I'd
been trying to like India and failing. I felt like a character in a post-
apocalyptic science fiction film. I couldn't help thinking that I
would be the one who would escape, while the locals were doomed.

With great relief, I read a sign announcing Ranthambhore. Minutes later, I was staring at a glistening white structure perched on top
of a hill, set blissfully high above the bustling town. After many
nights in central city hotels shrouded in thick smoggy air amidst
teeming streets, my sleep interrupted by the blare of car horns and the
barking of dogs, I'd be thrilled to be a guest of the local maharajah for
a few nights. But, no doubt, we'd be staying at a more modest establishment. Then the bus turned onto a side road heading directly toward the beckoning vision and entered through high gates.

At first glance, the Nahargarh Hotel resembles an eighteenth-
century Mughal hunting lodge restored with loving care. The path
from the bus to reception led us on a shaded walkway adorned with
frescoes, sculpture, and artful displays of marigold petals. We
passed through a courtyard in which a tinkling fountain, its basin
studded with floating lilies, conjured an illusion of cool. Around us,
golden silk banners affixed to high arches fluttered in the slight
breeze. My muscles, tense from two weeks of travel, loosened just a
bit. Though I felt guilty about it, this luxury was a facet of India
that had the potential to seduce me.

In addition to tourists flocking to the lovely illusion on the hill,
so do filmmakers. As we rounded the corner to cross yet another enticing courtyard, we were stopped by a sharp cry, "Quiet on the set!"

I took in the cameras, dollies, and crew. My perception shifted yet again—from maharajah's palace to exclusive hotel to what I now saw: Bollywood set. A dozen extras hovered just outside camera range. The most opulent of the flowers and silken drapes were clustered in the camera sightlines.

"Action."

A small girl in a swirling pink skirt raced across the courtyard toward a woman seated on pink pavement. Their costumes spoke of an earlier age, but their makeup was pure Bollywood: dramatic black-lined eyes, shocking red lips, rouged cheeks. A handler let loose a pair of doves. A line was uttered in Hindi.

"Cut."

We resumed our walk to the front desk, passing the film crew, a pair of spear holders resplendent in purple silk, and, in a courtyard adjacent to the main set, a small army of extras bedecked in richly colored saris. I couldn't help but wonder if the extras lived in the dusty village below. Assuming they did, what did they make of the Nahargarh? For someone raised in poverty-ridden, overpopulated India, the quiet, cleanliness, broad open spaces, and pseudo-opulence must have seemed like all Bollywood movies, a fantasy. For me, the hotel was a welcome respite but not totally out of my realm of experience. I felt more twinges of guilt, this time for feeling comfortable here. But guilt or no, I was glad to be able to remove myself for a few days from the daily reality of most of India.

Our room was spacious, decorated with comfortable furniture covered in sumptuous fabrics, and, most important for me, blissfully quiet. When I went into the bathroom, I noticed that the faucet leaked. The chairs wobbled. Later, walking around the property, I tripped several times on heaving, uneven sidewalks and stairways, where no two steps were the same height. When I looked closely, I observed cracks forming everywhere. The hotel was on the cusp of falling apart. What made this even more startling is that Nahargarh had been built less than ten years before. "It's all a wonderful fake," the guide told us. "No maharajah has ever set foot on the property." Like so much of India, even when the surface is glitzy, the infrastructure is on the brink of collapse.

That evening, a naturalist gave a talk about the area. In 1980 Ranthambhore was declared a national park and protected tiger sanctuary. Prior to park designation, the habitat and tigers were being decimated. Poachers wanted pelts, and villagers wanted firewood and land to graze cattle. In the 1950s there had been about forty thousand tigers in India. Currently the population is estimated at fourteen hundred, thirty-eight of which live in Ranthambhore. Given that India's population is now over 1.2 billion and expected to exceed China's by 2025, in a much smaller geographic area, pressure on all open land areas makes the tigers' future uncertain.

"Each tiger needs about ten square miles of hunting grounds," the ranger told us. He explained that they are solitary and shy creatures, and so, "It isn't likely you'll see more than one." He went on, "In fact, you may not see a tiger at all."

All around me people groaned. After a five-hour bus ride on rugged roads, we all felt we *deserved* to see a tiger.

The naturalist stressed that there are many other birds and animals—several varieties of deer, wild hogs, and lots of monkeys. "And the scenery is beautiful."

I was sure it would be lovely. By this point in the trip, my standards had tumbled pretty low; anywhere not strewn with piles of trash would be appealing. But I'd come to see a tiger.

Then the ranger gave a slideshow. Slide after slide of sleek, striped cats—hunting, sleeping, running. For the first time in days I was eagerly anticipating our next adventure.

As a parting gesture, the ranger distributed thin sheets of paper covered in dense, nearly indecipherable text. This "indemnity bond," he explained, must be signed and presented with your passport to be allowed permission to enter the park. What little I could read seemed to clear the park, the government, and even the tigers of any responsibility for absolutely anything that might happen.

At six fifteen the following morning, we made our way through dimly lit walkways in search of the promised coffee. In the central courtyard, two musicians greeted us with a song. They'd been there when we first arrived, when we'd finished our late dinner, and whenever we made our way through the space. They seemed to live there, often lounging about with no one to play for. Had it not been for their cheerful nods and smiles, they might have been mistaken for Disneyesque animatronic figures, triggered by motion detectors to play and sing.

We were ushered into an eighteen-seat open-topped bus. With our group of sixteen, plus the guide and naturalist, it was a tight fit. The bench seats were narrow and set close together; everyone struggled to get comfortable.

At the park gate, we queued up in a long line of vehicles while officials checked visitor identities and indemnity bonds. While we waited for entry, the hawkers were out in full force, almost combative in trying to sell us something, anything. Guidebooks. Baseball caps adorned with an embroidered tiger, listing slightly. T-shirts that smelled of camphor and probably wouldn't survive a single washing. Faded postcards. All around us, there was a flurry of negotiations, tourists nearly as frantic as sellers. You'd have thought they had never bought a souvenir before and would never have another opportunity.

An official in a natty khaki uniform climbed onto the bus. Long minutes passed while he scrutinized a list of names and matched them against passports and faces. Our guide, fearing that our time in the park would be shortened—there is a strict rule that visitors are only allowed from seven until ten and then again from four to seven—tried to assist. He was swatted away. The officer, in his bureaucratic way, dropped passports and the list and then became confused as he tried to match people with their photo. He called out, "Smith," and looked relieved when he got an affirming "Here." Since most names were probably unpronounceable for him, he just kept comparing photos and faces.

While this went on, the naturalist again emphasized that we might not see a tiger. But he reassured us, "Mornings are best." Then he explained, "How you spot a tiger is by listening to the other animals. When monkeys see a tiger they cough. Or you might hear birds screech." As our vehicle was finally given the go-ahead and lurched into the park, he continued, "Or you see movement—other animals fleeing the area, or the tiger rustling leaves and grasses." He told us that entry into the park is strictly controlled and that vehicles are assigned different areas in which to travel—this is supposed to reduce congestion and ease stress on the tigers. Despite his warning just a few moments before, he felt confident we'd spot a tiger: "Last evening we saw one near the lake. Each tiger roams a large area, but they tend to move during the day, not in the evening. So keep your fingers crossed she's still there."

Ranthambhore is described in guidebooks as a jungle. While it was a pleasure to be somewhere not crammed with humanity, it wasn't what I think of as jungle. In February, the land and vegetation are parched, and a thick layer of dust coats all surfaces. Still, it is considered the best time to visit because the grass and foliage have died back, making it easier to spot wildlife.

The potholes and bumps on the park road were extreme, even

by Indian standards. My friend Linda and I were on the rearmost seat—bad choice. As the bus bounced through one particularly large hole, we both screamed. A spring had broken, and our seat dropped about four inches, making an already rough ride even more uncomfortable. However, within minutes we were distracted by packs of deer, monkeys, peacocks, and dozens of varieties of lavishly hued birds. We all wanted the driver to stop so we could take photos, but the ranger insisted we should press on. "We'll see lots of these later on; now we must go look for a tiger," he explained. We kept moving.

"Hold on, we'll be going fast," the ranger warned us. "I think the tiger is at the other side of the lake." We asked how he knew; none of us had heard or seen a thing. "There are vehicles stopped over there; perhaps they see one." So we added another sign of nearby tigers to what he'd told us about animal warning sounds and movement—the presence of other tourists. We raced around the lake at bone-jarring speed, almost colliding with a couple of other vehicles. No tiger.

A guide in a nearby jeep leaned out and yelled, "Go up the hill!" Our driver stomped his foot on the gas, and we sped in the direction indicated, pursued by four other vehicles. No tiger.

"Go back," was the word passed from someone else. Two more jeeps had joined our convoy. Each of the eight vehicles tried to turn around and outmaneuver the others so as to be first at the possible site. When we arrived, no tiger.

On the rumor of yet another possible sighting, the pack wheeled around, kicking up a dust storm, and sped back, gathering more vehicles as we went. Even if the tiger had been there, we'd never have been able to see it through the dust. As we raced forward, two more jeeps flew over a ridge from the other direction.

After a few more back-and-forths, we were a pack of seventeen crazed groups of tourists.

Well, not all tourists; we were told that five of the jeeps contained government officials. The guides blamed them for the lunacy. Government employees are allowed to enter the park and go anywhere they like, at any time of the day or night. By my reckoning, that still left twelve tourist vehicles—a noisy battalion that would cause any sane tiger to head in the opposite direction. It also defied every rule and regulation that had been so painstakingly explained to us.

Eventually our guide said, "Let's just sit here and wait. Patience." That sounded great to me. I cheerfully watched the mob of jeeps, buses, and trucks race back down the hill. Within five minutes, we saw movement in the distant grass. The naturalist quieted everyone, and we glimpsed the tiger's distinctive stripes lurking in the woods. Sixteen cameras started clicking. A few more minutes and the tiger emerged from behind the trees into an open clearing, spotlit by the morning sun—an apparition made solid. She was magnificent with a brilliantly striped coat, sleek lines, obvious power and agility. Her stance was commanding: she *owned* this land. I could sense her watching us, ready to tense her muscular legs and spring should the need arise. We were allowed to visit only because she permitted us to do so. In the wild, it was easy to see why these creatures are revered by so many cultures. For about ten minutes she prowled the area, marking it. Then, with perfect grace, she headed back into the thicket.

Although we saw no more tigers during the next two hours, we did see lots of tiger food—the wild deer. There were birds by the hundreds, monkeys, and crocodiles. Still high from our tiger sighting, we were content to observe these lesser creatures.

On the road leading back to the hotel, elephants adorned in swirls of pastel colors and camels bedecked in ribbons stood awaiting their cue. The day's filming was beginning. As we entered the main gate, the extras were getting off a battered bus. Out came sword bearers, lady's maids, and servants—all resplendently clothed. In the courtyard the musicians resumed their song.

Twenty-four hours later, after another game drive and a lot of filming, we were headed to yet another Indian city. Back to the dense population, the filth, the noise, the crumbling crowded roads, the chaos. But then we'd never really left the chaos, had we?

I hoped the Taj Mahal, which we'd be visiting in a few days, would finally do the trick of winning me over to India. It didn't. Though the architecture is stunning, for me, the crowds of tourists and hawkers, the overflowing trash bins, and the distressing poverty just outside the confines of the compound bled the beauty away.

Before I'd left home, a friend had told me, "You'll see some of the most beautiful sights and some of the ugliest, and they're often right next to each other. Focus on the beauty." I tried but couldn't. It wasn't just the poverty that upset me; I've traveled in many poor countries. It was the relentlessness of too many people and what, to me, felt like utter pandemonium all the time, everywhere.

Built over a lifetime of exploring the world, my self-image as an intrepid traveler had been shattered. The enormity of India's problems left me feeling inadequate and depressed. By the end of the trip, I didn't even want to try to help; I just wanted to go home, to escape. That made me feel even worse.

In India nothing is what it seems to be; even the most beautiful, serene places are but illusions. The tiger was the single exception. It was pure, powerful, and without artifice—and is about to become extinct.

BERLIN REVISITED: GERMANY, 2011

In early 2011, my friend Judy emailed me, "Just found a really cheap airfare to Berlin. Any interest in going?"

I almost never say no to a travel invitation, and recent magazine articles about the changes to the city were intriguing. Judy's added sweetener, "I'll make all the reservations; all you have to do is show up," made the offer irresistible.

'd first visited Berlin in 1992 because of Michael, whom I'd met while traveling in Borneo. Michael, a native West Berliner, and I had roamed the island together for a couple of weeks. When we parted he'd invited me to visit him. Berlin had never been on my radar as a can't miss destination. As a Jewish woman born not long after World War II, tales of the Holocaust were still fresh, and Germany was painted as a country to avoid. Berlin, the epicenter of Nazi power, was considered especially repugnant. But I was curious as to where my romance with Michael might go. Shortly after I returned to New York, I'd landed an assignment that took me to Brussels frequently. The relatively short flight to Berlin made for an easy decision.

When I flew into Tempelhof Airport in 1992, it was the main Berlin airport. It didn't provide a warm welcome, though Michael certainly did. I remember disembarking the plane into a huge and solid building, feeling very tiny in the cavernous space. It seemed built to last through an apocalypse, or at least a bombing. When Michael told me that the structure had been designed by Hitler's favorite architect, Albert Speer, I wasn't surprised. But Michael was proud of it, not because of its Nazi history but because of its role in the 1948-49 Berlin Airlift. While he was too young to remember the airlift, his parents had talked about it frequently and were pro-American as a result. Tempelhof had been the main point through which West Berlin obtained food and fuel for eighteen months after the Russians sealed the city's rail, road, and water routes. If not for the airport, West Berliners would have perished or been swallowed by the Eastern Bloc.

On my recent trip, Judy and I flew into Tegel, Berlin's current central airport. It's a bright, airy building filled with eye-catching shops, restaurants, and lots of activity. It was surprising to hear that an even newer airport is being built, slated to replace Tegel. The contrast to my recollections of Tempelhof made Tegel seem the epitome of customer friendliness. This push to change, improve, and expand was a foreshadowing of what I'd find throughout Berlin in 2011. Everything in the city was getting a facelift or being replaced.

When I first visited in early 1992, the wall had only been down for about eighteen months. The East seemed frozen in time, while the West had been keeping pace with progress in the developed world. Though the wall had been demolished, it was easy to see where the demarcation had been, even without Michael pointing it out. In the East, piles of rubble from World War II remained heaped in empty forlorn expanses of land. Bullet holes and scorch marks from firebombs still scarred buildings. Shops and consumer goods were sparse. Squatters lived in buildings that looked as though they hadn't been repaired or maintained since being bombed fifty years earlier. The newest buildings were Russian minimalist—utilitarian, utterly devoid of ornamentation or anything else to brighten the human spirit. Even on the sunniest days, the East felt gloomy, dark, a bit ominous. With little effort, it was easy to imagine the crushing horror of the Nazis, the Russian oppression, and the terror of the Stasi (secret police).

Twenty years later, on the short ride to the hotel, I strained to see anything familiar. Here and there were buildings that maybe had been there when I had visited Michael. Was that the shop that two decades earlier Michael had insisted made the best ice cream in Berlin, if not the world? Was this the boulevard that had been the main shopping street in West Berlin? I couldn't be sure. Two clear symbols from my earlier trips were still evident: the many Turkish restaurants and the satellite dishes that sprouted from every window in some neighborhoods. Michael had told me about the large number of Turks who had recently come to Berlin as "guest workers." He pointed out that satellite dishes allowed them to get news from their homeland. He also correctly predicted that Germany's immigration policies would create future problems.

My affair with Michael brought me to Berlin three times in 1992. Each of those journeys reinforced my childhood prejudices. Michael showed me many remnants of Hitler's influence—numerous Nazi structures remained in the city. As a young man, Hitler had wanted to be an architect, and perhaps if he'd become one, the

world would have been spared much grief. The style he had preferred was heavy, square, dense. I remember the buildings as having
few windows, as if each were a prison-in-waiting, which perhaps
was the case. That dark period of history seemed omnipresent in
Berlin—the Olympic Stadium where the African American Jesse
Owens embarrassed the Germans with his triumphs, the apartment
blocks where Kristallnacht began, a desecrated Jewish cemetery,
and the single remaining wall of an apartment house that had once
housed Jewish families who had been forcibly removed and had
later in the war been destroyed by an Allied bombing raid. Small
placards affixed to the wall named each person who had lived in the
building and what had happened to them. Michael translated,
though I could easily read and understand the significance of
Buchenwald, Treblinka, and Auschwitz.

One day Michael and I headed to a quiet suburban area where he
pointed out a railroad station that had been a major departure point
for the concentration camps. There were no signs, no memorials,
nothing to identify the importance of this place. That especially
chilled me: a simple commuter station surrounded by a green leafy
neighborhood, not so different from my own. That so ordinary a
location could have been a place of such inhumane cruelty reminded
me that atrocities can happen anytime, anywhere. That there was
nothing to remind current residents of what had occurred there
seemed like an attempt to deny its history, or worse yet, erase it.

In 1992 the German capital was still in Bonn, though plans
were already in place to move it back to Berlin. Berlin displayed
little of its previous glory, but during its heyday between the World
Wars, the city had been among the most effervescent in Europe, a
center for art, literature, music, philosophy. Despite that heritage, it
felt subdued, with people doing errands more at the pace of a small

town than a major city. If not for my growing affair with Michael, one short trip would have sufficed. I went to Berlin to visit him, not the city.

In 2011 Judy brought an architecture guide to Berlin that included many walks around the city. On our first afternoon, we followed a route that took us through a mix of neighborhoods; for three hours it all felt like new territory to me. It was only at the end of our walk that we finally came upon buildings I recognized—the TV tower that had previously been a prominent symbol of the might of the East, and the Reichstag, home to the German parliament.

The new glass dome atop the historic Reichstag glowed from within, a visible symbol of the new transparency of the German government. All other government offices were totally new, having been built in the two decades since I'd last been in the city. Most line the Spree River. On the day we explored the area, the sky was a perfect blue, and the buildings, a wonderful geometry of glass and steel, shimmered in the sunshine. The reflected light and views into the interiors created a sense of brightness, air, and space that was both calming and uplifting, not what I typically associate with government. Across the river is the Hauptbahnhof—the central railway station, an intricate steel and glass puzzle building that screams movement. Trains run both above and below the main concourse, their arrivals and departures creating a constantly changing pattern of colors and people.

On the river passed a never-ending flotilla of tour boats. The number of boats was startling to me; they passed by every minute or so, each filled to near capacity. It was as if the world had come to look at the new Berlin. What visitors found in 2011 was stunning architecture, buildings designed by the best talent in the world, stores filled with merchandise, more than a hundred museums brimming with art and history and science, parks, restaurants, theater, music, and vibrant nightlife. The city was returning to its renowned past as the crossroads of Europe.

At the Brandenburg Gate, the most recognizable symbol of the city, the tourists were so densely packed it was impossible to get a single photo without including a mass of people. In photos from my earlier trips the gate stands pristinely and majestically alone, not a single person even on the perimeter of the scene.

One of our must-see attractions was the Jewish Museum, designed by Daniel Libeskind, opened in 2001. In all descriptions, the museum is lavishly praised—both for content and architecture. The goal is to not just show exhibits about Jewish history but to make visitors feel the pain and disorientation of Germany's Jewish population.

The lower galleries that describe the lead-up to Nazi power and the Holocaust have no windows, and the floors are slightly tilted. They made me a bit woozy and semi-desperate to escape. Throughout the museum, the galleries are long and narrow and zigzaggy; despite a map and good signage, it was often difficult to know exactly where I was. There are three empty spaces in the building, set aside as memorials. These areas define great architecture for me; without a single word of explanation, I understood the meaning of each space.

In the Garden of Exile, there are tall, broad concrete columns surrounded by greenery set in a grid, with pathways between them. At first glance it looks green and while not exactly inviting, not especially threatening either. The columns are set at a slight angle, opposite to the angle of the ground. The effect was disorienting; while I easily walked around, everything seemed off. It took a while to figure out why it felt so peculiar. This garden represents the difficulties those who escaped the Holocaust had in reorienting their lives.

The elongated walls of the Holocaust Tower reach inwards. The only light source is a narrow window at the top of the tower through which a meager slice of sunlight filters in. Within seconds it felt as though the walls were closing in on me, and I had to flee the room.

The final empty space is a long hallway that seems to reach to infinity as the walls and ceiling narrow. The floor is covered with the work of an Israeli artist: thousands of cast metal faces. These are round disks with holes for eyes, nose, and mouth—they look like screaming Munch skulls. When people walked in the hallway, the faces clattered. This was, despite the photographs of Auschwitz, Bergen-Belsen, and horrific scenes from the ghettos, the most disturbing imagery in the museum.

Curious to see how areas outside of the center fared during the city's twenty-year transformation, Judy and I boarded several buses and trams headed into sections far from the tourist areas. Most of the neighborhoods that had formerly been deep in East Berlin still looked down-at-the-heels—lots of graffiti and buildings in need of cleaning and repair. Constructed mostly in the 1950s and '60s, when housing was urgently needed to replace bombed-out homes, the structures were utilitarian and dull. They had no ornamentation and were in uniformly drab colors.

Despite the architectural blandness in Berlin's Eastern neighborhoods, things had changed for the better; the shops were lively, and outdoor cafés were filled with people. Small touches brightened the scene, like trompe-l'oeil images of sky and fields on the blank wall of an apartment block or a mural of brightly colored geckos climbing up the side of a building. It all had a very different feel than what I remembered from my trips twenty years before when everything in the East appeared gray, tired, depressed, and depressing.

At the end of one tramline, Judy and I came upon a large area set aside as a memorial to the Cold War. A section of the wall, lights, and guard towers had been left in situ, along with a broad expanse of no-man's-land. Photos and explanations told the story of this chapter of Berlin's history. The initial barrier was barbed wire; it was erected in 1961 in just twelve hours and surrounded the entire Western sector. Russian officials decided to create the physical partition to staunch the flow of people leaving the East—they'd lost one-fifth of the population in the years following political division. Over the next three decades, the barbed wire was replaced by ever higher and more solid barriers. Inner and outer walls, lights, ditches, and armed guards with orders to shoot to kill made the wall nearly impenetrable. It was a vivid reminder of how recently and harshly the city had been divided. The photos of the people killed while trying to escape reinforced the brutality.

I remember Michael telling me that when the wall had first come down, it was possible to look at someone and know, in a glance, whether they were from the East or West by their clothes and complexion. Easterners, having been malnourished for decades, looked pasty and ill. By the time I visited, eighteen months after demolition, that was no longer true. However, Michael said that he could still tell where Berliners had lived by the way they spoke. In fifty years of partition, East and West had developed different slang and spoke distinctly. I wondered what had happened to the language between then and now but had no one to ask.

Of all the sights in the city, for me, Potsdamer Platz in center city summed up Berlin's trajectory over the past hundred years. Prior to World War II it had been one of the largest, liveliest intersections in the city, indeed of Europe. The area was home to a major railway station, luxurious hotels and shops, many theaters, dance halls, bars, and restaurants. It was the heart of the city's cultural life, but it also housed government and business offices and was a focal point for innovation—Germany's first electric street lights and traffic lights were introduced there.

Later, it had been an important symbol for the Nazis. The government took over many of the offices, and in photos from that era, swastikas adorned most buildings. Toward the end of the war, the Allies bombed it relentlessly. What remained postwar was a vast pile of rubble that had then stagnated for fifty years.

During the Cold War, it had been an untouched, barren no-man's-land bisected by the wall. When I visited in 1992, the wall was down, but nothing else had been done. Despite Michael's quest to show me as much of Berlin as possible, I don't remember visiting Potsdamer Platz—there simply hadn't been anything to see.

Judy and I were in awe of the new Sony Center in Potsdamer Platz. It's a collection of buildings encircling a large open area covered by a "dome" that resembles a vast glass circus tent. Light and airy, it is an architectural gem that hummed with activity. The area, as much of the rebuilt city, was designed to blend residential and commercial enterprises so that people have a reason to be there 24/7. Festivals and concerts frequently take place under the dome, restaurants line the perimeter surrounding a fountain, and there's a film museum, cinema, theaters, and clubs. A major railway station and shopping mall, as well as apartment and office towers, are clustered nearby. Whenever we passed through the area, the liveliness seemed to epitomize the rebirth of Berlin.

When I first agreed to go to Berlin with Judy, I considered

tracking down Michael. He and I had not been in contact since 1993. The four thousand miles between our homes, as well as the oppressive dullness of Berlin at the time, had given a whole new meaning to geographically undesirable. Our romance fizzled out when the practicalities sank in. As fascinated as I was with the changes in Berlin, I wasn't interested in reconnecting with my personal past—I did not try to locate him.

Had my relationship with Michael flourished, I would have seen the incremental steps that transformed the city from gray to glitzy. Instead, the reconstruction seemed like a rebirth that happened in an instant.

IN TRANSITION: BURMA, 2012

As I've gotten older and have seen the world grow ever more homogenized, I've begun to yearn for destinations that have managed to hang onto their identity. At the time I visited Burma (Myanmar), it was at the cusp of transitioning from isolation to joining the global community. Traveling through the country, I was transported not only to a new and beautiful place but to the Asia I remembered from my earliest trips there.

BIRTHING BUDDHAS

The name "Mandalay" has always conjured up intrigue in exotic locales for me, maybe from seeing the Bob Hope–Bing Crosby *Road to Mandalay* movie as a child. In 2012 the city was peaceful but, walking down the street in the marble-carving district, I experienced "exotic" without a single dastardly plot as in the film.

As I ambled along, I kicked up the powdery white substance that covered every surface. For someone glancing at a photo, the sea of white might easily be mistaken for a dusting of snow. But in Burma, it surely wasn't snow. The fine particles mixed with sweat to form a paste on my skin, my lungs struggled to take in air, and the substance seemed more sinister than a mere movie villain.

This one street, maybe six or seven blocks long, supplies all of Burma, plus a large swath of China, Thailand, and other Southeast Asian countries with an endless army of marble Buddhas. Workers create small Buddhas, towering Buddhas, thin ones, fat ones, smiling, somber, pure white, and painted ones. Lining the road were small workshops, each crammed with sculptures, some in process, others completed and presumably awaiting shipment. Many statues stood in neat rows, looking like the terra cotta warriors that protect the emperor's tomb in Xi'an, China. Others lay jumbled as if tossed there like pick-up sticks. A few random horses, dragons, dancing women, and other fanciful creatures kept the Buddhas company.

Both sides of the narrow street buzzed with activity while buses, cars, and motorcycles sped between them, each stirring up a cloud of white particles. Tourists wandered through work areas, picking their way around workers and trying not to get hit by a vehicle or twist an ankle on the uneven surface of marble debris. Using power saws, Dremels for fine carving, grinders, and sanders, workers hunched over bulky blocks of marble or semi-finished forms. Women washed and hand polished nearly completed figures, the newly clean surfaces glinting in the filtered sunshine. Tools screeched, radios played, people called out to each other. Truck and bus motors added to the cacophony. It seemed a brutal setting for the creation of spiritual icons.

Using my camera as a way to focus myself, I homed in on small scenes within the chaotic activity.

Two women squat next to a reclining Buddha, intently scrubbing his back. Dusted in white, their appearance is ghostlike, ethereal. Their full attention is on the task, their hands smoothing and buffing the surface. They couldn't have been gentler or more reverential. A pair of angels, perhaps. They are surrounded by a dozen or more identical statues, each awaiting its turn.

I wondered if being Buddhist gave these women patience and instilled meaning in this repetitive, dull task.

Across the road was a small temporary storage area. I was enthralled and took endless photos of rows and rows of seated Buddhas, their bodies fully carved but faceless. Instead of a gentle smile and soulful eyes, their heads are formless blocks of roughened stone.

In the guidebook, I'd read a long explanation of how the master marks the outline on the large block of stone and makes the first cut after prayers have been chanted and solemn rituals performed—everything done ritualistically to ensure pure energy and auspicious life. Apprentices make rough cuts while the master looks on and advises. The master does the final, fine shaping. I see none of this, but perhaps I am there at the wrong hour of the day or don't know where to look.

I had always assumed that the Buddhas I'd seen in pagodas had been carved by artists, my frame of reference being Michelangelo and the Pietà. I imagined years, maybe even decades, of apprenticeship with a master to learn techniques and acquire an understanding of proportion and grace. Then a single artist would spend months carving a perfect Buddha, the end result a personal creation. Instead, this appears to be an assembly line, with each person assigned to a different body part. Perhaps the face alone is reserved for the most skilled craftspeople. So, are the makers of these figures gifted sculptors or merely skilled workers?

A short distance down the road, I photographed a young man power-grinding flowing folds into Lord Buddha's robes. I know he's young because of the baseball cap turned backwards on his head and the jeans he wears. The older generation dresses more traditionally. But his hair, covered in marble dust, looks prematurely gray. His face, arms, shirt, and jeans seem to have had all color bleached out. He is, of course, simply covered in dust from the piece he's working on. He wears no respirator or face mask; no one I see working does. I imagine his lungs must be white too, and I don't suppose he'll live a long life. In fact, as I move further up the street, I don't see anyone who looks to be much older than their mid-to-late thirties. Who knew that sculpting could be more dangerous than coal mining?

Set back from the work areas are shops, each salesroom displaying a slightly different variety of figures. In one I take photos of Buddhas with ruby-red lips and what appears to be a splash of eye shadow and rouge. Some of their carved robes are edged in gold, and others are adorned with a golden sash. My guide sees me looking and tells me these sculptures are bound for China. He points out the chubbier cheeks, fuller lips, and hair design. No one in Burma, he tells me, likes that style—it's too ornate.

In front of another shop I quickly snap a photo of a young man, perhaps the salesman or the owner's son, sitting on a folding chair next to a Buddha for sale. He could easily have been the model. His passive, plump face, staring into space echoes Lord Buddha's calm countenance. On the young man's face, it could be total peace . . . or boredom. He's got large ears, eyebrows high and arched, and neatly shaped hair; they all mimic the style of the statue. A white T-shirt, loosely covering his ample belly, has a row of soft folds that could have been carved by one of the craftsmen I'd just observed.

After thirty minutes and less than half the district, I've seen more Buddhas than I'd seen in my entire life, and I've traveled extensively in Buddhist countries. Who buys all these? They aren't tourist trinkets. This walk has given me much to think about. Where do all of the Christ figures in American churches originate?

How much do they cost? Does the serenity of a Pietà also emerge from a chaotic workplace? I cannot stop wondering.

"Exotic" is defined as "of foreign origin or character" or "strikingly unusual or strange in effect or appearance." The sea of white and all who work in it, birthing an army of Buddhas, was about as exotic a sight as I've ever come across.

IT'S ALL ABOUT THE MONEY

On the morning we'd arrived in Yangon from the US, our guide took us to a money changer. "This is a good one," he said. "They'll take your money without any problems." We didn't know what he was talking about, but everyone in my group dutifully took out some of their crisp American dollars and lined up. Prior to leaving for Asia, the tour company had sent instructions about bringing new dollars—no rips, tape, or writing on them. One by one we handed over two hundred-dollar bills, and in a quick exchange we received, complete with a brown paper sack in which to store it, a two-inch stack of well-worn bills. The exchange rate was roughly eight hundred kyat (pronounced "chat") to the dollar. The most common denomination—and the only one they had—is thousand-kyat notes. Clutching our thick wad of money, we all felt very wealthy. We also wondered how to carry the cash around; the pile was unwieldy.

The money situation for tourists is tricky. Before arriving, I'd read a lot about the Burmese political and economic situation. I'd learned that, because there were no diplomatic ties between the United States and Myanmar, US dollars were illegal. Euros were also unacceptable, as were British pounds. There were no ATMs anywhere in the country. The banks wouldn't exchange US or European currency. Credit cards weren't accepted, and travelers' checks were out of the question. I was glad I was on a tour and the bulk of my expenses had been prepaid, uncertain about how one would pay for high-priced items, like hotels or domestic plane tickets. I supposed one brought rolls of hundred-dollar bills, which the guidebook stated could be exchanged on the black market. That sounded a bit scary; I felt uncomfortable carrying around even a relatively small amount of cash.

While the inconvenience of being unable to easily use dollars was obvious to me as a tourist, it was only over the course of two weeks of traveling that I began to understand the greater impact for the Burmese.

On the second or third day in the country, once I'd acclimatized, I noticed something peculiar—the bus in which we traveled, new and very comfortable, had a right-side steering wheel but was driven on the right side of the road. In most of Asia, especially in former British colonies, traffic stays to the left. Our guide explained that when Burma declared their independence in 1947, they immediately changed to driving on the right, a demonstration of their break with British traditions.

"Okay," I said. "That makes sense, but why don't the vehicles have left-side steering wheels?"

"Well," he started, then paused. "None are manufactured here, and no one will sell them to us. Kyat isn't a very useful currency," he added ruefully.

I looked at the busy road. They were obviously acquiring vehicles somehow. "So how do you get all of these cars and trucks?"

"We barter for them."

I suddenly got it. "And everyone you barter with drives on the opposite side." I knew that India, China, and Thailand, the countries with which Burma shares its borders, had all stayed with the British standard. He went on to say that China was especially interested in minerals and wood and was their largest trading partner. Since most countries wouldn't deal with Burma, the Chinese could charge whatever they liked for items the Burmese needed. Many Burmese were becoming alarmed that their country was being "pillaged" by the Chinese, but they couldn't do anything about it. And though there was plentiful cheap and willing labor, because of the currency problem, no foreign companies would build factories or manufacture anything in the country.

After a few days, I began seeing other signs of the closed economy. There were very few banks, even in the biggest cities; Burma was a strictly cash economy. So no mortgages, no loans of any kind, no savings with interest—in fact, none of the financial services most of the world takes for granted. I also noticed that all of the computers in use at hotels and stores were in English. Although everyone in Myanmar is taught English in school and English has become the language of international trade, the real reason for English-language computers is that Microsoft and Apple did not recognize Burmese as a language. Because there was no legal way for the Burmese to pay them, they refused to translate their programs into Burmese.

Surprisingly, street vendors loved taking dollars and didn't much care about the condition of the bills. The reason, I finally deduced, was that many make illegal trips over the border into Thailand or India to buy goods, and there dollars are easier to use than kyat. The street vendors' English was, however, minimal. I was never sure if it was a language or math problem when I heard them cheerfully calling out to me, "One for two dollars, two for five dollars!"

About a week into the trip, a few people in my group needed to exchange more money. This time, in Mandalay, the exchange didn't go so well. The person behind the desk scrutinized each bill with the care of a gem appraiser. He handed two out of every three notes back. "But it's a clean bill," one fellow traveler protested.

"Smudged, no good."

Another bill required only one quick glance before the money changer handed it back. "Folded, no good."

"But it's brand-new."

"Folded, no good," he repeated.

Now everyone was becoming concerned. In the security of the bus, money emerged from hidden pouches and the bottoms of carry-on bags. We traded bills so that a few people who didn't have "perfect" dollars could get kyat. All of us were experienced travelers and had seen money examined carefully in other countries, but never anything quite like this. We asked the guide why the pickiness about the condition of the bills. He explained that money changers personally take the bills to Singapore for exchange into Chinese yuan or Indian rupees, acceptable currencies in Myanmar. Because there are so many counterfeit dollars, the Singaporeans are scrupulous in their examination of all currency. Burmese money changers, with no recourse, want to be certain they don't get stiffed. I never quite understood why a new bill was any guarantee against counterfeits.

Near the end of the trip, I started to think about how to tip our guide and bus driver. While I had enough kyat to give the driver, I'd need to exchange a lot of money to tip our guide. I decided manners be damned and asked him, "I know this is a bit forward, but would you prefer to have your tip in kyat or dollars?"

"Dollars. Definitely."

"I'm happy to do that, but if you don't mind, I'm really curious. Why? How do you deal with the dollars?"

He went on to tell me that he has a secure safe at home and that's where he stores most of the money. The rest is stowed at his parents' and in-laws' homes, "to make sure that at least some of it stays safe."

"Why not at a bank?"

"I wouldn't even consider putting it into a bank. I'm not sure I'd ever see it again." And, he continued, "With elections coming up, who knows what the government will do? They could decide overnight to devalue the currency. Or close the banks. Or who knows what?" He continued, "At least I know dollars are a stable currency."

I knew that officially it is illegal for Burmese citizens to have US dollars. So I pursued my interrogation. "But how do you use them?"

He explained that there is an official exchange currency, not kyat but "pseudo dollars," that are bought at banks and can only be used by the Burmese. These "pseudo dollars" can be exchanged at the border for real dollars. "And I do travel, so I could use them. But you never know what exchange rate they'll decide to give you." He pulled one out of his pocket to show me. It looked like badly printed Monopoly money. No wonder he wanted real dollars from real Americans. And, according to him, many Burmese have become frustrated and increasingly vocal about the problems associated with being cut off from the global economy.

This was February of 2012. Burmese elections were held two months later, and the international community declared the elections had been fair. Hillary Clinton visited the country twice, and plans were underway for reestablishing diplomatic ties. Change, massive change, was about to start. Having seen firsthand the impact of being excluded from the global marketplace, I understand that political change is all about the money. I just hope the country can make the transition without losing its unique charm.

YES, WE HAVE NO BANANAS:
CUBA, 2014

The island of Cuba is lush, with glistening white beaches, mountains, and fertile land. Free health care and education are accessible to everyone. People seem to be well-fed and are unfailingly polite and friendly. Because crime is almost nonexistent, it is possible to walk anywhere and feel safe. Music, dance, and the visual arts are thriving. It's a pretty impressive list. But it is just a piece of the story.

Before I visited Cuba, my impressions were gleaned from distant memories and the scantiest of touch points. The Bay of Pigs crisis was a major event in 1961, when I was ten years old. What I took from the news and the fear I perceived in all the adults around me was that we'd come close to global annihilation—though I'm not certain I really knew what that meant. Several years later the news focused on boat people—Cubans desperate to escape Castro's hold on their lives. My lingering impression was that Cuba was a dangerous place, so dangerous even for Cubans that people would do anything to come to the United States.

Over the next fifty years, I visited East Germany, Russia, China, and Vietnam, places that gave me a sense of living under Communist rule—some aspects grim, others not. I always felt that these countries were somewhat cheerless because they were totalitarian states rather than because of their economic policies. My assumption was that Cuba was a tropical version of those countries. But in truth, apart from an occasional visit to Little Havana in Miami to eat a Cuban sandwich, headlines about Elián González, and seeing Ricky Ricardo on reruns of *I Love Lucy*, I rarely thought about Cuba. That is, until I read that the US State Department had greatly loosened restrictions on tourism to Cuba. Because I'd seen how fast things had changed in Eastern Europe after the collapse of the Soviet Bloc and the sudden changes in Myanmar, I wanted to visit Cuba before the Castros died. My assumption was that within a very short time Cuba would revert to being a playground for American vacationers.

Though it was easier to travel to Cuba, American citizens could legally visit Cuba only on educational tours. I suspected the State Department believed the tours would demonstrate to Americans that Communism doesn't work.

After my friends and I selected a tour, we began to receive details about the trip, including booklets from the US State Department. The information provided made it clear they didn't want Americans traveling to Cuba to sip margaritas and sunbathe.

On a mandatory pre-departure phone call a few weeks before we left, the tour operator told us that unless we were deathly ill, we were expected to participate in every activity, every day. In Miami, the night before the tour, we met our group and were reminded once again of our obligation to attend every event on the itinerary. Our first night in Havana, our tour guide emphasized, yet again, that we had to do everything. I was convinced of the seriousness of this when she said, "My company had their license yanked temporarily because we became lax about enforcing the attend everything rule. It has happened to most American tour operators here. So we make no exceptions except for illness." In practical terms, this meant eight or nine hours daily of listening to lectures, attending performances, or walking around historic sites. It sounded exhausting.

My first surprise upon landing in Havana was that, despite repeated warnings from the tour company about searches for unmarked prescription drugs, banned reading materials, and a host of other restricted items, no one showed the slightest inclination to search our luggage or question us about our possessions. We whizzed through immigration and customs.

In the parking lot stood a shiny new tour bus—it was the only new vehicle in sight. We all immediately began snapping pictures of the Fords, Chevys, and DeSotos from the 1940s and 1950s that surrounded us. As Penny, one of my traveling companions who is a car-loving native of Detroit, said, "I haven't seen this many vintage autos since I was young, and those would have been new."

The thrill of seeing so many cars that we recognized from our childhoods never waned. But what was for us a quaint novelty was a time-consuming necessity for Cubans; these cars were just about the

only transportation available for locals. Creativity and resourceful-
ness are needed to keep the cars running; their owners are masters of
repairing and recycling. I couldn't help thinking that whenever the
US embargo ends, antique car collectors will swarm onto the island
and buy every vintage car they can get their hands on, even if they are
equipped with, to use Penny's phrase, "very nonstandard parts."

Ladas, Russian-built cars imported during the period of Soviet
support during the 1970s and '80s, had been so poorly constructed
that most rusted out or couldn't be repaired. Nearly all had been
scrapped, not something Cubans do unless they are forced to. The
few Ladas that managed to belch their way around Havana were
scary looking—sagging chassis with headlights or door handles
duct-taped on, their bodies rusting and generally looking as though
a single large bump or pothole would cause bits to fall off. Or, for
no reason at all, they might just quit moving. The government has
recently loosened restrictions on selling cars in Cuba, but they are
so heavily taxed and expensive that in the first six months a mere
fifty cars had been sold.

Public transportation is infrequent, especially outside of Havana. Buses are scarce and uncomfortable, often converted trucks
with almost no air circulation. Our Cuban tour guide told us that
trains do exist but are unreliable, not air-conditioned, and generally
unpleasant. He described a five-hundred-mile trip he took from
Guantanamo to Havana that was supposed to take ten hours but
ended up taking more than twenty-four. As time passed, the car
became stifling, the bathrooms overflowed, bodies reeked, and
there was no food or water available except for what people hawked
while the train idled at stations. He vowed to never again ride a
train in his homeland.

We had picked our tour because it was one of the few that traveled the length of the island—from Havana to Baracoa at the eastern tip. The further we traveled from the capital, the more we noticed the country's dysfunction and deterioration. Roads were reasonably good, but there was almost no traffic—there were few working vehicles outside of the capital. We'd see crowds of people standing at most four-way intersections waving fistfuls of pesos, hoping to hitch a ride. In remote areas, we saw as many horses and carts as cars.

Camagüey is the third-largest city in Cuba. In celebration of its five-hundredth anniversary, it had been newly painted and scrubbed, giving me a sense of the intricacy and beautiful lines of the architecture. But in the majority of towns, nearly every building had peeling paint, rotting or warped window- and doorframes. Whole buildings were listing. Worse yet, many were covered by black mold. Because of poverty and the US embargo—the two often seem to be linked—there are no supplies for repairing the ravages of time and nature. The mold, in addition to being unattractive, has resulted in many people having at least a mild case of asthma. I found myself continually clearing my throat.

Along one stretch of the national highway, there was a line of what looked like telephone poles—but no wires. Our guide explained that in 2012, Hurricane Sandy had swept through this part of the island, leaving a path of destruction. The government didn't have the resources to restring the phone wires or construct cell towers, so whole towns were without service. Along the same road, we passed endless fallow fields. These days, with a scarcity of modern equipment, almost no one is interested in pursuing farming as a career. Most people receive a college degree. Why would any well-educated college graduate want to plow fields with a mule? We were told sugar production was currently at 10 percent of the peak growing years during the time of Batista. As a result of this much-diminished farming, Cuba, which can ill afford it, must now import much of its food supply.

Even what they do grow languishes. Wherever we traveled, abundant bunches of bananas hung from trees. Yet, except for one hotel where we stayed, bananas were never available to us. When I asked why, our guide told me bananas are largely grown on private property—there are no "state banana farms." Hotels are all at least 51 percent government owned and forbidden to buy any goods or services that are not produced by other government enterprises. The banana growers have neither the contacts nor permission to export them.

"What do they do with all of the bananas?" I asked. "Surely a single family can't consume that many."

"Some sell them in local markets, but that's really a waste of time, since everyone grows bananas." He smiled. "Mostly they get fed to pigs."

I began to get the picture. Wandering through one of the few nongovernment markets, I saw that everyone seemed to be selling an almost identical array of produce: pineapples, onions, tomatoes, potatoes, peppers, cucumbers, and garlic. I imagined that in the state markets, the choices were even narrower. Though no one is starving, unless you grow it yourself, food options are limited. This was borne out by the meals we ate—variations on the same pork, chicken, rice, and vegetable combo with few seasonings. I fondly remembered the tasty sandwiches and chicken and rice meals I'd eaten in Little Havana in Miami and wondered if people ate better in private homes than in local restaurants. I hoped they did.

Based on what I'd read, I expected medical care, much touted as a model for the world, to be a highlight of what the revolution had accomplished. It is free for everyone, and the training doctors and nurses receive is promoted as world-class. Countries all over Latin America send students to Cuba to be trained. I got a very different picture when one of the members of our group became extremely ill, so ill he ended up in a clinic, and then the hospital. His wife told us the medical staff was large and caring. But they had almost no supplies. Rooms were crammed with patients and were hot, as there was no air-conditioning. Equipment looked to be many decades old. So, while well trained, the medical staff is limited in what they can do for patients. Fortunately, after a few days our tour mate recovered enough to be able to fly home.

Still, physicians are one of the country's major exports. Medical school is free. In return, newly minted doctors are sent all over the developing world in repayment for their education. The Cuban government charges host countries a large fee for the services of the doctors. But the doctors themselves are only given room and board and a meager stipend that barely pays for necessities. It sounded like indentured servitude. My impression was confirmed when I learned that after their term of service has been fulfilled, nearly all the doctors who are sent overseas defect, never to return to Cuba.

Doctors aren't the only ones defecting. Baseball, a sport that most Cubans follow avidly, has lost some of its top players to American teams. I am a dance aficionado. For years I'd been noticing that many of the best dance companies included at least one or two Cubans, frequently as principal dancers. Reading their bios, I noticed they'd often been members of Havana's renowned Cuban National Ballet company.

During our trip we saw several astounding contemporary dance companies. Entredans performed for us in an old theater in Camagüey, a city famous for nurturing the arts. Accompanied by a scratchy recording, dancing on a well-worn floor in a steamy room, they moved with energy and grace. I was enthralled by the choreography and a skill level that was as high as the best of world companies. After their performance we spoke, through a translator, with some of the dancers and the choreographer. The choreographer told us that they'd recently had a three-week visit from a principal dancer with the Alvin Ailey Dance Theater company. "We learned so much from him," she said. "He brought videos of many dance companies, and what I saw gave me many new ideas." She went on to say, quite candidly, that the visiting American dancer had opened her eyes to the narrowness of Cuba's worldview. Foreign performers rarely came to Cuba. The Internet was so slow that videos of dancers couldn't be streamed or downloaded.

Because isolation is stifling sources of creative inspiration, dancers feel cut off and restricted, and they have been leaving in droves. Before I visited, I'd read that in 2013, seven dancers had defected. No one in Cuba said a word about it. When I returned to New York, I researched and learned that Cuba's immigration laws punish those who abandon delegations or official work contracts by banning them from returning to the country for a minimum of eight years. Despite this, four months after I visited, six more dancers defected while they were on tour in Puerto Rico.

Even though there have been so many defections, the arts continue to thrive. All Cubans, from doctors to street sweepers to musicians and actors, earn a salary of ten to thirty dollars per month, plus food coupons. Housing is subsidized. This makes it possible for anyone to get by as an artist as easily as in any other profession.

Fabulous murals adorn many walls in every town, sometimes spouting propaganda, but most simply celebrating life. They were fanciful, colorful, and altogether charming. Everywhere we traveled, we encountered joyful music—sometimes organized, often not. Young and old played in bands and sang in choruses. They played modern tunes on ancient instruments, while everyone within earshot tapped their toes, sang along, or got up to dance. The infectious music seemed a way to temporarily forget about life's many problems.

While they don't have access to contemporary world music, I discovered that many Cubans of all ages revered the Beatles. One man, about my own age, sang me a medley of Beatles tunes in nearly non-accented English, though his spoken English was poor. Another much younger man proudly showed me his CD collection. Several times I heard Beatles tunes wafting from open windows.

The band has been a cultural touchpoint in Cuba. In the 1960s, while Beatlemania swept the globe, Fidel Castro banned Beatles music, believing they represented the worst of vulgar consumerism. His pronouncement didn't stop Cubans from adoring the band or from smuggling and copying tapes.

The atmosphere is changing. Our guide showed us a park in central Havana named for John Lennon. The dedication ceremony for the renaming of the park and the unveiling of a statue of John Lennon was held on the twentieth anniversary of his 1980 murder. Castro attended the ceremony and spoke of his respect for the former Beatle. "What makes him great in my eyes is his thinking, his ideas," he said. "I share his dreams completely. I, too, am a dreamer who has seen his dreams turn into reality."

By the end of two weeks, I'd spoken with many Cubans, both officially and not, and was glad to discover that people were willing, even anxious, to speak with me and felt free to do so. They recognized both the good and bad in their country. They praised and cursed the Castro brothers.

I'd always assumed the Cubans blamed Americans for most of

their economic problems. During the Batista years in the 1950s, the Mafia and the United Fruit Company had a stranglehold on the country, while the US government turned a blind eye to the situation. It is something that I, as an American, am ashamed of. Yet Cubans spoke more virulently about Russia. During the so-called "special period" after the Russians withdrew financial support in 1989 (after the dissolution of the Soviet Union), Cubans didn't have enough food, fuel, or basic supplies to meet even minimal needs. Most of the population spent several years at near-starvation levels.

I wondered why the embargo was still in place—what harm could Cuba possibly do to the US? When I asked a professor who was lecturing us on Cuban history, I got my answer. According to him, Jimmy Carter would have lifted the embargo during his administration. Carter realized that Cuba was no threat to the US and learned of the humanitarian need for food and supplies. However, wealthy Cubans who had fled the revolution and settled in Miami convinced him otherwise. They let him know that, while Cuba was not a threat to the US, they, as Cuban Americans, were a threat to Carter.

The wealthiest of the original Cubans who fled to the US at the beginning of the revolution have a vendetta against the Castros. Despite the fact that they escaped with their money, Cuban Americans blame Fidel and Raul personally for forcing them to leave their land and homes. This animosity has been passed down from generation to generation. The families do not want either of the brothers to have the satisfaction of seeing the embargo lifted. The hatred is as strong as between Palestinians and Israelis.

Ultra-wealthy Cuban Americans have been threatening Republican and Democratic leaders for decades. They have made it clear that the families will spend every penny they have making sure that any party that supports lifting the embargo will lose Florida in the presidential election. If these Cubans had settled in Alabama, they'd have no power. Living in a key swing state, their threats carry a lot of weight.

So the embargo continues. It has resulted in a profound lack of technology, machinery, medical supplies, and basic construction materials. American companies are banned from trading with Cuba. EU and Asian companies are afraid of doing business with Cuba for fear that it will make dealing with the US more difficult. Given the relative size and wealth of the two nations, it is obvious which country companies would prefer to do business with.

My trips to Russia, Vietnam, and China all happened after the fall of the Soviet Union, when each of these three countries had moved to a more market-driven economy. While not wealthy, their standard of living was improving and there appeared to be enthusiasm for the changes, as well as significantly increased access to material goods. These countries demonstrated what I thought of as "Communism light."

For me, Cuba demonstrated the impact of being a "pure" Communist state. The country's talent and brain drain across a broad swath of professions has been increasing from a trickle to a near waterfall. There are few challenging work opportunities for young adults. Those who are lucky enough to have found meaningful jobs are poorly paid and have little incentive to work hard. There is a lack of suitable housing; many homes are packed with multiple generations—out of necessity, not choice. The crumbling infrastructure makes even the most mundane of tasks difficult. Loosening strictures on travel to and from the US, by both the American and Cuban governments, have added to the exodus. From what I observed, the US truly represents the land of opportunity for many young Cubans. They view America as a place where, unlike their homeland, ambition and hard work really can change the quality of lives.

Our guide told us he wouldn't leave: "Cuba is my home." He went on to say, "But my children are talking about it, and I'm sure that in time they'll both end up in the States." He told us that numerous nieces, nephews, and children of friends had left, settling in such unlikely locations as Albany and Fargo. He was also furious at the Castros because his parents, who had wholeheartedly supported the revolution, were managing to stay out of desperate poverty only because he was able to support them.

Cuba is a country with resources and great potential—beautiful, with a perfect climate and an educated, talented, and naturally upbeat population. But it has been exploited by external interests and restricted by internal policies, rules, and regulations. By the end of the journey, I had a new appreciation of the power of world politics to impact individual lives. And, for the first time, I profoundly understood why the Soviet empire crumbled—Communism doesn't work. The State Department had accomplished its goal.

Yes, we have no bananas.

I'VE SEEN THE FUTURE:
DUBAI AND ABU DHABI, 2017

When I visited South Korea in 2012, I came back marveling that I'd seen the future. At that time South Korea had the world's fastest average Internet connection speed. It was available everywhere, even in the deepest tunnels of Seoul's subway system—commuters watched the morning news on their phones while on their way to work.

No one used cash—a quick swipe of a smartphone paid for coffee or a packet of gum and provided entry onto the metro. When I offered cash to pay for dinner, servers would appear baffled; you could almost see them thinking, Who uses cash? Most taxis and buses were electric, with charging stations scattered around the city. The contemporary architecture and interior design were stunning.

But after reading about Dubai, I understood South Korea represents the near-term future. Dubai is a vision of the distant future.

I'd seen photos of the city that emerged from the desert and read about Burj Khalifa (the world's tallest building), the mall with an indoor ski slope and artificial islands shaped like a palm tree. But I'd also heard about the Emirates' downside. One friend claimed Dubai had been built by slave labor. Another told me she'd been there several times to visit her nephew and had hated it. "Too beige," she'd said. "No green. Boring."

When my friend Sue was planning a trip to the UAE and asked if I'd like to travel with her, I jumped at the chance. I needed to experience Dubai for myself.

I am a fan of science fiction, avidly watching *Star Trek,* going to sci-fi films, and reading countless visions of the future. They taught me that for humans to survive on distant, hostile planets, we need to learn to terraform, or to transform alien environments into ones suitable for human habitation. Dubai is a terrestrial demonstration of how terraforming might be successful.

Our flight arrived in Abu Dhabi at night. We transferred by taxi to Dubai, about a ninety-minute drive. The highway was twelve lanes wide and smooth. We silently sped through the night in near darkness, exhausted from our thirteen-hour flight. As we neared Dubai, skyscrapers lit up in fanciful colors stretched across the horizon. We perked up, our adrenaline flowing at the prospect of exploring a city new to both of us. The fantastical skyline made us wonder if one week would be sufficient to see it all. Though this was my first time traveling with Sue, our mutual excitement gave me confidence we'd be okay.

Dubai's Sheikh Mohammed bin Rashid Al Maktoum is a benevolent dictator with vision. His goal was for the emirate not to be dependent on oil. He's led the transformation of Dubai into the center of Middle East commerce and finance. He's also the one who understood that infrastructure and tax policy would be the underpinnings of progress.

A few years prior to this trip, I'd worked with an organization whose mission is to bring together government officials who could not otherwise meet due to the political climate and policies. Behind-the-scenes facilitated sessions allowed them to tackle difficult problems. My assignment was to help my client identify the next set of strategic issues to address. The government officials, journalists, NGOs, and corporate executives I interviewed across the globe identified two interlinked issues. They were not, as I'd supposed, terrorism and political instability. Instead these thought leaders pointed to climate change and lack of water. Terrorism and regime change has been going on for centuries; those were viewed as short-term issues. Global warming and lack of water are long-term issues humanity has never faced. Nearly a sixth of the world's population now lives in areas afflicted by water scarcity, and that number is expected to grow significantly.

One of Dubai's first major investments was a massive desalination plant. I saw it from a distance and was impressed by the size of it—many acres of tubes and holding tanks emerging from the sea with massive pipes snaking toward the shore. I immediately grasped the reality that nothing else in this futuristic society could exist without it. The plant provides enough water to support the emirate's growing population, currently around two million and expected to grow by 5 to 8 percent annually. In early 2017, a solar-powered addition was completed, and an even larger expansion is planned; Dubai still looks toward the future.

Roads are being built at a frenetic pace as desert is transformed into arable land and gobbled up by new development. Brand-new, heavily traveled highways are smooth and well maintained. I compared Dubai's pristine thoroughfares with New York's pot-holed, worn, and garbage-strewn highways and wondered if Americans will ever have the will and resources to repair and rebuild in a meaningful way.

Offshore, islands have been created where none existed. On a walk through the Emirates Mall, we came upon a model of a new development being planned.

"This will be the most luxurious development in the world. One half will be residential and the other half a paradise for visitors." The salesperson pointed to the detailed model. "This is where the luxury villas will be, each one with fabulous views of the sea and city." Sue and I murmured our appreciation. "And this side will be for tourists, with lots of entertainment, including a theater reserved for Cirque du Soleil."

"Have they started building yet?" Sue asked.

"The island is being built now, but there aren't any structures as of yet."

"What's the timeline?" I wondered aloud.

"Dubai is hosting World Expo 2020, and it will be complete and inhabited by then."

"Wow, two years is all it will take?" This was remarkable. I recalled building projects in the US that had taken decades to complete.

"Plenty of time," he assured us.

Sue tried to get information about the pricing for the villas. The salesman hedged. "It isn't available at the moment, but if you give me your e-mail, I'll send it as soon as I can." My guess was that given how fast the market is shifting, prices wouldn't be set until a moment before the units go on sale. The display was simply to start collecting information for future marketing. I shied away from providing any personal information, but Sue had no reluctance in giving her e-mail. I surmised as a travel executive, she had a professional reason for wanting follow-up.

I've seen massive construction projects in China, even in Seattle and New York, but Dubai is like nowhere else. In the one week we were there, the city seemed to expand before our eyes. It struck me that while I'm unlikely to see new civilizations on distant planets, this was a reasonable surrogate for how things might evolve.

Dubai's metro stations looked like sets for a sci-fi movie, sleek shiny tubes with angled glass entrances. I wasn't surprised to learn they're featured in a new *Star Trek* flick. It took little effort to imagine extraterrestrials mingling with humans on the moving walkways approaching some stations.

Two lines are operational now, with three additional lines planned. The metro system, like so many things in Dubai, set a new world record when it opened—the longest driverless metro system on the globe.

When we visited Dubai, the temperature remained in the comfortable high eighties, but during summer months it often hovers in the 120–130 degree range. We were told there are two seasons, hot and hotter. The first time we rode the metro, we'd walked several long blocks in the moderate heat to reach a station. It was both a relief and a surprise to enter an air-conditioned environment. Every station is climate-controlled and spotlessly clean, as were the trains. Countdown clocks were prominently placed and unfailingly accurate.

Whenever we took it, the metro was packed with office workers, construction workers, shoppers, tourists, and students. When the train pulled into a station, people moved aside to let others off and on. On most trips, younger riders offered us seats. Despite the density, it was a calm, almost soothing environment, something I've never experienced on public transportation in any city.

What makes Dubai's system distinctively local are the "pink cars" designated for women and children. What surprised me most about the pink cars were women in tank tops and shorts standing side by side with women in headscarves and abayas (a loose black robe-like floor-length covering). No one appeared to notice or care how anyone dressed.

We rode the metro to Burj Khalifa, at 160 floors, the world's tallest building. Like the Empire State Building in New York (a mere 102 floors), it is an unmistakable landmark. Center city, it towers over dozens of neighboring skyscrapers.

The path to the observation deck elevators was lined with pictures and explanations of the construction of the tower and photos taken at the grand opening. Photos and bios of the major architects, engineers, and others involved in the design and building were displayed with obvious pride in their achievement and the number and diversity of the team—men and women who hailed from all over the globe.

Riding to the 124th-floor observation deck took less than a minute, was totally silent, and didn't make my ears pop.

From that bird's-eye view, the city's rapid changes were even more startling than at ground level. In every direction, dozens of new buildings were rising, and highways were stretching further into the city's outskirts. Most of what we saw didn't exist in the photos from when Burj Khalifa first opened in 2009. In those photos, Dubai looked a lot beiger—the desert hemmed the tower in. Looking out now from this aerie, the desert is still visible, but you must peer into the distance to find it. There are even broad patches of green. I'm sure within ten years it will be difficult to see any sand at all.

Not only was the observation deck a great place to look at the city, it was a wonderful place to scrutinize the tourists. Visitors, young and old from every corner of the planet, crossed paths in this pinnacle in the sky, all in awe of the view. The juxtaposition of multiple cultures sometimes made me chuckle. Two monks in saffron robes gazed at the view beside a group of corporate executives wearing bespoke suits. A group of African schoolgirls eagerly posed with their tour guide, who wore a traditional robe and headdress. A chatty pair of middle-aged British women compared souvenirs with their Japanese counterparts.

Connected to Burj Khalifa is the Dubai Mall. In the US, malls are shriveling and dying away in the wake of online shopping. This upscale mall was the antithesis, vibrant with a huge array of high-end international retailers selling everything from groceries to haute couture, restaurants of every cuisine and price range, and an ice-skating rink large enough to play regulation hockey. It's partially a tourist destination—every guidebook lists the mall as a top attraction—but it's also humming with buyers; lots of people toted shopping bags. The building materials would be suitable in a castle, and the architecture provides both huge open spaces with expansive views and small intimate areas for sitting and relaxing. It's not the boxy, lifeless interior I'm accustomed to in American malls. At one fountain, Sue and I stood marveling at the cascading water and sculpted diving figures; it was museum worthy.

I'd read that only 10 percent of Dubai's population is native; walking around the mall, I believed it. The mall was packed with European, Asian, African, and Middle Eastern expats and tourists from across the globe. And, as on the metro, any type of attire seemed acceptable. A pair of young women in full burkas sat at a café, fiddling with their cell phones and discreetly lifting their veils to take sips of coffee. At the next table two other young women dressed in shorts and T-shirts were doing the same, though they had an easier time with their drinks.

Perfume and cosmetic counters did a brisk business with women in headscarves and abayas. I watched as a shop clerk stood outside a boutique spritzing every woman who walked past with a strong scent; none of the women objected. I struggled with that. My knowledge of Islam is limited, but I always understood abayas, burkas, djellabas, and the like were to help women maintain modesty. To me, being drenched in perfume and wearing elaborate makeup (which many did) defeated the purpose.

The nearby Emirates Mall is famous for having an indoor ski slope. I had a hard time visualizing a ski slope in a building. While the ski run isn't the Rockies, for the middle of the desert, it's pretty amazing—snowmakers and a super-air-conditioned space sustain a reasonable bunny slope. The admission fee gets you rental of skis and bindings, warm clothes, a ride in a ski lift, and a few runs down the slope. I laughed when I saw nearly as many people (with skis on their feet) riding the lift *down* the slope as going up. In theory, skiing must sound exciting, but when faced with the daunting downward gradient, many novices chose to stick with the thrill of safely riding over it.

English is used more often than Arabic in public places. Consequently, foreigners who speak fluent English are in high demand. Guest workers from India, the Philippines, Africa, and the Middle East are building Dubai and Abu Dhabi and keeping it functional, each nationality adding to the culture. At our hotel, part of an American chain, most of the staff were Indian. Their influence carried over to the hotel's cuisine—at breakfast there was a nearly equal representation of toast, eggs, and cereal and chutneys, curries, and dosas.

For professionals, Dubai has become a go-to career stop for young, tax-averse foreigners working at global tech, finance, and communications companies. Sheikh Maktoum understood that financial stability depends on a diverse economy, and he created tax-free zones to attract global businesses. Branches of prestigious universities are also flooding the city—NYU, Rochester Institute of Technology, and the Harvard Medical School are just a few of the American colleges now operating in Dubai.

Prior to our trip, Sue had contacted colleagues for itinerary advice. Many of their suggestions all tourists would be likely to discover, but they also clued us in to sites primarily of interest to travel professionals. On their recommendation, Sue made a reservation at the bar at Burj Al Arab, referred to in the biz as a "seven star" hotel. With room prices starting at two thousand dollars a night, it wouldn't have occurred to me to look further. But Sue wanted to see the hotel. The only way in was to eat or drink on the property. When she told me we'd each need to spend a minimum of eighty dollars on drinks at the bar, I was a bit startled but trusted her judgment that we'd be in for something special. Besides, hotel bars are just about the only place in the Emirates to consume alcohol, and I do like a glass of wine.

When the taxi pulled up at the gate, we wended our way through a throng of tourists snapping photos of the hotel. Security required proof of our reservation before we were allowed onto the grounds; it's how they keep gawkers at a safe distance.

Near the hotel entrance, a line of Bentleys stood waiting to whisk guests away. Inside, exquisite floral displays, elaborate tiled floors, subtle lighting, and elegant furniture combined to striking effect—understated but top-of-the-line luxury. In the gift shop, the goods on display were far out of my price range, including the diamond-encrusted pistol. The hotel is within reach of only the top .01 percent; it demonstrated the extraordinary wealth attracted to the city.

After walking around the property and oohing over the infinity pools and outdoor bars with views of the Arabian Gulf and city, we went to the Skyview Bar on the twenty-seventh floor of the hotel.

Even at the hotel's inflated prices, eighty dollars buys a lot of drinks. For two hours we munched almonds and got progressively drunker as we watched the sun set in the panoramic view. The service was impeccable—friendly and low-key, the staff anticipated our every need. Seated near us were tourists from Scandinavia, Europe, and Asia, none of them staying at the hotel, all of them also getting drunk on their allotted alcohol. It was a very happy crowd with no one begrudging the high prices. We concluded that at Burj Al Arab, the two-thousand-dollar rooms were on a low floor in the back with no view.

Sue also booked a "desert adventure" trip in the hopes of seeing what Dubai's landscape looked like prior to the building boom. Open desert and sand dunes, which was what all of Dubai used to be, are now reached after a forty-five-minute drive from the city center. On our way there, we passed several booming satellite cities.

"How long have these towns been here?"

"Brand-new; two years ago this was desert."

"Why are they building so far out of town?" I asked.

"It's less expensive, and some people don't like how crowded Dubai is becoming." He paused. "But now, these are becoming suburbs. Lots of people commute from here. They'll be going further; the construction boom isn't over."

The guide, an Iraqi who'd been living in Dubai for about ten years, told me that until recently he hadn't needed to travel so far to provide a similar adventure. But, as building increases, wild desert shrinks. He didn't express pleasure or displeasure with the city's expansion; he accepted it as the norm. I thought about how difficult it is for many Americans to adapt to new technology and the changes it creates. In Dubai whole landscapes appear seemingly overnight. I wondered if our driver represented a new breed of humans—people who accept, even thrive, in constant, extreme change. Did his being an expat and willingly signing up for a whole new way of life contribute to his adaptability? I tried to imagine how middle Americans, many of whom would like to go back in time to a simpler age, would react to this tsunami of newness.

When we reached the "dune derby"—my term, not the tour operator's—we slowly drove onto the desert sand and then took a short break while the driver lowered the tire pressure on our Toyota Land Cruiser. Dropping from 40 to 15 psi stabilized it for driving on sand.

Sue insisted I ride shotgun in the hope I'd take great pictures. We took off sedately, but within a minute were on a hair-raising drive up and over the sand at high speed. We careened up dunes and then whizzed down them, navigating sharp turns at high speed. Mostly I held on for dear life and tried to keep from either whimpering or screaming on the adrenaline-charged rollercoaster-like ride. At the end of the ride, Sue crept out of the SUV and said, "I had no idea this is what a desert adventure would be. I *hate* rollercoasters. What was I thinking?" Still, the sunset over the desert followed by the starlit sky was breathtaking, and we appreciated being in a natural, undeveloped environment.

The next morning, Sue and I were introduced to Old Dubai, a part of the city and culture fast disappearing, at the Sheikh Mohammed Centre for Cultural Understanding. Our guide demonstrated traditional hospitality with coffee and dates offered by the "silent server." Until recently the silent server was a fixture in the homes of tribal leaders, making sure cups were always full but never interrupting negotiations. The guide then led us through the small fragment of the original city that remains intact, and we had a crash course on traditional architecture, clothes, local crafts, and religion. All but the religious customs are rapidly becoming extinct.

The cultural center is in the middle of the arts district, filled with galleries exhibiting contemporary art. At the calligraphy center, the only site for traditional art, we spent time chatting with the instructor. He was a longtime, but non-native, resident who told us, "I often walk down a block I thought I knew well, and it doesn't look familiar at all." He, unlike our desert safari driver, seemed distraught by the changes. He hoped to preserve a tiny fragment of a traditional Islamic craft.

While we were in Old Dubai, many Fashion Week events were scheduled to take place, complete with fashionistas and tech crews setting up with ultramodern technology. Walking through narrow alleys lined by stucco walls, I tripped a couple of times on cables winding their way to fashion shoots—even in this preserved enclave, the modern world was encroaching.

During our last two days in the Emirates, we toured Abu Dhabi, the capital of the UAE, largest of the Emirates, and the area with the greatest concentration of oil. Given its natural resources, it should be the wealthiest of the seven Emirates, but it isn't. Dubai's urban development has left Abu Dhabi looking like a poor relation. The center city is modern but small, and the pace of building has slowed down during this period of low oil prices.

But the emirate has developed a vision for itself as the cultural and entertainment hub of the UAE. The Louvre Abu Dhabi debuted one week prior to our trip. There are plans for the Guggenheim to open a museum in the same area and for a massive performing arts center to be built. A water park and Ferrari World already draw in tourists, and in the coming year, Warner Brothers planned to open a theme park.

In keeping with the vibe of the Emirates, the Louvre Abu Dhabi is the largest museum on the Arabian Peninsula and futuristic—it represents a new museum experience. One week after opening, the crowds were enormous. When we arrived early morning before official opening time, the entrance line stretched far from the building. When we left several hours later, the line remained equally long.

Designed by French architect Jean Nouvel, the building features a "floating" domed roof made of overlapping layers of metal with cutouts casting shards of light into the courtyard. It is meant to represent "rays of sunlight passing through date palm fronds in an oasis." The glints of light resembled a galaxy of stars. Galleries, spread out below the dome, are airy and connected by light-filled passageways.

Even the exhibits represent a new way of thinking. Displays are arranged by historical period, not geography, so European, Middle Eastern, Asian, African, and South American paintings and sculpture are displayed side by side. It was enlightening to see artwork created during the same time frame but thousands of miles apart. In some cases, without the explanations, it would have been difficult to determine the geographic origin. It made me wonder if humans evolved at the same rate in different parts of the globe, or if there was more cross-cultural sharing going on than I'd realized.

The other site every tourist to Abu Dhabi must visit is the Sheikh Zayed Grand Mosque, one of the largest and most beautiful mosques in the world. And, like everything else in the region, it is new, having been completed in 2007. While it is a functional mosque, the tourists far outnumber the people coming to pray. Hundreds of tour buses filled the massive parking lot.

Women must wear an abaya and headscarf to enter the grounds. The abayas lent to us were dark brown polyester. Within minutes of donning it, sweat trickled down my back. After an hour of walking the grounds, it felt as though I'd just emerged from a steam bath. As a feminist, I resented that women were forced to be uncomfortable while men were permitted to wear anything they liked.

Although we'd been told many times the UAE is safe and there is no crime *at all*, we had to pass through a metal detector to enter the grounds of the mosque.

The exterior of the mosque is breathtaking, with white marble minarets raking a perfect blue sky. Pathways covered by delicate arches lead past a tiled reflecting pool to the domed interior. Inside, the first sensation was awe—I've never been in such a large open building before; it can accommodate over forty thousand worshippers. And, because there is no furniture, the space seemed even larger. I had a sense of déjà vu, reliving the sensation the first time I entered Notre Dame Cathedral. If there is a God, this would be the place to speak with her.

On the way from the Grand Mosque to our hotel, the taxi driver pulled off the highway. He turned off the meter, murmured an apology, pulled out a prayer rug onto the sidewalk, slipped off his shoes, and knelt down to pray. This was the first and only time we'd had this happen while in the Emirates. A few minutes later he returned, and we continued to the hotel. When I asked him to turn the meter back on, he ignored my repeated request.

When we arrived, he demanded an exorbitant fare. While I sat in the taxi refusing to pay or get out, Sue went to find someone from the hotel to help. When the doorman appeared, he threatened to call the police; it is illegal to turn off the meter. The driver sullenly offered to leave without payment. While tempted to stiff him, we paid what the doorman told us was a fair price, and the cabbie sped away from the hotel. So much for being godly.

But he was the exception. In Abu Dhabi, which lacks public transportation and where tourist destinations are spread out, we took a lot of taxis. Friendly, talkative taxi drivers taught us how the city functions. Without exception, the taxi drivers were guest workers. They come to the Emirates on a two- or three-year contract, work long hours—usually ten to twelve hours a day seven days a week—and live in dormitories. To a person, they relayed positive sentiments about this arrangement. With a couple of years of hard work, they could send money home to support their family, and when they returned home, they'd have saved enough to start a business. All said it afforded them economic security they could not have achieved at home.

We asked if many people arrived, decided this wasn't for them, and left. A few, all agreed, but they were the minority. Because there are so many guest workers, everyone found others from their country of origin and banded together for support. Taxi drivers, construction workers, people in the hospitality industry, even people running government offices were all on a similar arrangement.

On our final morning, a young Ethiopian woman drove us to the airport in a pink taxi. She explained that she had a degree in accounting and was hoping to work for the UAE government. Eighteen months to two years working in a service industry was a requirement for sitting for the entrance exam. She thought this was reasonable given the need for unskilled labor. I couldn't help thinking that the government had tackled and solved a lot of issues in a thoughtful way in which most everyone did well. I wanted to bottle this seemingly magical formula and bring it back with me.

HEAT: PARIS, 2018

I've traveled to Paris many times, both for fun and work, and have always loved the city. The last time I'd been there, in February of 1997, was immediately following my father's death. On that trip I was alone, the first stop in a tightly scheduled, multi-city business trip. Everything about that visit had mirrored my mood. The meetings were somber; my client had just announced major layoffs. Granite skies and frigid temperatures made for near-empty streets. People swathed in coats, hats, and scarves raced through the city seeking shelter from icy blasts.

Even before I boarded the plane, this trip to Paris promised to be very different. Pacific Northwest Ballet, a long-term client, had invited me to attend the summer dance festival they were headlining. I'd be there as a guest, not working, and they'd included me in festive celebrations surrounding their performances. I'd asked my friend Judy to travel with me, and we planned to eat great food and enjoy the city. We'd rented what looked to be a comfortable apartment; I anticipated a leisurely, luxurious stay in a beautiful, magical city.

"Let's go sit in the lobby of the Ritz," I said to Judy. The apartment we'd rented was a mere six stops on the metro from central Paris. I hadn't anticipated that the short ride and walking the few blocks to Place de la Concorde would deplete my energy. The city was in the throes of a major heat wave and scorching hot.

Judy chose to wait outside while I slogged inside. I didn't much care about the decor or "ritzy" ambiance. What I craved was the air-conditioned lobby that a five-star hotel would certainly have. It didn't. Instead of blistering, the air was tepid. Sweat continued to drip down my face, my skin was sticky, and without the hoped-for coolness, my energy dropped a notch.

Whenever I travel to hot climates, I carry a folding fan, a tip I learned decades ago. It has often been a lifesaver. I pulled it out, hoping to create some semblance of a breeze. Since arriving in Paris, I'd been fanatically waving the fan, attempting to move stagnant air. It's amazing that I didn't develop carpal tunnel syndrome. Is there such a thing as "fan wrist"?

A bellman approached me politely but inquisitively. I could read his mind—why was this sweating woman occupying one of the few prized chairs in the lobby?

I didn't wait for him to ask. "I'm meeting members of Pacific Northwest Ballet."

"Of course, madam."

With that, he retreated. A few minutes later he approached again. "I thought you might like this."

"Oh. Merci!" I reached for the bottle of water. In two enormous swigs I downed the cool contents. Moments later he returned with another bottle. Parisian five-star hotels may not have sufficient air-conditioning, but they do have classy service.

I was unprepared for the heat. Before packing, I'd checked the forecast—low eighties during the days, mid-sixties at night, no rain. The meteorologists got it wrong. Almost every day was in the mid-nineties. At night it didn't cool down much. The only thing they got right was no rain. For our entire stay there wasn't so much as a cloud, though the humidity was high.

Nothing in Paris is adequately air-conditioned, if at all—not the metro, restaurants, museums, theaters, or stores. For the ten days of the trip, I wilted in the heat, drank gallons of water, and sweated profusely. I beseeched the gods for cooler weather and cursed the French for their lack of air-conditioning.

"But this is unusual. It almost never gets this hot here." I heard that from nearly every Parisian who spoke with me. I believed none of them.

Paris wasn't the hottest destination I've visited, but in the jungles of Borneo or the Saharan desert, I'd anticipated intense heat and was (sort of) prepared for it. In Borneo, I'd hiked with a guide to experience the dense canopy of vegetation in a national park. When we met, it surprised me that she carried a machete. Two hundred steps into the jungle, she began to hack at the dripping foliage.

"Isn't there a path to the lake?" I asked.

"This *is* the path."

"Really! When was the last time anyone walked on it?"

"I'd guess yesterday. Things grow very fast in this climate."

"Oh." I believed her but couldn't wrap my head around plants growing a foot or more a day. When I looked carefully, the path was evident: some muddy shoe prints, a few bare patches of dirt and cairns, small piles of rocks marking the way.

The leaves on the plants were huge; when they arched over the path, they provided a modicum of shade. Though it wasn't raining, the accumulated moisture from the oversaturated air formed fat droplets that steadily drizzled onto me.

After fifteen minutes in the claustrophobic greenery, it was as if someone had dropped a sodden, heavy blanket over me. I didn't know it was possible to sweat this much, every pore a dripping faucet. With each step, my shoes sank slightly into the ooze, and my pace slowed. As we walked further, the blanket became a straitjacket. The hike was just over a mile each way, but it felt as if I were in a Kafkaesque landscape, with the destination always out of reach.

When at last we reached the lakeside, I pulled my shoes off and jumped in fully dressed. What the hell, I was already soaked through.

Paris wasn't that hot or humid, and walking outside, in the shade, was tolerable. But any inside space was stifling. We deemed the Louvre, Musée d'Orsay, and other iconic collections off-limits. Ten minutes in the gift shop of the Decorative Arts Museum seemed like punishment for some past transgression. There was no AC, no fans, and the stagnant hot air sucked out any interest I might have had in purchasing anything. I came out almost as damp as I'd been in Borneo.

The ballet had arranged a private cruise on the Seine for the dancers, production team, and donors. This was to be a special treat to celebrate the company's Parisian debut. The invitation to join them thrilled me. As we pulled away from the dock, most people were visiting the inside buffet and bar. Wine flowed freely. Plates of appetizers, salads, breads, and charcuterie were presented as only the French can. Caviar and sour cream in wafer-thin crepes resembled a bouquet. Rolls of meat and cheese formed flowers. Smoked salmon set on a bed of greens appeared to still be swimming. But after surveying the offerings, I noticed it was the chilled soups that were most often selected. Icy cantaloupe soup and gazpacho seemed appropriately light for the scorching day.

Done eating, most people, clutching a delicate stemmed wine glass, headed to the top deck. We glided past the Eiffel Tower, the Grand Palais and Petit Palais, Notre Dame, and dozens of other historic buildings. It felt a bit unreal, even magical, like a scene from a 1940s romance movie.

In the old days, these would have been Kodak moments. Now cell phones captured and shared selfies and groups posing against the fairyland setting. In many of the pics, the hats worn as protection cast long shadows that obscured faces.

Because the boat cruised sedately, it created almost no breeze. The only shade was directly in front of the pilot's quarters. Every few minutes, he'd sound the horn to alert a shade-seeker to get out of his line of sight.

I lasted about an hour on the top deck then went below for relief from the sun and heat and to get a drink. The line for the bar wrapped snakelike through the space. No one ordered wine; the combination of alcohol and heat would have been suicidal.

"Two glasses of water, *s'il vous plait*," one guest requested. He gulped down the contents and asked for an immediate refill. The bartenders had a tough time keeping up with the demand for water.

While in the queue, I moved next to one of the few air vents. Paltry wisps of air emerging from the vent made it the coolest spot onboard. I abandoned my quest for water and planted myself there. Several acquaintances soon joined me. Imagine gliding past one of the world's most beautiful cityscapes and choosing to remain indoors with limited views. But, views be damned, this was the most comfortable place we could find to chat.

That night, the hottest since we'd arrived, we returned to an oven-like apartment. We flicked on the industrial-strength fan that vibrated and roared as if ready for takeoff. The apartment had large windows at opposite ends and good cross ventilation, but only if you were directly in the path of the breeze. That night I took a sleeping pill. Without it, I would have remained awake, drenched in sweat and miserable.

When I'd inquired about the apartment, I'd asked about air-conditioning. The owner, an American transplant, replied, "You won't find an apartment in Paris with air-conditioning; we just don't need it. Especially in June. Heat just isn't a problem then. You've picked one of the nicest months." In person she told us a different story. "When I first moved to Paris thirty years ago, it never got this hot. But every year it seems to get hotter and hotter. We have two, three, even four heat waves every summer, each one with higher temps and longer than before. I don't know how any-one can deny the climate is changing." Her apartment, located above us, was on the top floor of the building. Heat rose from below and baked from above. She told us she planned to be out of Paris for the month of August. "I don't think I can bear to be here. If it's this hot in June, imagine what August will be like."

"Why don't people install air-conditioning?"

"These are old buildings, and the wiring isn't adequate."

"Couldn't they be rewired?"

"I guess. But everyone prefers to spend their money to just get out of the city. They forget that every summer, the heat starts earlier and lasts longer."

Several people who'd come for the dance festival told us they'd rented what had been advertised as air-conditioned apartments, only to find out that "air-conditioned" meant fans. Many rental apartments don't even offer fans. I would have packed up and left.

While we visited, France's national weather agency placed Paris on orange alert; it's their second-highest warning for heat waves.

They advised the public to spend at least three hours per day in a cool area (I wondered where people could find one), drink water regularly, and avoid going outside when the sun is at its hottest. What they didn't say was that inside spaces were equally hot. Eighty-plus degrees in lifeless air doesn't provide much relief. They made no reference to the 2003 heat wave in which hundreds of people died.

Despite the heat, the luxury part of the trip was as wonderful as anticipated. Our day trip to Bordeaux included consuming decadent food and wine at a private vineyard with a blissfully cool dining room. In a slight alcoholic haze, we toured and tasted yet more wine at Château Rothschild. Starting in 1945, Baron Rothschild traded cases of wine with Picasso, Miro, Andy Warhol, David Hockney, and a host of others for permission to use their art on his wine bottles. I could have stayed in their gallery for hours, looking at the original paintings and drawings and how they had been transformed into labels. What made it even more appealing was that the gallery was air-conditioned; the ultra-wealthy have enough experience to understand the value of AC. I wondered when this notion would trickle down, but perhaps like their wealth, it will never happen.

Getting ready for the first pre-performance party, I fussed and fretted, internally debating if I should wear the elegant silk clothes I'd brought or switch to the looser, thin cotton outfits that were cooler but decidedly less chic. After much consideration, I opted for casual but cool. I was self-conscious when I walked into the venue. I needn't have been. Everyone else had also abandoned wearing "party" clothes in favor of their most comfortable outfits. I was relieved that I wasn't alone in my heat-induced misery.

The washer and dryer in our apartment proved to be lifesavers.

Most days we changed our clothes *at least* twice—not for fashion's sake, but because they were damp with sweat. We also took multiple showers every day.

This was France, not a developing country. It's an innovator in nuclear, solar, and wind power. It has introduced high-speed trains and is aiming to be the start-up capital of Europe. They could introduce air-conditioning in a flash if they focused on it, as the Rothschilds had done. I didn't understand their reluctance to make themselves more comfortable.

It's not as if Parisians don't get as hot and sweaty as Americans. On the metro, other riders looked as miserable as I felt. Bodies glistened, clothes looked damp, some people smelled. When I pulled out my fan, people near me leaned in for whatever breeze I generated.

The more I investigated the Parisian aversion to air-conditioning, the more confused I became. "It's not necessary, and it's bad for your health." "Abrupt swings in temperature cause colds. And coughs. And the flu." Funny, I've moved from frigid movie theaters and offices into steaming streets and don't recall ever getting sick as a result. The French smoke far in excess of Americans, yet they claim we're wimps and AC is bad for your health?

Friends had provided a list of recommended restaurants, but Judy and I went to none of them. The heat decreased our appetites, and the thought of riding on the metro to and from a restaurant made them even less appealing. When we weren't with the group, we ate at local brasseries and bistros. Food was less important than location.

I didn't buy a single souvenir; there was nothing tempting enough for me to venture into stifling shops.

In a city known for museums, the one we most enjoyed was the Rodin Museum—much of its collection is outdoors.

I spent a lot of time, especially on nights I couldn't sleep, ruminating on what makes or breaks a trip for me and on how expectations and reality rarely coincide. This trip was a study in contrasts: extreme luxury and extreme discomfort, often at the same time. The heat took some of the luster off the luxury, while the luxury in part mitigated the heat. On balance it was a great trip, but the enduring memories are likely to be about heat, not luxury.

When I returned home, I reveled in my cool apartment. I now have a deep appreciation for air-conditioning.

TRAVEL IN THE TIME OF COVID: LONDON, 2020

"Are you really going to go?"

"Yes." I nodded. "But just in case I get quarantined, I've packed a month's worth of medication. If I need anything else, I can certainly get it in London. It's not like I'm going to an underdeveloped country."

I really wasn't worried. I don't scare easily. And the news reports, while serious, focused on China, not Europe or the US. The Chinese were clamping down, and the spread appeared to be slowing. That was on Sunday, March 8.

On Tuesday, the day I was to leave, the news bulletins had shifted from China to Italy. Cases there were mounting and the death rate rising. The stock market was in free fall. I debated the wisdom of proceeding with my plans but rationalized London would be no more dangerous than New York.

Even more than the riskiness, I kept coming back to the fact that I really wanted to go. About eighteen months earlier, I'd reconnected with Michael, a dear friend from when I lived in London. We'd been chatting on FaceTime and messaging frequently. This trip was to be our in-person reunion after nearly fifty years. He'd be taking the train from Yorkshire and meeting me in London. This seemed a compelling enough reason to board a plane.

The trip to Kennedy airport, though just past rush hour, was eerily fast. What I'd presumed would be an hour-and-fifteen-minute drive took thirty-five minutes. Instead of the usual jockeying for a place to allow me to get out, the taxi pulled up directly in front of American Airlines' main entrance. No cops shooed anyone away for taking too long; there were no cops in sight.

There was no one on the line for Platinum-status flyers. I walked directly to a bored-looking agent; they may not like it when there are weather problems and crowds of frustrated passengers, but this seemed to be equally crazy making.

I handed over my passport.

"Where are you headed?" she asked.

"London."

"Lucky you; I'd like to get out of here now."

"Oh?"

"It's just so uncertain, and it seems like every hour or two we get new instructions." Then, perhaps realizing she'd said too much, she flashed a dazzling smile. "But no worries for you. Your flight is on time and nearly empty. Are you checking any bags?"

I rolled my carry-on suitcase to the TSA PreCheck line. The TSA agent glanced at my boarding pass and waved me through, stifling a yawn. Not a single person was ahead of me on the Pre-Check line. The normally jam-packed general security screening line had ten people, bunched near the X-ray machines. At this time, no one had heard of social distancing.

That was all strange, but walking to the gate, I had my first moment of *What the hell are you doing, Karen?* The corridors to the gates were devoid of passengers. A few employees leaned against shop entrances, not a customer in sight. I thought, *How come you're one of the only people flying out of JFK tonight? Has the zombie apocalypse settled upon New York City?*

Because the drive to the airport and getting through security had been so fast, I had a lot of time to kill before departure. For the first half hour I sat alone in the boarding area. Posting a photo on Facebook of the deserted corridor with the caption "Welcome to Ghost Town" brought an immediate response. Ten responses, twenty, thirty. At least the zombie apocalypse was confined to the airport.

Ever so slowly, people, mostly Europeans who seemed to be heading home, trickled towards the gate. Then the gate agent and crew arrived. Usually people crowd around the entrance, hoping to get onto the plane early to secure space for carry-on luggage. This flight everyone remained seated until they made the boarding announcement.

"Executive Platinum and Concierge Key members may board now." No one moved. "Group One boarding now." Again, no movement. "Group Two?" No one. With that, I walked over. I was Group Three and the first person to walk down the ramp.

The flight attendant said, "Sit anywhere you like in economy."

"Anywhere?" I echoed.

"This is going to be a nearly empty flight."

"How many people?"

"Two in business and fifty-five in the back." This on a plane that seats 396. "Take this row; it'll be all yours." She smiled, and with her gloved hand, pointed to a row of four seats. "This is going to be a very easy flight for all of us."

I've been on at least thirty to forty flights each year since 1982, some years many more—in total, well over fifteen hundred flights. I'd never seen anything like the terminal or the aircraft. But I decided rather than running off the plane in a panic, I'd enjoy the weirdness and the space. Before settling in, I opened my cache of sanitizer wipes and disinfected every surface for the row of seats. Then I made myself comfortable and, as is my usual pattern, fell sound asleep immediately after takeoff. I woke only as a crewmember announced preparations for landing.

Heathrow is typically as bustling as JFK. But the emptiness had followed me across the ocean. I breezed through immigration and, with zero hassles or delays, by eleven in the morning arrived in central London on the Heathrow Express train.

The minute I exited the train station, normalcy seemed to reappear. Paddington streets were filled with pedestrians and cars. Restaurants and shops were open. The only noticeable difference was the endless line of taxis awaiting nonexistent passengers.

Before checking in, I took advantage of the large dispenser of hand sanitizer at the front desk. I expected that the hotel would be semi-deserted, but the front desk clerk told me the hotel was fully booked. Leaving my bag at the hotel, I walked across Hyde Park to visit my friend Pascale. Belgian, she had been a client in the 1990s when I was working there frequently, and we've remained good friends. She'd been living in London for the past twenty years.

With the sun shining, trees haloed in pale green sprouts, daffodils and crocus blooming, and loads of people and dogs enjoying the perfect day, any lingering anxiety oozed away. The walk revived me, both physically and psychically. A cup of freshly brewed coffee and the company of a good friend and two mischievous kittens doubled down on my feeling of well-being.

That cocoon lasted until I returned to the hotel and foolishly checked for news. The stock market continued its precipitous drop, the federal government was issuing mixed messages about just about everything, including the closing of borders, and social media had exploded. Though I was jet-lagged and exhausted, random gnawing thoughts flashed in my consciousness. What if all borders closed? What would I do if I had to stay in London? Who would take care of my dog? In desperate need of rest and to silence those demons, I took a sleeping pill.

At breakfast, having had a decent night's sleep and a couple of cups of coffee, the world seemed brighter. The weather cooperated too, with bright sunshine and a warm temperature. Pascale and I had agreed to meet at the Victoria and Albert Museum, one of my favorite places in the city. Apart from the slow-running underground, nothing seemed amiss getting there. Very few people wore face masks, and no one seemed overly concerned about keeping their distance. Wearing gloves and carefully staying at least a few feet from other people, I felt both foolish and wise. At this point, there had been only a few isolated cases of COVID-19 reported in London.

Pascale and I visited several exhibits at the V&A, had lunch in the museum's lovely tearoom, and gabbed. Pascale reported some breakdowns in England's supply chain. As in the US, toilet paper and cleaning supplies were difficult to find. She told me that other basic foods and health-care items, like Band-Aids, were also missing. Still, our conversation and the setting couldn't have been less dramatic.

Returning to the hotel, I looked at my phone. My stomach sank as I read headlines, saw the stock market tanking further, and read dire warnings on social media. This time I made a conscious decision to shut off the phone and take a nap.

That evening I met up with Michael. My first thought when I saw him, fortunately not spoken aloud, was *Oh, my God, you've gotten old*. But when his blue eyes twinkled, I could see the transformed eighteen-year-old Michael. Our first half hour felt a bit awkward. Where does one start to fill in a gap of fifty years? Then it was as if time disappeared.

For the next three days, Michael and I roamed the city, chatted endlessly, and went to restaurants, pubs, and museums, all of which seemed normal. Though theaters in the West End announced greatly reduced ticket prices for all shows, we preferred to talk.

The reunion exceeded my expectations. I had brought a very dear friend back into my life. And when we checked recollections of ancient events, it delighted me to discover we had similar memories. We laughed about things that had happened when we were young and about the craziness of the world now. We shared the difficult times we'd gotten through. No subject was off-limits, which, to me, is the sign of a true friend. I regretted we'd missed so many years, especially since I've been in London dozens of times over the years, and was thankful for the technology that had allowed us to reconnect.

But each time I looked at the phone, I whipsawed back to the global reality of the pandemic. All Broadway theaters went dark. Then everything in New York City, except for the essentials, started to be shuttered. European borders were closing, except the UK. Next, I read UK flights to the US would be closed to everyone except returning Americans.

Continue the reunion or go home? News reports of it being

extremely difficult to get through to airlines on the phone kept me from trying. Video of returning travelers waiting for hours to get through immigration in the US scared me into thinking I should probably return home earlier than planned.

Along with my American Airlines' Platinum status, they had given me a special phone number for elite flyers. I got through to an agent in less than five minutes and arranged to return to New York a day earlier than scheduled.

My final day was divided between saying farewell to Michael and Pascale. It was bittersweet because both promised to come to New York to visit when the world returned to normal. I wondered how long that would take and what the new normal would be like. My optimism was wavering.

On departure day, as I walked to Paddington Station for the Heathrow Express, there were far fewer people out and about than when I'd arrived five days earlier, though it was at roughly the same time. As with the trip into London, this journey was fast, efficient, and empty. Checking in was a breeze, though the security line appeared a bit longer and the terminal busier, though far from what a normal day would have been.

While I waited for my flight, I sent out an SOS to friends in my building for some basic foods—milk, eggs, tomatoes, and such. My neighbor planned to go to the supermarket and said she'd be happy to get what I needed, though she wanted to know what substitutions I'd be willing to accept if the store didn't have everything, something she'd already experienced. I wandered around the airport shops looking for edibles to bring home. Other than chocolate and cookies, there wasn't much available except at Harrod's mini-food hall. Though I'm sure it was excellent, I wasn't willing to spend thirty-five dollars for a small chunk of cheddar. So, chocolate it was—a huge shopping bag full. I figured it would make great tips for people working in my building.

In the boarding area, I spoke with several other Americans returning home. Some stories were harrowing. One family, with three children under age six, were returning from a mission in Romania. When they heard the borders would be closing, they tried to get a flight out. There were no seats available. They hired a taxi to take them into Hungary. At the first small town across the border, the taxi driver dropped them off, apologizing but saying he had to get home while he still could. Another taxi took them to Budapest. They waited two days for a flight, not to the States but to Paris with connections to London, New York, and finally home to Virginia. Two women had been in Poland and told a similar tale of hastily rearranged plans. Others were returning from Germany, the Netherlands, and Spain.

We boarded in an orderly fashion, and the plane, while fuller than the one I'd arrived on, still had many open seats. Business class had only three people, and economy was about half-full.

The flight was uneventful, though every time I heard someone cough, I cringed. There was a lot of coughing. I didn't have a mask; there were none to be had in London.

As the plane began its descent, the flight steward made an announcement. "We will be handing out health questionnaires to everyone. Please make sure you fill one out for each member of your party, even infants."

Fair enough. When I scanned the questionnaire, it was woefully out-of-date. It asked only about travel to China and if we'd experienced any severe breathing problems. By this time Italy was in crisis, and other European countries were reporting escalating cases of COVID-19.

Upon touchdown, another announcement: "When we arrive at the gate, everyone please remain in your seats. Do not take anything out of the overhead bins. Personnel will come on the plane to review the questionnaires and take everyone's temperature. We'll call you up row by row." I assumed this was to minimize the kinds of scenes shown on TV of people packed tightly together in hallways waiting to get through immigration. Staying seated on the plane for a while seemed a great alternative.

We taxied to the gate. The bell dinged, signaling we had parked. No one got up.

Five minutes after they had opened the aircraft doors, another announcement: "Authorities will be checking temperature and questionnaires in the terminal. You're free to deplane." *Great*, I thought. Then those scenes of travelers in hallways waiting for hours reappeared. *Maybe not so great.*

Seated in the first row of economy, with only three people in business, I was one of the first people off the plane. Empty hallways, devoid of passengers and personnel, stretched before me. American Airlines has its own immigration area at Kennedy airport. Completely empty, I walked to a check-in machine and then directly to an immigration officer.

"Welcome home. I bet you're happy to be back."

"I am, thanks. I wasn't sure I'd be able to get back."

He scanned my passport and waved me through.

With no checked luggage, I walked directly through the baggage area, out through customs, and to the taxi line. No one had collected the questionnaire, asked me anything, or taken my temperature. A friend who'd flown on that same day and also hadn't had her temperature taken had asked an immigration officer about it.

The officer answered, "The only thermometers left around

here are rectal ones." At least there was an explanation for what seemed to be a gaping health security hole.

I, as well as my fellow coughing passengers, was being let loose unchecked in New York and, through connecting flights, across America. I decided it was important that I self-quarantine, but I shuddered to think how many people from my flight might transmit the virus. I'd just had a vivid example of how pandemics spread.

AFTERWORD

London was my final trip before staying at home became an imperative. I cancelled four planned trips and resigned myself to fantasy rather than real travel.

After two months of slowly going ever more stir-crazy, I hit on the idea of being a traveler in my own city. Even though I grew up in Manhattan and Queens and thought I knew the city well, New York has many hidden treasures. I challenged myself to explore as many as possible. I saw Manhattan from a dozen different vantage points and discovered lush gardens and unusual architecture. Street art became a new passion.

All of which is to say, you don't need to travel to distant locations to be adventurous. Still, I can't wait to once again board a plane and find somewhere new to walk around, photograph, meet people, eat great meals, and see live theater and wonderful art.

I hope my book has put you in the same mindset and will launch you on your own adventures.

To see photos from the journeys described, as well as pictures from my other travels, please visit my website: www.karengershowitz.com

You can also find me at:
https://www.facebook.com/karengershowitzauthor/
https://www.instagram.com/karengershowitz/
and @karengershowitz
https://twitter.com/KarenGershowitz/
and @karengershowitz
https://www.linkedin.com/in/karen-gershowitz/
https://www.youtube.com/channel/UCaPItU6rOKfJiW9j-RxA_TYQ/

ACKNOWLEDGMENTS

I've been writing this book my whole life, or at least it feels that way. Someone, most likely my mother, Mary Lotker Gershowitz, encouraged me to keep a travel journal for each trip I took. Recently I came upon one describing a trip to Florida, written when I was eight years old. Thank you, Mom, for the encouragement and for instilling me with endless curiosity.

There are two huge groups of people who need to be thanked: travel companions who helped to make trips more enjoyable and members of my writing community who read through endless material.

Travel companions include Lisa Ernst, Diane Mitchell, Martin Fager, Linda Leonard, Michael Meiners, Helaine Daniels, Gary Berman, Marcia Anderson, Maggie Anderson, Pascale Erseel, Kim Pophal, Penny Manning, Vicki Resnick, Judy Plows, Giovanna Schurr and George Schurr (who lives on in memories), Stephanie Feingold, Sue Shapiro, Helaine Meyers, and all the many people who have been kind and generous when I've been away from home.

Writing community members who encouraged me and helped to improve the quality of this book include Liz Burk, Cynthia Ehrenkrantz, Paul Phillips, Werner Hengst (who is much missed), Jean Halperin, Aileen Hewitt, Jennifer Lang, Cathleen Barnhart, Jennifer Chen, Judy Rabinor, Phyllis Melhado, Carol Hymowitz, Jack Eppler, Wendy Davis, Coree Spencer, Elvira Gonzalez, Elizabeth Tingley, Theresa Campion, Laura Petrecca, and Kathy Byrnes.

A special shout-out to two people who read the manuscript and encouraged me to go for it: Michael Taylor and Geri Kaplan.

Thanks, too, to the team at SheWrites Press for all of their help, especially Lauren Wise and Brooke Warner.

If I've forgotten anyone, many apologies. A complete list of people to thank could be a whole book.

ABOUT THE AUTHOR

Karen has been traveling solo since age seventeen, when she flew to Europe and didn't return to the US for three years. She got severely bitten by the travel bug and since then has traveled to nearly ninety countries and visited all fifty states—many of them multiple times.

photo credit: Diane Mitchell

After studying ceramics in college and graduate school she abandoned that career and switched to marketing so that employers would pay for her travel. In her new career as a marketing strategist and researcher she traveled the world conducting thousands of meetings, focus groups, and interviews. Her skills as an interviewer have persuaded total strangers to talk candidly about the most intimate of subjects: personal bankruptcy, illness, and religion. When traveling for pleasure, those same skills help her to draw out people's stories. She learned about their lives, as well as local customs and fashions and what makes them laugh. These conversations often led to invitations for dinner and personal tours.

Her hope is that each story can be read and enjoyed independently, but together they convey the profound impact travel has had on her life. Even more, she hopes these stories tickle the travel bug in readers and set them off on their own adventures.

Karen lives in New York City.